VICTORIAN THEATRICAL BURLESQUES

For Joseph Bristow

PN 2595.13.
B9 VIC

Victorian Theatrical Burlesques

Edited by
RICHARD W. SCHOCH
University of London

ASHGATE

Published by
Ashgate Publishing Limited
Gower House
Croft Road
Aldershot
Hampshire GU11 3HR
England

Ashgate Publishing Company
Suite 420
101 Cherry Street
Burlington, VT 05401-4405 USA

Ashgate website: http://www.ashgate.com

British Library Cataloguing in Publication Data
Victorian theatrical burlesques
    1. Burlesque (Theater) 2. English drama - 19th century -
    History and criticism 3. Burlesque (Literature)
    I. Schoch, Richard W.
    822'.0523'0808

Library of Congress Cataloging-in-Publication data
Victorian theatrical burlesques / edited by Richard W. Schoch.
    p.cm.
 Includes bibliographical references (p.)
  Contents: Miss Eily O'Connor (1861) / by H.J. Byron – 1863; or, the sensations of the past season (1863) / by H.J. Byron – The very latest edition of Black-eyed Susan (1866) / by F.C. Burnand – The Corsican "bothers" (1869) / by H.J. Byron – The poet and the puppets (1892) / by Charles H.E. Brookfield and James Glover.
 ISBN 0-7546-3362-4 (alk.paper)
 1. Burlesques. 2. English drama–19th century. I. Schoch, Richard W.

PR 1259.B87 V53 2003
822'.05230808–dc21

2002026188

ISBN 0 7546 3362 4

Printed and bound in Great Britain by MPG Books Ltd, Bodmin, Cornwall

Contents

List of Illustrations

Illustration 1 is reproduced by courtesy of the National Portrait Gallery, London; illustrations 2-5, 7 and 8 by kind permission of The Harvard Theatre Collection, The Houghton Library; and illustrations 6 and 9-13 courtesy of The British Library.

Acknowledgements

During the period in which this edition was prepared I had the good fortune to be a recipient of a Leverhulme Research Fellowship. It is a great pleasure to thank The Leverhulme Trust for the gift of extended time for research, reflection, and writing. This work could not have been completed without the generous assistance and expertise of librarians and curators at The British Library, The Folger Shakespeare Library, The Harry Ransom Humanities Research Center, The Harvard Theatre Collection, The London Library, the Theatre Museum, the University of London Library and the Widener Library at Harvard University. Annette Fern and Julia Collins deserve particular thanks for guiding me through Harvard's spectacular resources in nineteenth-century British theatre. Permission to publish excerpts from manuscripts in The Harvard Theatre Collection has been generously granted by The Houghton Library, Harvard University. At Ashgate Publishing, Erika Gaffney has been an exemplary commissioning editor. She has also been a courageous one, and is to be heartily commended for agreeing to publish an edition of little-known nineteenth-century plays. Thanks are due to Alan Stewart and Kirk Melnikoff for helping me to frame the entire project—and, more importantly, for believing that it was worthwhile. Alan kindly offered much-valued advice on editorial procedures. For their superb hospitality, Annabel and Richard Cellini have my sincere gratitude. My time in Boston was made most agreeable through the companionship of Ari Lipman, George Marcotte, and Christine Smith. To this volume's dedicatee, a generous friend and colleague, belongs my affectionate admiration.

Note on Stage Directions

Closed in	Masked by a piece of scenery moved onto the stage.
Down or Downstage	Toward the audience.
L.C. ('Left Centre')	The actor stands to the left (from his or her perspective) of centre stage.
L. 1 E. ('Left 1st Entrance')	The actor enters from the stage left side of the first set of wings—that is, the ones placed farthest downstage. An entrance through the next set of wings was notated 'L. 2 E.' and so on. A typical nineteenth-century 'wing-and-drop' set consisted of three or four wings. The number of wings varied according to the size of the stage.
L.U.E. ('Left Upper Entrance')	The actor enters from the farthest upstage entrance on the stage left side.
R.C. ('Right Centre')	The actor stands to the right (from his or her perspective) of centre stage.
R. 1 E. ('Right 1st Entrance')	As above, but from the stage right side.
R.U.E. ('Right Upper Entrance')	As above, but from the stage right side.
Up or Upstage	Away from the audience.

Introduction

'You might call [burlesque] rubbish, buffoonery, vulgarity, anything you liked, but your temperament must have been abnormally phlegmatic if you could resist the influence of that riotous mirth and not be carried away by it'.
                    Augustin Filon, *The English Stage* (1895)

'I abominate Burlesques'.
                    W.B. Donne, Examiner of Plays (*c.* 1855)

In the spring of 1865 a London drama critic imagined the judgment that theatre historians of the twenty-first century would hand down on the burlesques popular with nineteenth-century audiences. His conjecture was not particularly encouraging. Any 'right-thinking scholar' of the future, the critic predicted, would be hard pressed to reconcile 'the nature of the works which he disinters with the high degree of pleasure' they once afforded.[1] The regrettable, yet inescapable verdict would be that 'much of the rich and refined humour which was common on the stage in the reign of Victoria [would] no longer be understood or appreciated'. Nonetheless, the journalist still hoped that future historians might 'discover some point in the dashing burlesques of our time'. In the same spirit, this edition of Victorian burlesques invites its readers to recover the satiric 'point' of this most spirited form of theatrical vulgarity.

From J.R. Planché's *Orpheus in the Haymarket* (1865) to F.C. Burnand's *Tra-la la Tosca* (1890), and from E.L. Blanchard's *The Merchant of Venice (very far indeed from the text of Shakespeare)* (1843) to Robert Reece's *Faust in a Fog* (1870), the burlesque exempted no area of polite culture from its parodic assault. Nineteenth-century playgoers enjoyed burlesques of Shakespeare, Greek tragedy, melodrama, classical mythology, English history, Arthurian legend, Arabian tales, *bel canto* opera, the novels of Sir Walter Scott and Edward Bulwer-Lytton, the poetry of Goethe, and the plays of Henrik Ibsen, Arthur Wing Pinero, and Oscar Wilde. Burlesque playwrights and performers were nothing if not indiscriminate. Robert Brough, for example, wrote burlesques of *The Tempest*, *Ivanhoe*, Daniel-François Auber's opera *Masaniello*, and Euripides' tragedy *Medea*. John Robert O'Neil, writing psuedonymously as 'Hugo Vamp', devised the equestrian burlesque *The Siege of Troy; or, the Miss-Judgment of Paris* (1854). Frederick Robson, the greatest stage comedian of the Victorian era, was equally acclaimed for his starring performances in Francis Talfourd's *Macbeth Somewhat Removed from the Text of Shakespeare* (1853) and Brough's *Medea; or, the Best of Mothers, with a Brute of a Husband* (1855). Shakespeare was the most frequently burlesqued playwright, and *Hamlet* the most frequently burlesqued play. From John Poole's *Hamlet Travestie* (1810) to W.S. Gilbert's *Rosencrantz and*

Guildenstern (1891), more than a dozen parodies of Shakespeare's immortal tragedy appeared on the nineteenth-century stage. Burlesque dramatists also satirized contemporary plays. Sheridan Knowles's *William Tell* (1825), an almost entirely forgotten historical drama, was burlesqued six times within twenty years, from Burnand's *William Tell* (1856) to Reece's *William Tell Told Over Again* (1876). Dion Boucicault's melodrama *The Corsican Brothers* (1852), a more remembered play, occasioned no fewer than nine burlesque versions. One of them—H.J. Byron's *The Corsican 'Bothers'* (1869)—appears in this volume.

Wildly popular in their own day, burlesques are now little read, scarcely studied, and rarely performed. Yet since they are inherently metadramatic—that is, plays about other plays—burlesques offer us an unparalleled opportunity to understand not only how drama changed throughout the Victorian age but also how popular culture *responded* to those changes. It is precisely the metadramatic qualities of burlesques which enable the best of them to function not as idle mockeries but as searching critiques of dramatic form. And thus the principal aim of this edition is to highlight the ways in which nineteenth-century burlesques of nineteenth-century plays—*Black-Ey'd Susan* (1829), *The Colleen Bawn* (1861), *The Corsican Brothers* (1852), *Lady Audley's Secret* (1863), and *Lady Windermere's Fan* (1892)—can be read as a sustained critical commentary on such theatrical forms as sensation melodrama, society comedy, and modern realism.

Despite their unique perspective on the aesthetic and social dimensions of drama, burlesques have been largely neglected by scholars, students, and theatre practitioners alike. Such neglect is due partly to a longstanding academic prejudice against all forms of nineteenth-century drama. The abundance and strength of scholarship written over the past decade, however, has shown just how wrongheaded that prejudice was. Even so, burlesques still suffer from neglect because the texts themselves are relatively scarce. While more than a thousand burlesques were performed in the nineteenth century, the vast majority of them survive only as manuscripts originally submitted to the Lord Chamberlain for licensing.[2] Several hundred burlesques survive in contemporary scripts published for immediate use by provincial theatres and amateur troupes. Once plentiful, these texts are now typically found only in the rare books collections of major research libraries. In their own day, however, such inexpensive acting editions were not regarded as valued 'literary' publications. Indeed, almost no nineteenth-century burlesques were ever published in the handsome, well-laid out editions which memorialized the legitimate dramas of Knowles and Bulwer-Lytton. The five-volume collection of Planché's extravaganzas published in 1879, for which the author himself wrote the preface, strikingly departs from the decidedly casual treatment of burlesques by the Victorian literary establishment. Posterity has shown a similar disregard. This volume is the first critical edition devoted exclusively to Victorian burlesques.[3]

What is a Burlesque?

In compiling an edition of burlesque texts, a judicious editor might well begin by asking 'What is a burlesque'? The question is deceptively simple for it has never admitted a single, easy answer. Historically, burlesque has been defined as a subset of literary or theatrical parody that inverts form and content.[4] As Joseph Addison observed in *The Spectator* nearly three hundred years ago, a burlesque either 'represents mean Persons in the Accoutrements of Heroes' (i.e., low to high) or 'describes great Persons acting and speaking like the basest among the People' (i.e., high to low).[5] In the first instance, the burlesque preserves the original text's style yet applies it to inappropriate characters and circumstances (e.g., a footman who speaks like Cardinal Richelieu); in the second, the burlesque deforms the original text's style yet retains its characters and circumstances (e.g., a Cardinal Richelieu who speaks like a footman). This definition boasts staying power. Charles Cowden-Clarke, in 1871, explained that a theatrical burlesque either 'elevat[es] a daily occurrence...into a situation of classic dignity' or 'invest[s] subjects or events of "great pith and moment" in the costume and dialect of vulgar life'.[6] More recent critics have argued much the same. Simon Trussler, John Jump, and Simon Dentith, for example, all maintain that the high treatment of a low subject constitutes a 'classic' burlesque while the low treatment of a high subject is better termed a 'travesty' (or 'low' burlesque).[7] According to such definitions, most Victorian burlesques should be called travesties since, to borrow Trussler's definitional terms, they 'vulgaris[e]' an 'elevated or classical theme' (*Burlesque Plays*, p. ix).

　　While such fine distinctions between 'burlesque' and 'travesty' carry their own logic, they do not conform to nineteenth-century theatrical practice. As theatre historians know only too well, the terms 'burlesque', 'travesty', and even 'extravaganza' were used interchangeably by playwrights, managers, actors, critics, and spectators alike. As confirmed by the all-encompassing title of Maurice Dowling's *Othello Travestie, an Operatic Burlesque Burletta* (1834), the nineteenth-century stage did not insist upon precise differentiations among various theatrical forms and styles. While for the sake of convenience I use the term 'burlesque' throughout this edition, I do not thereby exclude from discussion certain kinds of plays and performances. Indeed, the often overlooked term 'travesty' carries the important metaphorical—and frequently literal—sense of cross-dressing implied in all instances of theatrical parody. While we now tend to think of 'burlesque' as a synonym for 'striptease', the word conveyed just the opposite meaning in the nineteenth century: not stripping off, but dressing up. Quite simply, a burlesque for the Victorians was a play which self-consciously 'dressed up' as another play (or poem or novel, etc.). Robert Reece nicely captured this essential quality of burlesque in the title of his own *Richelieu Redressed* (1873). The title also carries the equally important meaning that a burlesque 'corrects' its source text. Whether originally labelled burlesques, travesties, extravaganzas—or some combination thereof—the plays included in this edition all present themselves as comic misquotations of original 'legitimate' plays and performances.

Burlesque and Metadrama

Instead of relying on generic categories which wrongly attempt to impose retrospective order on unruly theatrical practices, we would do better to focus on the essential activity of burlesque as a sustained, self-conscious comic interpretation of a source text. In other words, let us concentrate less on the formal properties which burlesques 'possess' and more on the metadramatic work which they actually 'do'. The specific, almost technical questions we might ask about a burlesque (e.g., how does the stage Irishman Myles na-Coppaleen appear in a burlesque of *The Colleen Bawn*?) are useful only to the extent that they lead us to pose more searching questions about the play's critical dynamics (e.g., what does it mean that burlesque Myles deconstructs the conventions of the stage Irishman?). This shift in definition—form to function, if you will—recalls the theoretical principle which the Russian Formalists first articulated that parody 'refunctions' canonical literary forms once they have become rigid or mechanistic. Although it appears counter-intuitive, parody in fact preserves the continuity of literary (or theatrical) traditions by endowing overly-familiar texts with new capabilities. Because a parody comically distorts an original text it is always understood by reference to its original. Parody thus provides an exemplary instance of intertextuality. This is what Mikhail Bakhtin meant by the inherent dialogism of parody: 'another's speech in another's language'.[8] A burlesque, like other parodic forms, necessarily remains equivocal toward its sources, whose value it simultaneously affirms and denies.

    Contemporary literary theory may help to explain the fundamental ambivalence of nineteenth-century burlesques, but it certainly did not invent that ambivalence. More than a century ago Burnand asserted that an effective burlesque

> publicly exposes on the stage some preposterous absurdities of stagecraft, which may be a passing fashion of the day, justly ridicules some histrionic pretensions, parodies false sentiment, and shows that the shining metal put forward as real gold is only theatrical tinfoil.[9]

For all its doggerel, painful punning, and licentiousness, the burlesque—the 'candid friend of the Drama', as Burnand insisted—styled itself as the norm to which transgressive theatrical practices should revert. Drawing a shrewd distinction between classic dramatic texts and inept *performances* of those texts, the future editor of *Punch* explained that burlesques are themselves a response to the unfortunate occasions when legitimate drama was 'injured by the misinterpretation of self-complacent mediocre actors' or 'rendered ridiculous by extravagant realism in production'. With the drama thus besieged, the burlesque's 'legitimate employment' was to 'hold the mirror up, not to Nature, but to such distortion of Nature' in order that those very distortions might be rectified. Burlesque sought, then, not merely to criticize contemporary performances, or so its advocates enjoined, but to *correct* them. The burlesque was as much prescriptive as it was diagnostic. Let us look at some examples of how the Victorian burlesque staked its claim to legitimacy through constructive ridicule.

    A principal target of burlesque mockery was 'blood and thunder' melodrama. Burlesque effectively 'killed' this outmoded genre, Burnand elaborated, along with its 'broods of empty-headed, stilted, third-rate Macreadys, who looked upon themselves as legitimate successors of the great Kemble school' ('Spirit of Burlesque', p. 176).[10] A stinging satire of old-fashioned melodramatic villainy occurs in Byron's *Ali Baba; or, The Thirty-Nine Thieves* (1863) when the robber Abdalla, originally played by Ada Swanborough, encourages the murderous Hassarac to renounce 'vulgar violence' and 'become more polished in [his] style'.[11] The villain, acted by George Honey, proudly defends his allegiance to melodramas produced at the 'old Coburg' (the south London theatre now called the 'Old Vic'). Yet Hassarac's description of those supposedly 'exciting' performances turns out to be obviously satiric, with its emphasis on overloaded scenery, ill-timed special effects, and ponderous music:

> Give me the tangled wood, or stormy ocean—
> A knife—dark lantern—lots of horrid things,
> With lightning, every minute, at the wings;
> A pistol, big enough for any crime,
> Which never goes off, at the proper time;
> Deep, rumbling, grumbling music on the drums—
> A chord whenever one observes 'she comes;'
> An opening chorus, about 'Glorious wine;'
> A broadsword combat every sixteenth line;
> Guttural vows of direct vengeance wreaking,
> And thunder always when one isn't speaking.
>
> (p. 11)

The even more extreme production values of 'sensation' melodramas were regularly derided in burlesques of the 1850s and 1860s. Much like contemporary sensation novels, the genre popularized by Wilkie Collins, sensation melodramas organized themselves less around plot or character development than around the enactment of such thrilling events as horse races, train wrecks, shipwrecks, or avalanches. Tom Taylor mocked the entire genre in *Sense and Sensation; or, The Seven Saints of Thule* (1864). The prologue to John Halfourd's *Faust and Marguerite* (1854) similarly jeers at the theatrical public's desire for sensation. A 'Dramatist' disdainfully refuses to accept the brute authority of 'Public Taste':

> ...Don't mention it, I pray;
> To 'Public Taste' I can no homage pay;
> It hurls the Poet from his lofty station.
> To wallow in the quagmire of '*sensation*.'
> Never will I my mission so profane,
> Nor sell my creed for mercenary gain.[12]

It would be wrong to assume that the legitimate drama escaped burlesque censure. When Charles Kean managed the Princess's Theatre in the 1850s, he was mercilessly attacked in parodies of *The Corsican Brothers*, *Faust and Marguerite*, *Hamlet*, *Macbeth*, *Richard III*, *Sardanapalus*, and *The Winter's Tale*. 'We have been done to death with burlesques', *The Spectator* entreated in the spring of 1853.[13] A bemused *Lloyd's Weekly London Newspaper* reported that a 'Charles Kean mania [was] breaking out like a rash upon all [burlesque] actors', making it impossible to 'go to a theatre without hearing the continual imitation' of Kean's performance as Macbeth.[14] Robson, a few years later, impersonated the Italian

1 Frederick Robson in the title role of Robert Brough's *Medea; or, the Best of Mothers with a Brute of a Husband*, Olympic Theatre, London, 1855

classical actress Adelaide Ristori in the role of Medea (illustration 1). The tragedienne herself, who performed only in her native Italian, witnessed the opening night performance at the Olympic Theatre. So slyly ingenious was Robson's impersonation that the admiring Ristori, unaware that she had just enjoyed a burlesque upon herself, embraced the comic actor as a '*uomo straordinario*'.[15] Later in the century, Ellen Terry found herself repeatedly burlesqued. Marie Linden, in Burnand's *Faust and Loose* (1886), mimicked the actress's portrayal of Marguerite, while Nellie Farren somehow incorporated a burlesque of Terry as Portia in *Ruy Blas and the Blasé Roué* (1889). (Farren's other impersonations in the play included a toreador and a chimney sweep.) Much to his consternation, Henry Irving was frequently the target of ridicule, whether in parodies of Shakespeare, *The Corsican Brothers*, or *Faust*. On occasion a burlesque ensemble impersonated the entire cast of the 'legitimate' version of the play being parodied. In Burnand's *Stage Dora; or, Who Killed Cock Robin?* (1883) the actors at Toole's Theatre mocked the London cast of Victorien Sardou's *Fédora*. The burlesque ensemble, as *The Theatre* detailed, took particular aim at Charles Coghlan's 'reserved force', Squire Bancroft's 'supercilious sedateness', and Mrs. Bernard Beere's 'passionate fervour'.[16]

Just as burlesques were quick to attack other kinds of plays, performances, and performers, they were quick to defend the legitimacy—the necessity, as they saw it—of their distinctive humour. A particularly memorable instance occurs in Planché's *The Camp at the Olympic* (1853), the topical revue which Alfred Wigan commissioned to inaugurate his management of the Olympic Theatre. Wigan, playing himself, enlists the aid of Fancy to help decide which play he should produce first. The scene quickly changes to the 'Camp of the Combined British Dramatic Forces' with the tents of Tragedy, Melodrama, and Opera arranged on one side of the stage and those of Comedy, Farce, and Pantomime on the other. Personifications of the various theatrical genres appear before Wigan, each hoping to be selected by the Olympic's new manager. The 'Spirit of Burlesque' boisterously interrupts the scene in the person of Robson dressed as King Arthur from Henry Fielding's burlesque *Tom Thumb*. The overwrought 'Spirit of Tragedy' falls onto a *chaise lounge* as the sound of 'penny trumpets' heralds Burlesque's arrival. Singing to the tune of 'Here we go, up, up, up', Burlesque merrily taunts Tragedy that

> Your Hamlet may give up his Ghost,
> Your Richard may run himself through,
> I'm Cock-of-the-Walk to your cost,
> And I crow all over your crew!
> For Burlesque is up! up! up!
> And Tragedy down! down! down! O!
> Pop up your nob again!
> And I'll box you for your crown, O![17]

This is all too much for Tragedy, who, ventriloquizing Macbeth, implores such 'unreal mockery' to 'quit [its] sight'. Burlesque steadfastly retorts that it must

....fling your follies in your face,
And call back all the false starts of your race,
Show up your shows, affect your affectation.
And by such homeopathic aggravation,
Would cleanse your bosom of that perilous stuff,
Which weighs upon our art—bombast and puff.

An act of theatrical reform which aggressively compensated for the 'follies' of other people's productions—as so vividly testified in *The Camp at the Olympic*—the traditional burlesque became part of the very performance history upon which it cast a reproachful eye. Yet it thereby became responsible for its own dissolution. Because a parody 'belies the concept of a definitive or authoritative work', as Michele Hannoosh has remarked, 'it cannot legitimately propose itself as the definitive [work]'.[18] Theatrical burlesques do not dismantle other performances in order to assume their vacated canonical positions. Rather, burlesques abjure the entire notion of canonicity by removing the ground for the meaning of *all* texts and performances, including themselves. Out of their necessary self-consciousness, then, burlesques become susceptible to their own critique. Such openness to self-ridicule, however, saves burlesques from the charge of being gratuitously destructive.

To be sure, Victorian burlesques frequently renounce the self-denying implications of their own rhetoric. Yet burlesques cannot have it both ways. And, ultimately, they do not. How does this happen? Typically, burlesques acknowledge that they possess no singular privilege by enacting alternatives to themselves. A burlesque artist's repertoire of 'knowing' winks, glances, and nudges allows performers to realize something (often a sexual innuendo) which they must immediately relinquish. '[S]aucy [Marie] Wilton winks her way', one theatrical wit observed of the burlesques performed at the Strand Theatre in the early 1860s, '[a]nd says the more the less she has to say'.[19] Through such embedded counter-performances, as it were, burlesques tease their spectators with glimpses of performances never to be fully realized. When a burlesque of *Hedda Gabler* resurrects dead characters in its finale, it thereby implies that burlesques do not remain committed to telling the same story the same way night after night. Characters whose fates are *not* pre-ordained by an underlying source text endow burlesques with an aura of unpredictability, as if tomorrow night Hedda might not put a pistol to her head.

Critical Responses to Burlesque

Let any one...who has undergone the penance—and it is no slight one—of going to see the burlesques, which, either alone or as introduction to pantomimes, are now filling the West-end theatres, ask himself if they are exhibitions which he can with propriety take any woman or child to witness. The sickening vulgarity of the jokes, the slang allusions, the use of words and phrases unknown in the vocabulary of ladies and gentlemen, the ridicule of associations which are all but sacred, the outrageous caricature of grave passions, the exhibition of crowds of girls in costumes only suitable for the *poses plastiques* of Leicester-square, above all, the way in which young actresses are made to say and do things which must destroy every shred of modesty and feminine grace in them, make these burlesques pernicious alike to performers and audience.[20]

This impassioned critical diatribe, from an 1858 article in *Fraser's Magazine*, is hardly exceptional. Because they took unabashed liberties with prevailing orthodoxies of theatrical practice, burlesques inevitably came under sustained attack for what an outraged William Archer similarly called their 'indescribeable puerility of wit and vulgarity of tone'.[21] He scorned the 'lame metres, cockney rhymes, [and] inane puns' of burlesque scripts no less than the 'lofty disregard of metre, meaning, punctuation, and H's' shown by burlesque performers'.[22] To be sure, not all critics were hostile. Cowden-Clarke, for example, praised the 'genuine humour, and wit' of *Hamlet Travestie* ('Comic Writers of England', p. 572). Most critics, however, were decidedly unfriendly to burlesque. W.B Donne, when he was still Acting Examiner of Plays in the Lord Chamberlain's Office, likened burlesque to an 'impure flesh-fly' which 'battens upon the imagination' of genius only to slowly—but surely—devour it.[23] Writing to Fanny Kemble, he lamented the theatre's seemingly unstoppable impulse to 'burlesque whatsoever is good and beautiful... I want no stronger token of the decline, if not the utter decay of all dramatic feeling than this'.[24] Similarly, the critic E.S. Dallas maintained that the burlesque's 'strange prodigality of power' is 'but power all run to seed.' '[T]he dialogue is in the vernacular of the London taverns', he objected, while 'the plot is not simply improbable, it is impossible and incomprehensible'. One anonymous squib turned burlesque doggerel against itself, wondering whether 'High Art' could 'mak[e] a stand' at theatres where

> ...Robson, servile to the town,
> Discards the Actor, and adopts the Clown?
> Where Toole or Compton, perfect in his part,
> Touches each sense except the head and heart?
> Where mobs 'recall' [i.e., encore] the wit of Rogers' wig,
> Applaud a pun and recompense a jig.[25]
> (quoted in *Temple Bar* November 1871, p. 457)

As the hostility of these remarks confirms, nineteenth-century views on the perceived demerits of burlesque turned on reductive oppositions between 'high' and 'low' culture in which the burlesque could only ever be a debauched version of a classic original. Such comments, though ill-tempered, yield some insight. Admittedly, burlesques are not great plays—at least not in the ways in which their 'source' texts might be great. Their language, characters, and situations do not appear complex. Still less do they invite a compelling range of interpretation. However logical such pronouncements appear, they nonetheless conceal a flawed premise: that burlesques should be read—and judged—as 'rival' versions of their originals. Yet everything we know about parody tells us that we cannot read burlesques simply as mock versions of serious plays. Certainly, plays like *Giddy*

Godiva; or, The Girl that was Sent to Coventry (1883) are mocking; but they are neither redactions, adaptations, nor renderings—not even false renderings—of their originals. Here is the crucial distinction: an adaptation *is* the play it adapts; a burlesque *represents* the play it burlesques. A performance of Byron's *Miss Eily O'Connor* does not count as a performance of Boucicault's *The Colleen Bawn* because it is an interpretation—and not an iteration—of its source text.   The unwarranted hostility which many critics have shown toward Victorian burlesques results not from any inherent defects in the plays themselves but from a fundamentally misguided strategy of interpretation. This is not to say that no burlesque was bad. Certainly some were. But it is to say that a bad burlesque was bad in a way that has not been generally appreciated.

The Art of the Topical

For all their theatrical immediacy, burlesques nonetheless found their origins in poetry. The French satirist Paul Scarron popularized the comic genre of the mock-epic with his *Virgile Travestie en vers Burlesques* (1648-53), an adulterated classical text whose regal and aristocratic characters were transformed into stereotypes of the contemporary *bourgeoisie*. To employ the apt metaphor of travesty, we might say that Scarron's poems constituted a 'dressing down' of Virgilian heroes. In both Charles Cotton's translation of Scarron (1664-5) and Samuel Butler's *Hudibras* (1663), English burlesque authors found a poetic device easily translated into theatrical form. Yet unlike George Villiers' *The Rehearsal* (1671), which satirized the entire genre of heroic drama, nineteenth-century burlesques almost always focused upon specific plays and productions. Through a combination of the debased treatment of exalted characters as found in burlesque poetry and the self-conscious theatricality of plays like *The Rehearsal*, nineteenth-century burlesques emerged as a distinctively topical form of theatrical parody.
      By the 1840s burlesque scripts fell into a consistent pattern which remained largely unchanged until the end of the century: rhymed couplets in a parody of the original text; the transposition of characters from 'high' to 'low' (in *Tra-la la Tosca,* the painter Cavaradossi becomes Cameradossi, a photographer of *cartes de visite*); the contemporization of past events (the rock from which Arthur draws Excalibur in *Lancelot the Lovely* is a fairground 'try-your-strength' machine); the ludicrous re-enactment of classic scenes (Juliet's dog barks throughout the balcony scene in *Romeo and Juliet Travestie*); a pronounced theatrical bias, with an emphasis on stage business, sight gags, and special effects (Robson impersonated the French tightrope walker Charles Blondin in *King Alfred the Great*); relentless puns (Claude Melnotte is urged to 'pray raffle' his pre-Raphaelite painting in *The Very Latest Edition of the Lady of Lyons*);[26] and soliloquies and set pieces rewritten as lyrics to contemporary songs, whether popular, operatic, or even minstrel (the historically incorrect ditty 'Walking in the Zoo' is sung in *The Field of the Cloth of Gold*).[27]   Above all, burlesques trafficked in topical allusions, their 'catch penny stock-in-trade'.[28]   Characters, events, and scenic locations were regularly updated to conform to an audience's knowledge, if not necessarily to its experience. Burnand's mythological burlesque *Ixion* (1863) included references to Mary Elizabeth Braddon's sensation novel

Lady Audley's Secret, the racehorse 'Gladiator', Charles Kingsley's novels, and Mudie's Circulating Library. The entire plot of Robert Brough's *Medea* comically alludes to impending changes in divorce law.

As revealed in the opening scene of *Robin Hood and Richard Coeur de Lion* (1846), first performed at the Lyceum Theatre, cramming a burlesque full of topical allusions was supposed to guarantee its popularity.[29] In a parody of the witches from *Macbeth*, three playwrights (surrogates for the burlesque's three authors) encircle a large inkstand and recite their lengthy recipe for a successful burlesque:

> Tale of fairy, joke of Hood,
> Squibs from *Punch*, not understood.
> An evil Djinn, a host of sprites,
> By Coryphées in silken tights.
> Dissolving Views and Poses Plastiques,
> The Human Tripod—how unique!
> Mazourkas, Polkas, and Quadrilles,
> Keller's Muscles, Cockle's Pills
> Airs from Balfe on organ ground,
> Scraps from Shakespeare, once renowned.
> > Bubble, bubble, horrid trouble,
> > Stir up well, and Burlesque bubble.
>
> Railway jests of various uses—
> Workhouse tyrants and abuses—
> Surrey combats, scenes to tally,
> Parodies on opera-ballet.
> London slang and quaint dog-Latin—
> Ah! put that in. Yes, put that in.
> Sly allusion, only spare
> What the Licenser won't bear.
> > Bubble, bubble, toil and trouble,
> > Brains ferment, and Burlesque bubble![30]

The conceit of the *Macbeth* parody allows the writers of *Robin Hood and Richard Coeur de Lion* to compile a long list of amusing topical allusions without undertaking the much harder task of integrating those allusions into a dramatic scene. But that is just the point. The mere recitation of seemingly mindless topicalities—'Brains ferment'—suggests the additive quality of much burlesque dialogue in which allusions were heaped one upon the other without regard for logic, relevance, or narrative structure. Yet it must also be admitted that the range of topical reference in this extract is impressively varied: journalism ('*Punch*'), burlesque chorines ('Coryphées in silken tights'), panoramas and dioramas ('dissolving views'), theatrical performance ('Surrey combats'), freak shows ('The Human Tripod'), *tableaux vivants* ('Keller's Muscles'), opera and dance ('Airs from Balfe', 'Mazourkas, Polkas, and Quadrilles'), social ills represented in melodramas ('Workhouse tyrants and abuses'), literature ('Scraps from Shakespeare'), and censorship ('What the Licenser won't bear').[31]

After the dramatists' incantation, a 'small Robin Hood'—parodying the apparitions conjured for Macbeth—rises from the over-sized inkstand and presents a manuscript to Robert Keeley, the Lyceum's new manager (fol. 36b). Before vanishing, the spectre counsels him to '[b]e bold—play this, and prosper'. Not surprisingly, the script placed in Keeley's hands was a burlesque on Robin Hood—that is, the play which the Lyceum audience had come to watch. The manager agrees to produce the script and so the scene instantly changes to Sherwood Forest. This burlesque remains conscious, then, not only of topicalities and localizations but also of the circumstances of its own production. *Robin Hood and Richard Coeur de Lion* enacts its own myth of origins, assuring its audience that the performance they are about to witness will contain all the ingredients required to ensure its success.

Repetition, with Revision

Unlike more sedate theatrical forms, burlesques never rested comfortably on their laurels—if, indeed, they ever earned any. Written practically overnight, rehearsed in a week, and performed for a month or two, they were attractive only as long as they remained novel. So prized was a burlesque's novelty that theatre managers and playwrights repeatedly stressed the need to keep secret the topic of a forthcoming burlesque. 'If you have a subject in your mind for me to consider', Talfourd assured one London theatre manager from whom he sought a commission, 'it is a sacred secret with me'.[32] Similarly, when the young Burnand told Thomas Hailes Lacy that he was contemplating a burlesque on *Fair Rosamund*, he prudently reminded the theatrical publisher that the disclosure was 'strictly private'.[33]

Burlesque playwrights laboured under no illusion that their works would survive as theatrical masterpieces; rather, they laboured under a relentless pressure to churn out commissioned scripts. As Byron noted in the dedicatory letter which prefaced the acting edition of *Mazeppa* (1859), he wrote the piece 'at the eleventh hour, and in an inconceivably short time'.[34] When a burlesque's fresh topicalities and slang expressions eventually staled, productions 'updated' themselves through continual revisions, deletions, substitutions, and interpolations. In a letter to the comic actor John Clarke, the burlesque playwright Leicester Buckingham enclosed a new ending to a scene—a 'tag'—which he believed had a 'freshness about it which will be sure to make it go'.[35] Apart from newly written (or improvised) jokes, a burlesque production could be refreshed by inserting the latest popular song, imitating the idiosyncrasies of an eminent actor then starring in the West End, satirizing the stage business of a current hit production, or introducing the newest dance craze at the end of a deeply tragic scene.

Let us not, however, assume that such changes altered what was otherwise a fixed original performance. Rather, such changes *were* the performance precisely because they branded it as custom-made for its own audience. Every production was different because every audience was different. Since many of a burlesque's ever-changing novelties were left unscripted, it is difficult to compile a detailed record of how a production evolved over time. Whether in manuscripts, actors' sides, a published acting edition, or even a rare promptbook, a burlesque script provides only tantalizing hints of what the *Saturday Review* described as 'the grimace, the humorous inflections of voice, the quaint posturing, the graceful dance, light, sparkle, and colour' of the burlesque performer.[36] No burlesque text can approximate what was said, heard, or enacted in different theatrical stagings of that same text.

As its onslaught of topicalities would imply, the burlesque's principal appeal was its timeliness. Halfourd rewrote *Faust and Marguerite* at the last minute to include a parody of Kean's 'legitimate' performance as Mephistopheles in a production which had just opened at the Princess's Theatre. In the summer of 1879 the Comédie Française performed Victor Hugo's *Hernani* during its temporary engagement at the Gaiety, a playhouse better known for its devotion to the profane arts of burlesque. After the classical French troupe departed, the Gaiety's burlesque ensemble commemorated its own homecoming by staging Byron's devilish new burlesque *Handsome Hernani*. In 1884 Wilson Barrett's spectacular production of the 'toga play' *Claudian* inspired Burnand to dash off the burlesque *Paw Clawdian*, which the comedian J.L. Toole promptly produced to wide acclaim.[37] The parody was only too robust, as demonstrated by comparing a portrait of Barrett in *Claudian* with one of Toole in *Paw Clawdian* (illustrations 2 and 3). Reproduced in the sheet music for 'The Evergreen Chappie', a song Toole performed in the burlesque, the comedian's outrageous costume clearly mocks the stately classicism of Barrett's period dress. Like Barrett, Toole wears a white tunic, red cloak, and metal arm bands. But the comedian also sports a silk top hat set at a jaunty angle. Barrett's sturdy laced boots (not captured, alas, by the studio photographer) are transformed into the slender, high-heeled dancing shoes of a burlesque chorine. Notice, moreover, Toole's extravagant pose: right hand on hip, left hand extended, and left foot delicately turned out. Through Toole's incisive mimicry, the virile tragedian becomes girlishly comic.

As the foregoing examples attest, the optimum way to 'catch' some new point of topical interest was not to revive a once successful burlesque but to commission an entirely new one. While some of the most popular burlesques were revived, usually within a few years of their original productions, no single burlesque text acquired a permanent place in any theatre's repertoire. The theatre's compulsion to generate new burlesques need hardly surprise us since the very notion of a burlesque 'revival' is itself counter-intuitive. *The Theatre* compared reviving a burlesque to 'reopening a bottle of champagne that has been half emptied and corked up again. The effervescence and sparkle of the wine are found to have fled.'[38] Indeed, critical responses to revivals were generally negative. Burnand's *Diplunacy*, a parody of Sardou's *Diplomacy*, was revived fifteen years after its 1878 premiere. 'How brilliant all those mimics were in '78,' *The Theatre* happily recalled; yet 'how dull their imitators are in '93!' An 1889 revival of William Brough's *The Field of the Cloth of Gold* received only 'partial appreciation' despite having been enormously popular in its original production at the Strand.[39] 'Not a line has been cut', one reviewer tellingly observed, and 'scarcely one altered'. This reluctance to revise the text is all the more curious given that Samuel French's acting edition explicitly instructed future performers that songs 'on the Topics of the Day' are to be 'altered from time to time as

2 Wilson Barrett in the title role of W.G. Wills's *Claudian*, Princess's Theatre, London, 1884. Courtesy of The Harvard Theatre Collection, The Houghton Library

3 J.L. Toole in the title role of F.C. Burnand's *Paw Clawdian; or, the Roman Awry*, Toole's Theatre, London, 1884. Courtesy of The Harvard Theatre Collection, The Houghton Library. The image is from the sheet music for the comic song 'The Evergreen Chappie'

occasion requires'.[40] Yet no such alterations were made. To treat a burlesque as a classic—as an inviolable text—was to be false to the essentially disposable nature of burlesque. For no burlesque ever regarded anything as sacred, least of all itself.

Apart from infrequent (and often ill-advised) revivals, the more common fate of a burlesque was to have a London production lasting anywhere from a few weeks to a few months, followed by occasional spin-off productions in such provincial cities as Edinburgh, Birmingham, Manchester, or Liverpool. The two-year run of *The Very Latest Edition of Black-Eyed Susan* at the New Royalty Theatre remains a notable exception to the prevailing practice. The three-act burlesques performed at the Gaiety Theatre in the 1880s and 1890s, discussed in more detail later in this introduction, enjoyed long runs because they marked the gradual transition from old-fashioned topical burlesques to the new genre of musical comedy.[41] Yet even long-running burlesques were still updated in a calculated effort to entice back into the theatre spectators who had already seen a performance. The press, complicit in this marketing ploy, encouraged theatregoers to attend the same burlesque many times over. In an unlikely use of literary metaphors, the *Playgoer* urged those who had seen the 'first edition' of *Ruy Blas and the Blasé Roué* to see the 'second edition' because of its sprightly 'new songs, new dresses, new dances, [and] new jokes'.[42] '[I]t is like seeing a new play', the magazine rather disingenuously declared.

The Sense of Nonsense

Perhaps the most frustrating aspect of reading Victorian burlesques is that so many of their topical allusions are now unfamiliar. The perceived opacity of burlesque language has not been without consequence. Indeed, the scant scholarly attention which these comic plays have received is partly attributable to the enduring, yet erroneous perception that burlesque humour depends primarily upon comprehending long-outdated topical allusions, puns, and slang. For many students of nineteenth-century popular drama, burlesques do not warrant serious examination because over the intervening years they have become unintelligible. Consider, for example, James Ellis's view that while topicalities guarantee a burlesque's short-term notoriety they also make it 'utterly inaccessible' to later generations.[43] Indeed, many of the local references in these plays elude general comprehension. Hence, the ample footnotes which are a necessary part of this edition.

Perhaps the most incontrovertible example of how burlesques thwart our attempts to understand them is the pun. Audaciously, a pun makes a word's sound the basis for its meaning. According to the logic of punning, two words which sound alike (e.g., 'heir' and 'air') must also mean alike. In the wake of deconstruction, when the waywardness of language has been taken almost for granted, the long-reviled pun has come into its own. We thus might look upon burlesque puns not as irritations for the reader but as insights into the play itself. Whether in soliloquies or dialogue, puns were typically arranged in sequences. Such extended punning carried a cumulative effect in performance whereby each successive pun was more excruciating than the last. The audience thus experienced an ecstatic agony as the performance repeatedly carried itself to—and then retreated from—the brink of semantic collapse. The virtuosity of burlesque performers lay in their ability first to intercept a word before it landed on its accustomed meaning and then instantly to redirect it toward an entirely different meaning.

When reading a burlesque we have time to linger over its numerous puns. Since most of them were italicized in the original acting editions (to transform an auditory joke into a legible one) readers then and now could be more confident that they were not missing anything. Watching a burlesque, however, is a rather different experience. The frequency of puns and the rapid pace at which they are delivered make listening to a burlesque quite a challenge. For a burlesque aspires not to the self-congratulatory titters of spectators pleased with their own ability to 'get' the jokes (though such tittering there may be) but rather to the silence of spectators for whom the punning language of burlesque no longer signifies in a comprehensible manner. As contemporary accounts reveal, audiences frequently had trouble making sense of the dialogue. The burlesque playwright Andrew Halliday complained that '[h]alf of the puns' in burlesque performances were 'lost upon the audience owing to [the puns'] obscurity and the rapidity with which they follow upon each other's heels'.[44]

While it is undeniably true that many localizations in Victorian burlesques are no longer immediately intelligible in the twenty-first century, it is equally true that those same references have *never* been immediately intelligible. In other words, nineteenth-century burlesques began to date even in the nineteenth century. Toward the close of the Victorian era, *The Theatre* observed that as 'times alter' and 'fashions change' a burlesque's topical allusions grow 'less than pointless' (1 November 1891). Augustin Filon lamented that reading in middle age a burlesque he first enjoyed as a youth was like cutting through a 'thicket of allusions which had become enigmas'.[45] Nor should we presume that burlesques were uniformly intelligible to their original audiences. They were not. Actors flubbed their lines, authors crammed too many topical allusions into the text, and audiences did not always possess the requisite knowledge to understand all the local references. The *Era* declined to provide a plot summary of *King Queer, and his Daughters Three* (1855) because 'it would not be a very easy task to make it perfectly intelligible'.[46] Archer, after undergoing the 'penitential study' of reading several burlesque texts to learn if he had missed any 'clever writing' which had been injuriously 'gabbled' by the performers, smugly concluded that the performers had done him an unwitting favour by turning impoverished dialogue into indecipherable gibberish through their strong Cockney accents (*English Dramatists*, p. 113). The audience's awareness of its own inability to 'take in' the whole play has thus always been part of the burlesque experience. In consequence, then, any latter-day inapprehension of burlesque puns and topicalities does not depart from, but actually conforms to, historic patterns of spectating and reading. The ferocity with which critics like Archer and Dallas condemned the language of burlesque attests not to its degradation, but to its absurd exaltation. The burlesque was most splendidly itself when its word torture was most horrific.

To be sure, some spectators certainly understood some topical references and puns. It would be ludicrous to suggest that no audience ever understood anything. But I do suggest that there was never any original moment of complete spectatorial mastery which we must now struggle heroically to recover. We need not be intimidated, then, by seemingly irretrievable burlesque topicalities to the point where we forsake the plays entirely. Fragmentary, unstable, and hostile to the ascription of unitary meaning—a condition which the seeming fixity of the printed text conceals but does not overturn—burlesque language provides only the illusion of certain meaning.   In actuality, burlesques disperse meaning by implicating themselves in an extensive network of references and cross-references. The annotations provided in this volume will not—indeed, cannot—restore a burlesque's original meaning by clarifying all its references, solving all its puzzles, and answering all its riddles.   What they can do, however, is help us to engage with the texts in a more committed manner.

Life upon the Stage

Despite the enduring popular appeal of burlesques, not every London theatre wanted to stage them.   None of the nineteenth century's principal actor-managers—W.C. Macready (Covent Garden and Drury Lane), Samuel Phelps (Sadler's Wells), Charles Kean (Princess's), Henry Irving (Lyceum), and Herbert Beerbohm Tree (Her Majesty's)—ever staged a burlesque. (Early in their careers, however, both Irving and Tree had appeared in burlesques.) Covent Garden and Drury Lane, the old 'patent' houses, rarely produced burlesques, while the Haymarket did so only occasionally. Other venues which showed scant interest in burlesque were the minor theatres, saloons, music halls and penny gaffs of the East End and south London, whose repertoires were heavily slanted toward melodrama, sensation, and sing-alongs. 'Burlesques and extravaganzas have never been extremely popular on the south side of the river', a contemporary observer condescendingly noted, 'and the manager who would venture to place either of those innovations before a transpontine audience on Boxing Night would assuredly meet with the treatment that so daring an iconoclast would deserve.'[47] Indeed, an 1861 performance of Burnand's *Sappho; or, Look before you Leap* at the Standard Theatre in east London 'fell flat', one class-conscious reviewer noted, because it required a 'more erudite audience' which could be found only in a theatre 'west of Temple-bar'.[48]

The principal places where burlesques found a home in Victorian London were the handful of small theatres which occupied the 'outskirts' of the 'half-genteel' West End, most notably the Adelphi, the Olympic, and the Strand.[49] Toward the close of the nineteenth century, the Gaiety became the city's pre-eminent burlesque house.   The Adelphi, though known primarily for farce and melodrama, also regularly produced burlesques under the managerial regimes of Frederick Yates (1828-42) and Benjamin Webster (1844-74).[50]   In the 1840s, the Adelphi developed a formidable comic ensemble which included Paul Bedford, Edward Wright, and 'O.' Smith, whose gifts were displayed in such burlesques as the Brough brothers' *Frankenstein; or, the Model Man* (1849), Gilbert Abbott à Beckett and Mark Lemon's *Sardanapalus, the 'Fast' King of Assyria* (1853), and Burnand's *Helen; or, Taken from the Greek* (1866).   Despite acquiring a more respectable, middle-brow audience in the 1850s and 1860s, the Adelphi still attracted a sufficient number of London's 'fast' young men who comprised the burlesque's most loyal spectators. Wych Street, one of the dingiest thoroughfares in central London, was home to the Olympic Theatre. Under the acclaimed management of Madame Vestris (1830-9), productions of Planché's witty classical extravaganzas attracted an unexpectedly fashionable audience. After a decade of variable fortunes, the theatre prospered once more in the 1850s when Robson reached the height of his celebrity. '[N]oisome Wych-street', *Belgravia* reported, 'was crowded with West-end equipages' during the legendary comedian's 'brilliant career'.[51] Among those who crowded the theatre to see Robson were Charles Dickens, W.M. Thackeray, William Morris, Dante Gabriel Rossetti, and even Queen Victoria.

Under the lengthy management of the Swanborough family from 1858 to 1887, the Strand Theatre became more identified with burlesque than any other London theatre in the mid-Victorian era. A burlesque 'is no novelty at the Strand', one critic observed in 1864; '[i]t would be a novelty to find [the theatre] without one'.[52] In its heyday the small theatre boasted Byron as its house dramatist and a company which included such stellar burlesque artists as Marie Wilton, Ada Swanborough, Patty Oliver, James Rogers, James Bland and 'Lil'' Clarke. Marie Wilton was the Strand's principal burlesque 'boy' until 1865, when she and Byron left to assume management of the Prince of Wales's Theatre. The Gaiety Theatre stood on Wellington Street, opposite the much grander Lyceum Theatre. In 1868, on the first night of John Hollingshead's management, the theatre presented Gilbert's operatic burlesque *Robert le Diable*. Despite occasional forays into the legitimate drama, the Gaiety continued to keep alight the 'sacred lamp of burlesque' until the end of the century, even after George Edwardes succeeded Hollingshead as manager in 1886. The Gaiety's famed burlesque quartet—Farren, E.H. Royce, Edward Terry, and Kate Vaughan—reached the height of its popularity in such productions as *The Lady of Lyons Married and Settled* (1878) and *The Forty Thieves* (1880). In one ludicrous scene from *Ruy Blas and the Blasé Roué*, Farren and Leslie appeared dressed as schoolgirls. *Dramatic Notes*, in its review of *The Forty Thieves*, predicted that the four starring players 'would be remembered as pre-eminent examples of the grotesque powers developed in the modern school of extravaganza'.[53]

Through their slang, topical allusions, and domestication of character and situation, the burlesques staged at these (and other) theatres exuded a pronounced informality. How much solemnity could there be, for example, in the scene from Halliday's *Kenilworth* (1858) when Elizabeth I arrives at Greenwich as the captain of a paddle-box steamboat which bears the sign 'London Pride, One Halfpenny'?[54] Although the tone of burlesque was always informal there was never anything relaxed or casual about the performances themselves. Indeed, there were precious few moments of tranquillity in a burlesque, as confirmed by Henry Barton Baker's lively description of the end-of-scene 'breakdown' dance: a 'frantic outburst of irrepressible animal spirits' in which the performers had 'no more control over their legs than the audience had over their applause'.[55] A good burlesque possessed a certain 'go', he further explained, a 'riotous mirth' which embraced actors and audiences alike.

While a good measure of a burlesque's humour was written into the script, the success of any production rested primarily with actors who were called upon to execute an impressive range of histrionic skills in a comparatively brief performance. (Most burlesques lasted under an hour.) Burlesque actors created 'absurd effect[s]', Burnand observed, by 'uttering nonsense as if it were sense' and by effecting 'sudden transitions of manner and inflexion of voice as shall give a comic touch to situations which in themselves are serious' ('Spirit of Burlesque', p. 177). Formidable technique was required to embody this absurdity. In his 1864 series 'Theatrical Types', which first appeared in the *Illustrated Times*, T.W. Robertson offered a comprehensive appraisal of the intense demands made upon burlesque performers. Posing as the 'Theatrical Lounger', Robertson explained—not entirely facetiously—that the burlesque heroine must

> sing the most difficult of Donizetti's languid, loving melodies, as well as the inimitable Mackney's 'Oh, Rosa, how I lub you! Coodle cum!' She can warble a drawing-room ballad of the 'Daylight of the Soul' or 'Eyes melting in Gloom' school, or whistle 'When I was a-walking in Wiggleton Wale' with the shrillness and correctness of a Whitechapel bird-catcher. She is as faultless on the piano as on the bones. She can waltz, polka, dance a *pas seul* or a sailor's hornpipe, La Sylphide, or the Genu-*wine* Transatlantic Cape Cod Skedaddle, with equal grace and spirit; and as for acting, she can declaim à la Phelps or Fechter; is serious, droll; and must play farce, tragedy, opera, comedy, melodrama, pantomime, ballet, change her costume, fight a combat, make love, poison herself, die, and take one encore for a song and another for a dance, in the short space of ten minutes.[56]

Notwithstanding its hyperbolic compression of all the tasks an actress might undertake in the course of a single performance, Robertson's survey vividly captures the virtuosity required of burlesque artists. With a due degree of *amour propre*, Nellie Farren declared that burlesque acting posed unique challenges because its practitioners had to create their roles out of nearly nothing rather than simply learn them from a pre-existing script. As the star of *Very Little Hamlet* and *Monte Cristo, Jr.* proudly recounted, burlesque was

> much more difficult and exacting than the drama. In the latter an actress is given a part, and there are stage instructions and business ready for her at hand, which, after she has studied, are all plain sailing. In burlesque the actress gets a part. First there is the music, then the words of the songs to sing, and next she must make up her mind what she is to do with the song. Then there will be two or three dances to invent and learn, different to anything she has done before. Then comes the part which is frequently very sketchy, and has to be written up as you call it—'gagged,' we say. I think we deserve more credit for our work in burlesque than we get from those who know nothing of how hard we have to work to make a success.[57]

Given the singular importance of 'gagging', burlesque was never an enticing option for playwrights eager to preserve the integrity of their scripts. '[B]ut scant courtesy is paid to what authors write', *The Theatre* observed, by performers who 'introduce what they like in working up the characters, and often what originally consisted of but a few lines, develops into quite a long *rôle*'.[58] William Yardley's account of the frenzied rehearsals for his hastily-written *Very Little Hamlet* (1884) confirms the truth of that remark. When Hollingshead commissioned Yardley to write a burlesque in three scenes he stipulated that only the 'first and the third' were actually to be scripted. Yardley, to his surprise, learned that the 'second' scene

> is not to be written at all. It is to be sheer 'gag' by the Ghost, Polonius, and the King, 'with songs;' and it is required for several reasons. Firstly, there must be a 'front scene,' in order to allow the scene-shifters time to convert scene 1 into scene 3; secondly, Polonius has a topical song to introduce, and the Ghost a 'song and dance;' and thirdly, the principal boy [i.e., Nellie Farren as Hamlet] must have time to change her dress.[59]

The novice author, unaccustomed to such peculiar conventions, initially 'rebelled against the idea that [his] burlesque should be interspersed with songs, dances, and "business" from the music halls'. He found it curious that the actor playing Polonius decided to change his line 'very like a whale' to 'very like a crow upon the roof' simply to provide the cue for the interpolated topical song 'So I'm told by the Crow on the Roof'. Similarly, the actor portraying the Ghost wished to perform the music hall song 'Money'. He promptly informed the defenceless playwright that he would insert some additional business into the performance as a segue into the new musical number. Thus, the Ghost, walking downstage, explains to the audience that he haunts the battlements of Elsinore because the impoverished Danish royal exchequer cannot pay for his burial. 'Money, money is what is wanted', the still-to-be-interred Ghost insists, whereupon the orchestra strikes up the tune 'Money'. Distinguishing between the text he initially wrote and the production as it evolved during rehearsal, Yardley nervously awaited the opening of '*Very Little Hamlet*—or rather the burlesque whose identity is concealed under that title'.

Burlesque Audiences

In approaching the complex task of documenting the audience for nineteenth-century burlesques we would do well to recognize that the burlesque's 'double voice' encodes a definition of competent—and incompetent—spectators. Competent spectators possessed sufficient knowledge of the burlesque's 'sources', whether plays, novels, poems, operas, fables, history books, or contemporary events. Such knowledge enabled them to appreciate not just the manifest amusement of the burlesque's catchy songs, dances, and 'gags' but also, and more importantly, the cut and thrust of its pointedly topical parody. By contrast, incompetent spectators—that is, those who lacked the requisite foreknowledge—would be unable to fully appreciate a burlesque *as* a burlesque. If audience members had no knowledge of Irving's performance as the eponymous twins Fabien and Louis dei Franchi in *The Corsican Brothers*, for example, then they would not have completely understood Royce's performance in *The Corsican Brothers and Co., Ltd* (1880) as a burlesque on Irving. Other productions set the threshold for audience competence higher still. Richard Henry's *Lancelot the Lovely; or, the Idol of the King* (1889) featured not only parodies of Arthurian legend, but also satiric impersonations of popular music hall performers. Thus, the audience had to know something about Tennyson's epic poem *and* the latest music hall celebrities.[60] J.M. Barrie's *Ibsen's Ghost; or, Toole up to Date* (1891) incorporated parodic quotations of four Ibsen dramas: *A Doll's House*, *Ghosts*, *Hedda Gabler*, and *The Wild Duck*. A spectator unacquainted with the furore surrounding Ibsen's arrival on the London stage would have found Barrie's clever sketch both pointless and tiresome. Proponents of traditional 'high art' routinely criticize popular culture (or 'mass art') for offering an entertaining but fundamentally facile experience. By contrast, 'high art' supposedly makes more intensive demands on its audience. With respect to burlesque this distinction is hardly warranted. Although burlesques are a proudly popular form of theatre, the best of them are neither easy nor superficial. Burlesque audiences, to be sure, wore their learning lightly; but they were learned all the same.

The extent to which audiences met—or failed to meet—the various demands of 'knowingness' posed by Victorian burlesques remains unquantifiable. Yet logic alone tells us that no theatrical form can long survive if it attracts a predominantly incompetent audience. Burlesque's popularity throughout the nineteenth century indicates the continuing existence of a critical mass of knowledgeable spectators. That burlesques had little trouble finding a knowing audience need scarcely surprise us. Godfrey Turner's indiscriminate, but not atypical theatregoing in the 1840s and 1850s—he recalled attending productions at 'Drury Lane, the Haymarket, the Lyceum, the old Olympic, and the old Adelphi'—gives us a sense of just how broad the tastes of theatre audiences were.[61] Before the triumph of the 'long run' in the closing decades of the century, the repertory system enabled audiences to witness an enormous range of productions within a single theatrical season, let alone over a lifetime of playgoing. For spectators unable to keep up with every play and performance, second-hand experiences were just as valuable. Newspapers and periodicals, whose number increased exponentially in the second half of the century, featured theatrical reviews and extended essays on acting, playwrighting, and the morality of the stage. Actors and actresses were endlessly photographed for widely displayed and circulated *cartes de visites*. These popular items memorialized performances which their owners may never have attended. Similarly, the mass publication of acting editions of contemporary plays enabled stage-struck amateurs to pore over the scripts of plays they might not have seen in a 'legitimate' performance yet might see in a burlesque version. There were indeed many ways to become a competent burlesque spectator.

But just who were these competent spectators? Standard histories of the Victorian theatre generally claim that London's educated middle classes comprised the burlesque's core audience.[62] The claim is correct as far as it goes since the middle class was indeed likely to possess the knowledge needed to make them competent spectators. (Some nineteenth-century burlesque playwrights, including Burnand and Talfourd, were university educated.)[63] But it wrongly assumes that the Victorian middle class was itself a singular category. What social historians long believed was a stable, coherent entity actually comprised 'diverse social groupings', Patrick Joyce has explained, 'split among economic, social, political, and religious lines'.[64] Who belonged to the middle class was, moreover, a question not simply of demographics, but of ethics. Dror Wahrman has argued that the Victorian middle class, as a moral and cultural force, was principally an 'imagined constituency': a mythologized vision of how *all* members of society should conduct their private lives.[65] To think of the middle class as having a precise social referent would thus be to diminish the pervasive influence of its moral precepts. The variety of experiences, actual or imagined, which might all be termed 'middle-class' suggests that we cannot expect *any* class-based reception of Victorian theatrical productions to have been either uniform or predictable.

A further objection lies in the incongruity of the moral values associated with the middle class (presuming that we can still speak of such a group) and the burlesque stage. Perhaps the most cherished Victorian value was respectability, one which the legitimate theatre wholeheartedly embraced for itself as a cultural institution, for the acting profession, and even for the social standing of its audiences. Yet no nineteenth-century comic genre—burlesque, pantomime, extravaganza, or farce—ever respected the decorum of theatres managed by such eminent tragedians as Macready, Kean, and Irving. Unlike the productions which they satirized, Victorian burlesques never formed part of middle-class attempts to educate mass audiences through mass culture. Indeed, anyone sympathetic to burlesques would be more inclined to question—not affirm—the values associated with legitimate culture. Were it otherwise, there would be no need for burlesque.

As its detractors tirelessly asserted, burlesque contributed nothing to the education or morals of its audience. In fact, it was perceived as an agent of corruption. When W.B. Donne, as the Examiner of Plays, urged the government to provide 'recreations which may divert the masses from sensual indulgence and specious temptations', he regarded burlesque not as the wholesome cure but as the pernicious affliction.[66] These 'foul excrescences' of the stage, he insisted, jeopardized the theatre's mission to provide much-needed 'rational entertainment'.[67] A decade earlier, an outraged reader of the *Theatrical Times* raised the call to 'shame the public' out of the 'indecency' of burlesque.[68] The informality, mockery, and nonsense of the burlesque stage could only ever be at cross purposes with the legitimate theatre's stalwart efforts to be recognized as respectable. Even when the Olympic attracted an increasingly fashionable audience at mid-century it was still a 'nasty place to leave after the performance'.[69]

A key term for understanding the burlesque's refusal to endorse middle-class respectability is 'fast': Victorian slang for a flamboyant disregard of the conventional, the expected, and the customary. For those anxious to safeguard their own respectability, the epithet 'fast' implied more than a hint of moral censure. As one incensed reader of the *Theatrical Times* remarked in 1848, burlesques—the 'offspring' of 'Fast Men'—comprised nothing more than 'incidents at once absurd and improbable' and 'characters that are all outrageous and indecent caricatures'.[70]   As such impassioned invective presumes, 'fastness' was a toxin which quickly spread throughout the entire theatrical establishment, contaminating not only playwrights, but also actors and audiences.   Burlesque characters frequently identified themselves as 'swells', 'men about town', and other variants of the 'fast' man.   In Halfourd's *Faust and Marguerite*, the orchestra plays 'I love to be a swell' as Faust and Mephistopheles 'strut grotesquely across stage' (p. 17).   When Claude Melnotte, the hero of Byron's *The Very Latest Edition of the Lady of Lyons* (1859), disguises himself as the Prince of Como he assumes 'the modern fast-man's manner' (p. 16).

Demographic changes in the mid-nineteenth century effectively consolidated London's bachelor sub-culture, enabling 'fast' men to emerge as a highly visible urban constituency.   With a suburban railway network fully in place by the 1850s, middle-class families relocated from the West End and the City of London to the suburban regions of Islington, Highgate, Clapham, and even Richmond.   As these families moved out, single young men moved in.   These educated bachelors could also be the sons who stayed behind as the rest of their families decamped to the suburbs.   In consequence of these population changes, the West End and its environs housed a growing number of 'men about town' who had professional careers, disposable income, leisure time, and few domestic responsibilities.   Since many of these men lived in 'chambers and lodgings', as Walter Besant observed in his monumental survey of London, they had neither the means nor the desire to entertain at home.[71]   Their leisure pursuits were predominantly public, whether in clubs, theatres, or song-and-supper rooms like The Coal Hole and The Cider Cellars.   The *Era* described them as 'young gentlemen who float about town after nine o'clock cogitating where they shall invest their odd shilling in exchange for a little fun'.[72]   The magazine advised them to seek their 'fun' in attending burlesques.

The 'fast' young man's insatiable desire for pleasure certainly contrasted with the sober diligence of his more earnest elders.   It was by virtue of its own profligacy (immorality would be too strong a word) that the burlesque's core audience understood itself to be a dissenting one.   And burlesque itself was a favoured means for articulating that dissent from dominant cultural and social hierarchies.   Ultimately, the most distinctive feature of the burlesque audience was not its socio-economic profile, which can never be precisely documented, but the wayward disposition of its values.   Consider the following case, extreme though it is.   Edward Boulton and Frederick Park were arrested in 1870 under the Vagrancy Act as they left the Strand Theatre after attending a performance of Burnand's burlesque *St. George and the Dragon*.   Their crime was having appeared in public in women's clothing.   In the weeks leading up to their arrest Boulton and Park had attended several London theatres in drag, displaying a strong preference for burlesque: that is, for productions which nearly always featured cross-dressing.   Jim Davis, in a provocative essay, speculates that late-Victorian burlesques may well have attracted a 'specifically homosexual following'.[73]   The Boulton and Park case vividly demonstrates that the burlesque theatre conferred upon its spectators a license to transgress social norms, only one of which was heterosexuality.   To be sure, burlesque was both a cause and effect of social non-conformity.   And thus the *experience* of watching a burlesque needs to be set alongside other more or less disreputable practices as late-night carousing, attending illegal prizefights at secret locations outside London, smoking clay pipes in the streets, playing billiards, reading the gossip columns in *Bell's Life in London*, and public transvestism.

The unconventionality of burlesque spectators extended equally to the playwrights, almost none of whom derived a steady or substantial income from theatrical work. Most of them lived from hand to mouth, relying on the equivalent of dramatic and journalistic piecework: short plays, theatrical and literary reviews, essays and sketches. Talfourd, author of such burlesques as *Alcestis, the Original Strong-minded Woman* (1850) and *Shylock; or, the Merchant of Venice Preserved* (1853), was the 'most irregular of irregular livers' (Burnand, *Records and Reminiscences*, I, p. 387). The dashing young playwright, Burnand recalled, 'would dine when others breakfasted, and breakfast when other men dined'. A few months before his death, bedridden and coughing up blood, the impoverished author still tried to gain a commission to write a Christmas burlesque.[74] Robert Brough led an even more erratic life, having been born with a 'slop-work constitution'.[75] In Hollingshead's poignant character sketch, Brough appears 'as a lost soul, an awful example, a misguided being'. After his untimely death in 1860 at the age of thirty-two, Brough's fellow members of the Savage Club organized a charity performance of his burlesque of *The Tempest* (co-written with his brother William) to aid his destitute widow and three children. Talfourd, who played Caliban, would be dead two years later.

Censorship

Under the Licensing Act of 1737, no new play could be performed at a licensed theatre in Britain without the approval of the Lord Chamberlain. These powers of censorship, which remained in effect until 1968, were largely delegated to the Examiner of Plays. In the Victorian era, this office was held by Charles Kemble (1836-40), his son, John Mitchell Kemble (1840-57), W.B. Donne (1857-74), E.F.S. Piggott (1874-95), and George Alexander Redford (1895-1912). Donne also served as Acting Examiner between 1846 and 1856, thus making him the principal figure in the licensing and censorship of nineteenth-century drama. 'To strike out personal names, when they affect rank, office, or private character, I shall consider essential,' Donne asserted in 1872; '[w]hen allusions to, or censure on public measures, of *recent* date are introduced I shall direct them to be omitted in representation'.[76] The Victorian theatre was largely self-regulating, however; and the vast majority of plays submitted for licensing were neither censored nor revised. Theatre managers generally did not send the Examiner a script which included representations, whether serious or satiric, of biblical characters, the Queen and the Royal family, foreign dignitaries, contemporary politicians, or even theatrical celebrities. The unofficial, but more authoritative force of public morality no doubt wielded its own inhibiting power.

Of course there were exceptions. On the opening night of the Brough brothers' *Olympus in a Muddle; or, Wrong People in Wrong Places* (1855), the actors stumbled over their lines because so many had been cut at the last minute by the Examiner of Plays. The *Era* complained that the forced removal of the burlesque's 'political' jokes rendered the production 'almost useless as regards its primary intention'.[77] Also censored was the following satiric reference to Charles Kean in Buckingham's burlesque *William Tell* (1857):

> Tell me of something that will make one sad.
> See Kean play Hamlet, that will do it, lad.
> Oh! dear! that remedy's much too severe,
> My nerves would never stand the shock, I fear.[78]

Yet as everyone in theatrical world, including the Examiner of Plays, knew only too well, censoring a script was not the same thing as censoring a performance. Objectionable dialogue might be cut from the script yet could still be spoken on the stage. New dialogue, moreover, could be introduced at any time during a play's run. And the many non-textual elements of acting—pose, gesture, inflection, and expression—could never be effectively censored. Burlesques thus had a comparatively easy time of avoiding stringent censorship. 'There may be no immorality in the actual words of the burlesques', a disapproving Archer conceded, but actors would nonetheless 'introduce immorality into the chaste framework' of the otherwise innocent script (*English Dramatists*, p. 112). 'Any coarse allusion or personal insult to those in authority over us', Planché candidly admitted, 'may be, and *has been*, foisted into a burlesque or a pantomime after its performance has been sanctioned by the licenser.'[79] The allusions to General Sir Robert Napier's victory in the Abyssinian War that appear in the acting edition of *The Field of the Cloth of Gold* could not have been part of the script originally submitted to the Lord Chamberlain, as Martin Meisel has helpfully pointed out, because Napier's victory occurred two day *after* the play had opened.[80]

It was not so much that the censors were lenient, then, as that a burlesque script never fully correlated with the actuality of its performance. The constant updating of a burlesque's topical allusions could only frustrate any effort to censor the performance. The 'hits' of burlesque acting—the interjected asides and allusions—allowed satire, and especially political satire, to be easily incorporated into a performance. In 1871 the *Era* affirmed that the Examiner of Plays routinely eliminated 'personal and political allusions from our Burlesques and Pantomimes' *and* that 'no Burlesque or Pantomime has been produced which has not been full of such allusions'.[81] No sooner does the censor strike out political allusions in a burlesque script than the theatre manager restores them in performance. This is not to say that such performances were necessarily subversive or obscene. But it is to say that the essentially 'open' nature of burlesque endowed performances with an air of inhibition and unpredictability not found in other, more regularized types of theatre.

Sometimes objections were raised to various aspects of a performance which deviated from the licensed script. In 1869 Lord Sydney, the Lord Chamberlain, sent a circular to London theatre managers condemning the 'impropriety of costume' worn by pantomime and burlesque actresses.[82] The condemnation was in vain. The dresses of the ladies in the *corps de ballet* were not lengthened because the managers knew it was better to incur Lord Sydney's displeasure rather than that of the 'Johnnies' who purchased tickets night after night to watch burlesque. In a contrasting instance, the stage history of Gilbert's *The Happy Land* (1873) demonstrates the Lord Chamberlain's power to rescind a theatrical licence. Written under the *nom de plume* 'F. Latour Tomline', *The Happy Land* was Gilbert's parody of his own play *The Wicked World*. In many respects the burlesque was a non-stop political allusion since it featured personalized representations of the Prime Minister (W.E. Gladstone), the Chancellor of the Exchequer (Viscount Sherbrooke), and the Commissioner of the Board of Works (A.S. Ayrton). Donne, the Examiner of Plays, knew none of this since the script he approved was not the script which was ultimately used. The burlesque opened at the Court Theatre on 3 March 1873. Eighteen pages of unlicensed material were performed. The Prince of Wales, who attended the opening performance, complained to the Lord Chamberlain about what he thought were indecent political allusions. Four nights later, the Lord Chamberlain banned the play. Once revised, however, *The Happy Land* was put back on the stage. But even then the play's parodic edge was sharpened since, as one critic observed, 'increased power was given to the satire by the deferential tone in which the actors touched dangerous words and awkward subjects'.[83] Damned if you censor, and damned if you do not.

Objections were also voiced by 'legitimate' tragedians whose acting styles were mocked by burlesque impersonators. Disowning his own youthful burlesque performances, Irving was particularly sensitive to being imitated by low comedians. In the interpolated *Pas de Quatre* from *Ruy Blas and the Blasé Roué*, four burlesque actors dressed as ballerinas impersonated four leading actors of the day (Barrett, Irving, Arthur Roberts, and Toole) with their faces made up to look like the theatrical celebrities. Only Irving took offence at the Gaiety's production. In a stern letter to Fred Leslie, the comedian who burlesqued him, he objected to being 'put in women's clothes' and demanded the 'immediate withdrawal' of the insulting 'exhibition'.[84] Edwardes, the Gaiety's manager, generated free publicity for his theatre by leaking the story to the London press. Irving, in retaliation, persuaded the Lord Chamberlain to enforce the clause in the Gaiety's licence which prohibited impersonations of public figures. The squabble ended when Edwardes, under compulsion, agreed that Leslie would no longer appear in the *Pas de Quatre* made up to resemble Irving. A caricature of the time depicts the Lyceum actor-manager turning the megaphone of 'potted burlesque' upside down to silence Leslie's impersonation (illustration 4). All that remains visible of the Gaiety comedian are his dangling hands and his petticoats. Yet the burlesque enjoyed the last laugh since Leslie continued to mimic the distinctive mannerisms of the petulant Irving. He performed the dance wearing a veil—a blatant image of censorship—which only made his covert impersonation more amusing.[85] The Gaiety audience would clamour for Leslie to mimic Irving, whereupon the actor would peer out from his silken veil and slyly whisper—to even greater laughter—'No, I mustn't'. Irving, who did his utmost to muffle the burlesque, succeeded only in amplifying it.

From Burlesque to Musical Comedy

While burlesques performed in the mid-nineteenth century robustly engaged with contemporary drama, burlesques written later in the century began to retreat from

An Incident of 1889.

4 'An Incident of 1889' Henry Irving and his burlesque impersonator, Fred Leslie. Courtesy of The Harvard Theatre Collection, The Houghton Library

such pointed critical interventions. Indeed, a good number of late-Victorian burlesques grew increasingly detached from their ostensible source texts and so were less inclined to 'fling [the] follies' of the legitimate theatre in its face. To describe a performance as a 'burlesque' had become misleading, the *Gentleman's Magazine* complained in 1872, because in so many such performances 'nothing is burlesqued'.[86] These so-called burlesques 'entertain by mumming simply'. Burlesques gradually forfeited their critical capacities and rebranded themselves as eroticized 'leg pieces'. Byron punningly observed that such performances consisted of 'all legs and no tale' (quoted in Burnand, 'Spirit of Burlesque', p. 182). Farren's costume from *Little Jack Sheppard* (1885), depicted in illustration 5, seems little more than an excuse to accentuate the actress's tiny waist and to display her slender legs. Mary Ann Keeley, the original Jack Sheppard, enjoyed the Gaiety production but complained that it relied too heavily on 'up-to-date music-hall business'.[87] In a similar vein, Archer waspishly reported that burlesques had sunk to the level of 'music-hall imbecility'.[88] G.A. Sala, more stridently still, ranted that the new burlesque style amounted to little more than 'semi-obscene dances' performed by half-naked 'jiggling hussies'.[89] As the *Saturday Review* observed in its account of *Lancelot the Lovely*,

> [b]urlesque is the one species of dramatic work that seems to us to have lately fallen off. That its fall has been great we will not pretend, for the reason that its estate was never particularly high... The whole style of burlesque has completely changed of late years. Either audiences do not want, or else authors cannot provide, witty or pointed dialogue, comic situations or incident. These strong features, as they used to be considered, are now altogether ignored, the one object of writers being to find a character in which a favorite low comedian may display his eccentricities.[90]

No theatre contributed more to the transformation of burlesque from theatrical parody to something approximating musical comedy than the Gaiety. Starting with Hollingshead's successful management, the Gaiety produced such comic plays as *Ariel* (1883), *Faust up to Date* (1888) *Frankenstein* (1887), *Little Robin Hood* (1882) and *Monte Cristo, Jr.* (1886), all of which acknowledged a source text but none of which engaged in sustained parody. These increasingly nominal burlesques had effectively lost their 'double voice'. *Dramatic Notes* disappointingly observed in its review of *Ariel* that except for 'the name borrowed from Shakespeare's *Tempest*, no one would have known there was any connection between the burlesque and the poet's enchanting creation'.[91] There 'was certainly nothing even distantly Shakespearian' in Nellie Farren's starring performance; 'she might have been Aladdin as much as Ariel'. Similarly, the *Playgoer* protested that *Faust up to Date* should be called *Forced up to Date* because '[n]o effort is made to burlesque any one or anything at all'.[92] With particular reference to Gaiety productions, Percy Fitzgerald noted that because 'modern' burlesques no longer followed 'strict rules' they had become 'disconnected' and 'tedious'.[93] To be sure, not all critics espoused such a negative view. No one 'wants a plot in a

MISS FARREN.
AS "JACK SHEPPARD"

COPYRIGHT.

Stereoscopic Co

110 & 108, REGENT ST.
& 54, CHEAPSIDE.

5 Nellie Farren in the title role of Henry P. Stephens' *Little Jack Sheppard*, Gaiety Theatre, London, 1885. Courtesy of The Harvard Theatre Collection, The Houghton Library

Gaiety burlesque', *The Bat* freely declared; no one 'cares whether Miss Farren is called Frankenstein or Robinson Crusoe'.[94]   When Edwardes, formerly of the D'Oyly Carte company at the Savoy Theatre, succeeded Hollingshead as the Gaiety's manager, the movement toward musical comedy became even more pronounced.

In turning their backs on traditional parodic conventions some burlesques began to imitate the increasingly lavish production values of the legitimate stage. Burlesques lengthened from one act to three acts, and so became the main—and sometimes only—feature on an evening's bill.   The songs as well as the lyrics were composed especially for a particular production, the scenery became more elaborate, the dances more intricate, and the costumes more revealing.   As burlesque productions changed, so did their audiences.   Hollingshead's account of the Gaiety 'masher' who 'comes night after night, week after week, to see the burlesque' and who 'knows every line and every air in the piece' disclosed just how markedly audience expectations had changed.   Spectators of an earlier generation did not witness the same burlesque 'night after night' if only because no single burlesque held the stage for more than a few months.   Variety—not consistency—had been central to the audience's experience.

But all that was changing.   In 1883, the magazine *Time* observed with some equanimity that

> burlesques of the period, whatever their shortcomings as literary compositions, do well enough for the audience, for the simple reason that the *habitués* of the theatre at which these are produced go less to hear than to see. Effects of scene and costume, of pose and figure, blended with effects of sound, are quite enough to secure a stage success.[95]

By the turn of the century, burlesque had transformed itself from theatrical parody into theatrical entertainment in its own right.   That entertainment, as its own traditions and conventions developed, came to be known as musical comedy.   Cut off from its origins in satire, the label 'burlesque' survived as the poor relation of vaudeville and variety, eventually becoming synonymous with striptease and sleaze. Yet for most of the Victorian age, as this introductory essay has tried to document, burlesque ranked high among the most critically ingenious offerings of an irrepressibly popular theatre.

Notes

[1]Unattributed newspaper clipping, 6 May 1865, Theatrical Miscellany Scrapbook 10, Folger Shakespeare Library, Washington, DC.

[2] The manuscripts of plays originally submitted to the Lord Chamberlain for licensing are now divided between the Larpent Collection at the Henry Huntington Library (plays licensed between 1737 and 1823) and the British Library (plays licensed between 1824 and 1968). After the passage of the Theatres Act of 1968 plays have no longer been submitted to the Lord Chamberlain.

[3] Michael Booth's five-volume *English Nineteenth-Century Plays* (Oxford: Clarendon Press, 1969-76) contains only two burlesques—*The Enchanted Isle* (1848) and *The Field of the Cloth of Gold* (1858)—neither of which parodies a nineteenth-century

play. Stanley Wells' five-volume *Nineteenth-Century Shakespeare Burlesques* (London: Diploma Press, 1977) includes, as its title indicates, only parodies of Shakespeare's plays.

[4] For the sake of etymological precision, it bears remembering that parody is a Greek term (*parodia*) whose first recorded usage, in Aristotle's *Poetics*, refers to mock-epics. Burlesque, by contrast, is an early-modern term which derives from the Italian *burla*, meaning to ridicule or to joke. Travesty—meaning to dress up—is an even later term, first used to describe the mock-epic poetry produced in seventeenth-century France.

[5] *The Spectator* 15 December 1711; quoted in Donald F. Bond, ed. *The Spectator* 5 vols. (Oxford: Clarendon Press, 1965), II, pp. 467-8.

[6] Charles Cowden-Clarke, 'On the Comic Writers of England. VII.—Burlesque Writers', *Gentleman's Magazine* n.s. 5th 7 (June-December 1871), p. 557.

[7] Simon Trussler, ed., *Burlesque Plays of the Eighteenth Century* (Oxford: Oxford University Press, 1969); John Jump, *Burlesque* (London: Methuen, 1972); and Simon Dentith, *Parody* (London: Routledge, 2000).

[8] Mikhail Bakhtin, 'Discourse in the Novel', in *The Dialogic Imagination*, ed. Michael Holquist and trans. Caryl Emerson and Michael Holquist (Austin: The University of Texas Press, 1981), p. 324.

[9] F.C. Burnand, 'The Spirit of Burlesque', *The Universal Review* 2.6 (September-December 1888), p. 171.

[10] W.C. Macready and John Philip Kemble were, respectively, among the most prominent tragedians of the early-Victorian and late-Georgian theatre.

[11] H. J. Byron, *Ali Baba; or, The Thirty-Nine Thieves* (London: Thomas Hailes Lacy, n.d.), p. 10.

[12] John Halfourd, *Faust and Marguerite; or, The Devil's Draught* (London: Thomas Hailes Lacy, n.d.), p. 6.

[13] *The Spectator* 30 April 1853.

[14] *Lloyd's Weekly London Newspaper* 8 May 1853.

[15] G.A. Sala, *Robson: A Sketch* (London: John Camden Hotten, 1864), p. 49. Since Ristori did not understand English, the burlesque's puns and nonsensical dialogue were entirely lost upon her. Had she known English, she might not have been so easily duped.

[16] *The Theatre* 2 July 1883. 'With singular felicity [Burnand] sees the ludicrous points of every serious performance, and boils down the most tremendously tragic play into a concentrated essence of fun'.

[17] *The Camp at the Olympic*, in *Plays by James Robinson Planché*, ed. Donald Roy (Cambridge: Cambridge University Press, 1986), p. 182.

[18] Michele Hannoosh, 'The Reflexive Function of Parody', *Comparative Literature* 41.2 (Spring 1989), p. 114.

[19] Unattributed poem (*c.* 1861), quoted in *Temple Bar* (November 1871), pp. 456-7.

[20] 'A Word about Our Theatres', *Fraser's Magazine* 57 (February 1858), p. 233.

[21] William Archer, *English Dramatists of To-Day* (London: Sampson Low, 1882), p. 113.

[22] The 'disregard' of 'H's refers to the dropped initial '/h/' in the Cockney dialect which most burlesque performers used.

[23] W.B. Donne, 'Dramatic Register for 1853', *Quarterly Review* 95 (June 1854), p. 87.

[24] W.B. Donne, a letter to Frances Anne Kemble, 17 July 1856, W.b. 598, fol. 239, Folger Shakespeare Library, Washington, DC.

[25] The poem alludes to the actors Frederick Robson, J.L. Toole, Henry Compton, and James Rogers. Well-known for performing cross-dressed roles in Strand burlesques,

Rogers played the Nurse in Andrew Halliday's *Romeo and Juliet Travestie* (1859) and the title role in a revival of Byron's *Miss Eily O'Connor* (1861).

[26] H.J. Byron, *The Very Latest Edition of the Lady of Lyons* (London: Thomas Hailes Lacy, n.d.), p. 12.

[27] T.W. Robertson, in his series 'Theatrical Types', imagined an only too plausible *contretemps* during a burlesque rehearsal when the rival actresses Miss Gigwell and Miss Oddjaws fall out over who will introduce the new song 'Ribstone Pippins'. Both performers are enamoured of the absurd refrain: 'Rip-pip-pip, my rip-pip-pip,/ My rip-pip-pipstone pippins,/ Rip-pip-pip-pi-pip, rip-pip-pip-pi-pip-ip-pip-ip-pip,/ My ribstone pip-ip-pippins'. 'The "Ribstone Pippin" difficulty for a long time agitates the theatre', Robertson anxiously relates. 'Negotiations fail, a congress is held, and eventually a compromise effected. "Ribstone Pippins" is sung as a duet. On Boxing Night the audience demanded its repetition and its re-repetition.' Quoted in T. Edgar Pemberton, *The Life and Writings of T.W. Robertson* (London: Richard Bentley, 1893), pp. 115-16.

[28] Review of W. Davenport Adams, *A Book of Burlesque*, *The Theatre* 1 November 1891.

[29] Joachim Stocqueler, Shirley Brooks, and Charles Kenny, *Robin Hood and Richard Coeur de Lion* (1846) British Library Add Ms 42,994, fols. 34-53.

[30] Quoted in *The Theatre* 1 November 1882. The manuscript submitted to the Lord Chamberlain includes most of the second verse, but none of the first (fol. 36b). Since the script was never published, *The Theatre's* critic must have had access to a promptbook or an actor's 'side'.

[31] 'The Human Tripod' was a three-legged child on display at a bazaar in Regent Street. Keller was a male model who performed at the Vauxhall Gardens and the Egyptian Hall.

[32] Francis Talfourd, a letter, 5 August 1861, uncatalogued manuscript, Harvard Theatre Collection, Houghton Library.

[33] F.C. Burnand, a letter to Thomas Hailes Lacy, 13 January 1862, uncatalogued manuscript, Harvard Theatre Collection, Houghton Library.

[34] H.J. Byron, *Mazeppa! A Burlesque Extravaganza* (London: Thomas Hailes Lacy, n.d.), p. 5.

[35] Leicester Buckingham, a letter to John Clarke, 12 April 1867, uncatalogued manuscript, Harvard Theatre Collection, Houghton Library.

[36] Review of W. Davenport Adams, *A Book of Burlesque*, *Saturday Review* 18 July 1891.

[37] Toole impersonated Barrett. The burlesque was so popular that the Princess's company, under Barrett's leadership, attended a performance (*Under the Clock* 23 April 1884). Toole even took out an advertisement burlesquing John Ruskin's approving comments on Barrett's *Claudian*. In Toole's fanciful account from the fictitious *Mall Pall Gazette*, the erstwhile art critic confessed that he had 'been turned out of the house no less than three-and-thirty times, in consequence of the positive uproar of hilarity I have created out of pure enjoyment of it'. Toole's Theatre, advertisement, May 1884, quoted in *Under the Clock* 14 May 1884.

[38] Review of *Little Jack Sheppard*, Gaiety Theatre, London, *The Theatre* 1 September 1894. Seymour Hicks, who co-authored and starred in *Under the Clock*, made his Gaiety debut in this production.

[39] *The Theatre* 1 February 1890.

[40] William Brough, *The Field of the Cloth of Gold. An Original Grand Historical Extravaganza* (London: Samuel French, n.d.), p. 30. Among the original topical allusions were the trip of the Prince and Princess of Wales to Ireland, Queen Victoria's public appearances, the Oxford-Cambridge boat race, spirit rapping, and laws on the Sunday opening of public houses.

[41] *Monte Cristo, Jr.* ran for over a hundred nights, *Faust up to Date* for nearly two hundred, and *Carmen up to Date* for almost two hundred and fifty.

[42] *Playgoer* 15 May 1890.

[43] James Ellis, 'The Counterfeit Presentment: Nineteenth-Century Burlesques of *Hamlet*', *Nineteenth Century Theatre Research* 11.1 (Summer 1983), p. 29.

[44] Andrew Halliday, 'Burlesques', *Cornhill Magazine* 4 (August 1861), p. 176.

[45] Augustin Filon, *The English Stage* (London: John Milne, 1897), p. 95.

[46] *Era* 15 April 1855.

[47] Unattributed newspaper clipping, December 1864, Theatrical Miscellany Scrapbook 10, Folger Shakespeare Library, Washington, DC. 'Transpontine'—i.e., across the bridge—was the condescending epithet used by the West End theatrical establishment to describe south London theatres and theatre audiences.

[48] Unattributed newspaper clipping, F.C. Burnand file, Harvard Theatre Collection, Houghton Library.

[49] Otto Wenckstern, *Saunterings in and about London* (London: Nathaniel Cooke, 1853), p. 265.

[50] The comedian Charles Mathews was joint proprietor of the Adelphi between 1828 and 1835.

[51] Walter Thornbury, 'London Theatres and London Actors. VI', *Belgravia* 9 (1869), p. 466.

[52] Unattributed newspaper clipping, 27 December 1864, Theatrical Miscellany Scrapbook 10, Folger Shakespeare Library, Washington, DC.

[53] *Dramatic Notes* December 1880, p. 73.

[54] Andrew Halliday, *Kenilworth; or, Ye Queene, Ye Earle, and Ye Maydenne* (London: Thomas Hailes Lacy, n.d.), p. 26.

[55] H. Barton Baker, *History of the London Stage* 2nd edn. (London: G. Routledge & Sons, Ltd, 1904), p. 448. Michael Booth describes a 'breakdown' dance as an 'extraordinarily lively shuffle, with vigorous and often grotesque arm and body movements'. In a 'cellar-flap' breakdown, the dancer's feet remained fixed on the same spot while the arms and torso gyrated madly. Michael Booth, *Prefaces to English Nineteenth-Century Theatre* (Manchester: Manchester University Press, 1980), p. 187. The 'cellar-flap' dance was originally performed on the trap door which led to the cellar of a public house. The wood of the trap door set into the floor had better acoustic value than the floor itself.

[56] *Illustrated Times* 23 April 1864.

[57] 'Topical Interviews. No. 88. Miss Nelly Farren', unattributed newspaper clipping, bound in *The Theatre* n.s. 7 (July-December 1880), Folger Shakespeare Library, Washington, DC.

[58] Review of *Carmen up to Date*, Gaiety Theatre, London, *The Theatre*, 1 November 1890.

[59] William Yardley, 'My Burlesque', *St. James's Gazette*, clipping in the Folger Shakespeare Library, Washington, DC.

[60] Review of *Lancelot the Lovely*, Avenue Theatre, London, *The Theatre* 1 May 1889.

[61] Godfrey Turner, 'First Nights of My Young Days', *The Theatre* 1 September 1887.

[62] See, for example, Booth, *Prefaces*, p. 150.

[63] Talfourd's *Macbeth* burlesque was first performed in 1847 when its author was still an Oxford undergraduate. Burnand attributed the harsh reviews of his first burlesque, *Ixion*, to the presence in the opening-night audience of members of Cambridge's Amateur Dramatic Club, who, out of a misplaced desire to encourage the author, 'overdid the applause'. F.C. Burnand, *Records and Reminiscences* 2 vols (London: Methuen & Co., 1904), I, p. 375. By contrast, the Brough brothers were the products of

working-class Liverpool. Robert Brough, particularly, was sceptical of men who boasted a university education.
[64] Patrick Joyce, *Democratic Subjects* (Cambridge: Cambridge University Press, 1994), p. 164.
[65] Dror Wahrman, *Imagining the Middle Class* (Cambridge: Cambridge University Press, 1995), p. 263.
[66] W.B. Donne, 'Popular Amusements', *Westminster Review* (July 1856), reprinted in *Essays on the Drama* (London: John W. Parker and Son, 1858), p. 256.
[67] W.B. Donne, 'Plays and Their Providers', *Fraser's Magazine* (September 1853), reprinted in *Essays on the Drama*, p. 83.
[68] *Theatrical Times* 2 December 1846.
[69] 'One of the Old Brigade', *London of the Sixties* (London: Everett & Co., 1909), p. 64.
[70] *Theatrical Times* 28 October 1848.
[71] Walter Besant, *London in the Nineteenth Century* (London: A&C Black, 1909), p. 262.
[72] Review of *The Corkonian Brothers*, Strand Theatre, London, *Era* 12 March 1854. Like other aspects of 'fast' life, burlesque playwrighting was a young man's game. Robert Brough was twenty when *The Enchanted Isle* opened at the Adelphi Theatre in 1848, as was Talfourd when his *Macbeth Travestie* opened at the Strand that same year.
[73] Jim Davis, 'Androgynous Cliques and Epicene Colleges', *Nineteenth Century Theatre Research* 26.1 (Summer 1998), p. 59.
[74] Francis Talfourd, a letter, 5 August 1861, uncatalogued manuscript, Harvard Theatre Collection, Houghton Library.
[75] John Hollingshead, *My Lifetime* 2 vols (London: Sampson Low, Marston & Co., 1895), I, p. 84.
[76] Lord Chamberlain's paper, 1:263, 14 November 1872, quoted in John Russell Stephens, *The Censorship of English Drama 1824-1901* (Cambridge: Cambridge University Press, 1980), p. 119.
[77] *Era* 26 August 1855.
[78] Leicester Buckingham, *William Tell* (1857), quoted in Stephens, *Censorship*, p. 183 n. 4.
[79] J.R. Planché, *Recollections and Reflections* 2 vols. (London, 1872), II, p. 109.
[80] Martin Meisel, 'Political Extravaganza: A Phase of Nineteenth-Century British Theater', *Theatre Survey* 3 (1962), p. 23.
[81] *Era* 14 January 1872.
[82] Lord Chamberlain's Office, 28 January 1869, quoted in Theatrical Miscellany scrapbook 19, fol. 95, Folger Shakespeare Library, Washington, DC.
[83] *Manchester Guardian* 10 March 1873, quoted in Tracy C. Davis, *The Economics of the British Stage, 1800-1914* (Cambridge: Cambridge University Press, 2000), p. 146.
[84] Austin Brereton, *The Life of Henry Irving* 2 vols (London: Longmans, Green, and Co., 1908), II, p. 157.
[85] Seymour Hicks, *Twenty-five Years of an Actor's Life* (London: C. Arthur Pearson, 1912), p. 48.
[86] 'Players of Our Day. Burlesque Actors and Actresses', *Gentleman's Magazine* n.s. 9 (July-December 1872), p. 560.
[87] Quoted in Walter Goodman, *The Keeleys on the Stage and at Home* (London: Richard Bentley, 1895), p. 75. Mrs. Keeley first played Jack Sheppard at the Adelphi in 1839.
[88] William Archer, *About the Theatre* (London: T. Fisher Unwin, 1886), p. 22.
[89] G.A. Sala, 'On Stage Costume', *Belgravia* 8 (1869), p. 115.
[90] *Saturday Review* 27 April 1889.
[91] *Dramatic Notes* October 1883, p. 49.

[92] *Playgoer* November 1888, p. 6.

[93] Percy Fitzgerald, *Principles of Comic and Dramatic Effect* (London: Tinsley Brothers, 1870), pp. 183-4.

[94] Review of *Frankenstein*, Gaiety Theatre, London, *The Bat* 3 January 1888. Farren had played both roles in recent Gaiety productions.

[95] 'Burlesque: Past and Present', *Time* 3 (1880), p. 132.

MISS EILY O'CONNOR

H.J. BYRON
(1861)

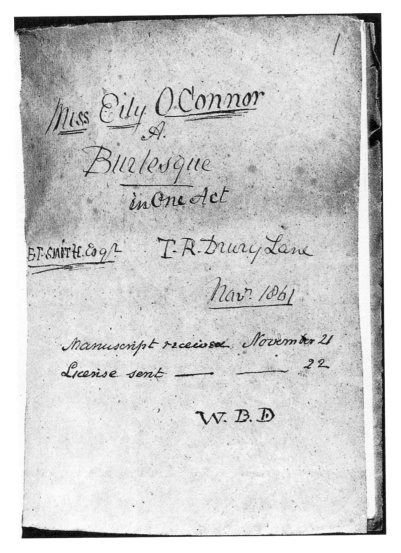

6 Title page of the original manuscript of *Miss Eily O'Connor* (1861)
(British Library Add Ms 53,009 I)

Editor's Introduction

Miss Eily O'Connor

Miss Eily O'Connor takes its name from the heroine of Dion Boucicault's sensation melodrama *The Colleen Bawn*. The original play opened at Laura Keene's Theatre in New York City in March 1860, and received its London premiere at the Adelphi six months later. The author and his wife, Agnes Robertson, took the roles of Miles na Coppaleen and Eily O'Connor in both productions. The play ran for nearly three hundred nights in London, earning the dramatist and his wife the princely sum of £23,000. Based upon Gerald Griffin's novel *The Collegians* (1829), the melodrama centers on the clandestine marriage of Hardress Cregan, an Anglo-Irish gentleman, and Eily O'Connor, an Irish peasant girl. Despising his wife's brogue and provincial dialect, the snobbish Hardress turns against her when he realizes that he must marry the wealthy Anne Chute to save his family estate. Although Hardress only contemplates killing Eily, his crippled servant Danny Mann—his sinister shadow, as it were—devises a murderous plot. Danny lures the distressed Eily to a remote lake, where, after she refuses to hand over the only copy of her marriage certificate, he tries to drown her. Miles, stumbling upon them, wounds Danny and pulls Eily out of the water. He keeps her in seclusion, biding his time until he reveals the full truth. Meanwhile, Hardress, who knows nothing of these events, mistakenly believes that Eily committed suicide after he deserted her. Only now does he realize the extent of his love for her. Tormented by guilt, he confesses everything to Anne Chute just as they are about to wed. The police then arrive to arrest Hardress for ordering Danny to commit murder. During the hastily arranged judicial proceedings Miles brings in the alleged victim herself. To everyone's astonishment, she is very much alive. Eily offers to renounce her marriage vows to Hardress, but at last he chooses to publicly embrace her as his wife.

    In a curious inversion of theatrical hierarchies, the burlesque *Miss Eily O'Connor* premiered at Drury Lane.[1] Despite its varied repertoire of tragedy, melodrama, farce, opera, and ballet, this venerable theatre did not generally stage burlesques. Indeed, its vastness must have been at odds with the intimacy and familiarity that characterized burlesque acting. In the summer of 1862, by which time Boucicault had become lessee, Drury Lane produced *The Colleen Bawn* with the author reprising his signature role. That production, in turn, led the Strand Theatre to revive *Miss Eily O'Connor*. This was an unusual turn of events. It was almost unknown for a theatre to produce a 'legitimate' drama *after* it had already staged a burlesque version. Yet this is precisely what happened at Drury Lane—and precisely what was ridiculed at the Strand. As the *Era* tartly observed, 'such are Time's revenges in the Theatrical world'.[2] Not surprisingly, the burlesque fared better at the Strand, where the 'smaller stage' allowed Byron's 'daring puns and exhilarating parodies' to be heard with 'increased effect'.

Both productions of *Miss Eily O'Connor* featured cross-dressing, with Eily, Miles, and Hardress acted by performers of the opposite gender. The Strand revival starred Marie Wilton as Miles and the exuberant James Rogers as Eily. With his parted hair and patterned tuck-up dress, Rogers unmistakably recalled Agnes Robertson's performance in the original melodrama (illustrations 7 and 8). In keeping with the frequent revisions made to burlesque scripts, the Strand's revival featured a new overture, different songs, and fresh topical references. For example, the finale was rewritten so that it no longer referred to 'foggy nights' (the original production had premiered in November) but to 'summer time' since the revival opened in August.[3]

Sensation melodramas of the mid-nineteenth century were roundly censured by high-minded critics for pandering to the debauched tastes of theatre audiences. In Byron's parodic version, the 'Water Cave' scene opens with Danny rowing Eily across the lake. Bumping against the rock placed at centre stage, the boat nearly pitches Eily overboard. No sooner is Eily forced out of the boat than it floats away of its own accord. Danny tries to drown her after she refuses to hand over her marriage papers. He repeatedly pushes Eily under water, but her head quickly resurfaces. She absurdly calls for the police and complains of having caught a cold. All this finely paced stage business is accomplished while singing the duet 'Sally, come up'—whose new refrain is, appropriately enough, 'Eily! go down'. As she disappears for the third time, a pop gun goes off and Danny falls into the water. Miles, imitating the acrobat Jules Léotard, swings across the stage on a trapeze. He pulls Eily out of the water, at first mistaking her for a fish. She falls back into the water, however, and Miles dives in after her. Singing the duet 'The Cure', they search for each other underwater, resurfacing at different places on the stage. Their movements are perfectly sequenced, since each character reappears just in time to sing his or her part of the song. This scene was created through the combination of a painted backdrop, a 'practicable' rock, painted gauze stretched across the stage to look like water, and trap doors cut into the stage floor. To seem to be underwater the actors slipped through a trap door. To reappear in a different part of the lake, they simply came up through a different trap door and raised their heads above the gauze masking. What the audience saw was a head floating above the water.

Another notable instance of burlesque humour in *Miss Eily O'Connor* is the shrewd parody of the 'stage Irishman', a theatrical stereotype exemplified by Boucicault's own portrayal of Miles na Coppaleen. Byron used Miles's first entrance to inventory the clichéd conventions of the 'dramatic Pat'. To the tune of 'Charley Mount', our man enters singing that the greatest charm of the picturesque vista before him is the charm lent by his 'small distilleree'. He cradles a 'small keg of whiskey' and carries a shillelagh. Turning to the audience, Miles declares himself to be a 'stock stage Irishman', a persona for which he possesses all the necessary qualifications: not only does he have the gift of blarney but he is also ragged, aimless, feckless, and drunk. 'For orb and sceptre', Richard Allen Cave has astutely observed, 'this King of Misrule carries those emblems of iniquity, the keg and the shillelagh, implying a life torn between the rival attractions of booze and violence'.[4] In a rhetorical *tour de force* of culinary puns, Miles emphasizes

James Rogers – Miss Eily

7 James Rogers in the title role of H.J. Byron's *Miss Eily O'Connor*, Strand Theatre, London, 1862. Courtesy of The Harvard Theatre Collection, The Houghton Library

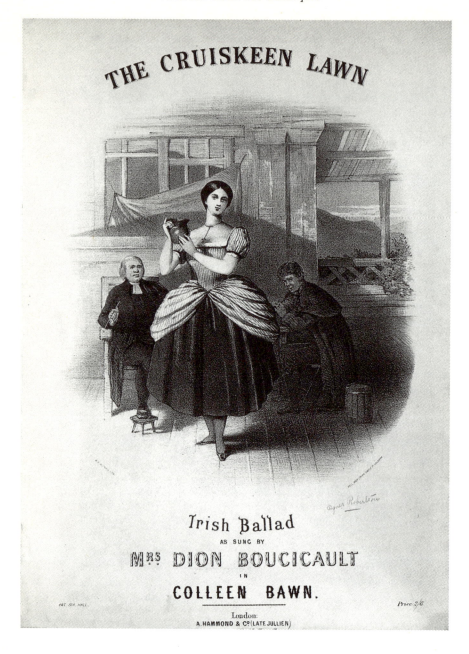

8 Agnes Robertson in the title role of Dion Boucicault's *The Colleen Bawn*, Adelphi Theatre, London, *c.* 1860. Cover sheet for the song 'The Cruiskeen Lawn'. Courtesy of The Harvard Theatre Collection, The Houghton Library

the stage Irishman's beastly nature by comparing him to an 'Irish hare' that has been 'caught' and 'seasoned'. This analogy gains depth through a pun on 'baste', which is both a cooking method and a homophone for how the Irish pronounced 'beast'. In his extended act of self-presentation, Miles speaks exclusively in the third person, thus highlighting the difference between himself as Miles and himself as Miles the 'stock stage Irishman'. For the original spectators this theatrical distancing acquires even greater resonance because the performance continually reminds them that a male character is being impersonated by a woman. The burlesque performer and the burlesque audience, equally alienated from acts of representation, are thus made equally complicit in the burlesque's metatheatrical criticism.

The text of *Miss Eily O'Connor* is taken from Lacy's acting edition, collated with the British Library manuscript (Add Ms 53,009 I). In this and all other scripts in this volume, obvious spelling and punctuation errors have been silently corrected. Alternative readings, usually taken from unpublished sources, are given in the notes.

H.J. BYRON (1834-84) was born in Manchester, the son of a former British consul in Port-au-Prince, Haiti. As a young man Byron studied medicine and law. Eventually becoming disenchanted with both subjects, he sought to establish himself as a playwright. After an early success with *Fra Diavolo* (Strand 1858), Byron received further commissions not only from the Strand but also from the Adelphi and the Olympic. Like other burlesque playwrights Byron was also a comic journalist. He was founding editor of *Fun* and also began the short-lived *Comic Times*—whose motto 'On his walk he madly puns' was a corruption of *Honi soit qui mal y pense*, the motto of the Order of the Garter. Byron was briefly co-lessee of the Prince of Wales's Theatre with Marie Wilton, and later managed the Criterion Theatre and, in Liverpool, the Alexandra Theatre. *Our Boys*, his most successful drama, premiered at the Vaudeville Theatre in January 1875 and ran for over 1,000 performances before closing in April 1879. Some of his better-known burlesques include *The Maid and the Magpie* (1858), *Miss Eily O'Connor* (1861), *Grin Bushes* (1864), *Little Don Giovanni* (1865), *Little Don Caesar de Bazan* (1876) and *Forty Thieves* (1878), the last co-written with F.C. Burnand and Robert Reece.

Notes

[1] Other burlesque versions include the anonymous *Oily Collins* (Soho 1861), Martin Dutnall's *The Cooleen Bawn* (Surrey 1861), and Andrew Halliday's *The Colleen Bawn Settled at Last* (Lyceum 1862).

[2] *Era* 10 August 1862.

[3] Many of the changes were published in a supplement to Lacy's acting edition. See 'The Introductions and Alterations in the Burlesque of *Miss Eily O'Connor*, as Represented by The Royal Strand Theatre' (London: T.H. Lacy, n.d. [1862]).

[4] Richard Allen Cave, 'Staging the Irishman', *Acts of Supremacy: The British Empire and the Stage, 1790-1930*, ed. J.S. Bratton *et al.* (Manchester and New York: Manchester University Press, 1991), p. 63.

Miss Eily O'Connor

First performed at the Theatre Royal, Drury Lane (under the Management of Mr. E.T. Smith), on Monday, November 25, 1861.

A new and original Burlesque Extravaganza, founded on the great Sensation Drama of THE

COLLEEN BAWN!

Written by H.J. Byron, Esq. and entitled

MISS EILY O'CONNOR.

Miles na Coppaleen (*a model stage Irishman, in fact a perfect Pat'un*)...Miss L. Keeley
Hardress Cregan (*Hard-up*)...Miss E. Arden
Kyrle Daly (*Soft-down*)..Mr. Barsby
Danny Mann (*a Ferry-man*)...Mr. Robert Roxby
Mr. Corrigan (*a Fore-closer, anxious for closer relationship*)
....Mr. Holston
Sergeant Torralooral (*a Passive and unintelligent. Officer*)..Mr. Tom Matthews
Eily O'Connor (*a Flower born to blush unseen and waste her sweetness on the desert[ing] heir*)..Mr. Atkin
Miss Ann Chute (*a Victim to Mis-An-Thropy*)........................Miss Stuart
Mrs. Cregan (*a Lady with a very strong will of her own, but a very unsatisfactory one of her late Husband*)........................Mrs. Selby
Bridesmaids, Flunkies, Friends, and Myrmidons of a Tyrannical Government, termed Police, &c., &c[1].

---

[1] *Myrmidons* Warlike Thessalonians who followed Achilles on the expedition against Troy. More generally, those who follow orders blindly.

Programme of Scenery and Incidents.

Scene I
MRS. CREGAN'S HOUSE, MUCKROSS HEAD IN THE DISTANCE.
How the Cregan family appear to be in a bad way off, and Corrigan
appears to be a good way on—How Mrs. Cregan grasps at Hardress's one
glove, but rejects Corrigan's entire suit—Universal suspicion, doubt and
discomfort.

Scene II
A MOUNTAIN PASS.
How the audience is shown to what extreme length Irish Miles may
go—How Corrigan proceeds to pump, and Miles (it is hoped) to draw
well.

Scene III
THE COTTAGE AT MUCKROSS HEAD.
Scene of mutual recrimination between husband and wife—How Hardress
gives up Eily, and how Eily nearly gives up her marriage certificate—How
Miles comes on to his cue and to rescue—How Danny becomes the bearer
of a pacific message, and how Eily starts on her trip down the river.

Scene IV
EXTERIOR OF MILES'S LODGINGS.
Which being concocted simply to allow Miss Keeley to sing a charming
song, and the Carpenters to set the next scene, is necessarily a very
important though short one.

Scene V
THE DIPPING CAVE.
The incidents of this remarkable scene must be seen to be
appreciated.—*Verb. Sap.*

Scene VI
A PASS AMONG THE MOUNTAINS.
Tremendous meeting of re-peelers—How Corrigan and his myrmidons go
on and go off.

Scene VII
INTERIOR OF MRS. CREGAN'S HOUSE.
A REAL SENSATION JIG, by the LADIES OF THE CORPS DE BALLET.
Arranged by Mr. Cormack.
Preparations for Hardress's marriage—How Corrigan stops the proceedings and commences them—How Hardress is protected from handcuffing by the muslin, and how Eily makes a grateful return for her husband's conduct—How everything is set square—How Mrs. Cregan comes round, and the curtain comes down straight.

SCENE FIRST.—*The Exterior of Mrs. Cregan's—same as in the Drama of the 'Colleen Bawn.'—House, L.—rocks, set waters, moonlight.*

*Music—Rising of the curtain—*HARDRESS *enters from house, L., looks stealthily about.*

Hard.   I can't find Danny Mann—it's very odd I
Can't when I'm pressed for time find any bod-y.
Danny, my man, you haven't told the truth.
What's come to that most animated youth?
*Music.—*DANNY *enters cautiously from back*, L.U.E.
Oh! here you are at last: well, really, Danny—

Dan.   Whist, Mr. Hardress Cregan, speak *pianny*.

Hard.   And why *pianny*? what have we to fear?

Dan.   In case there should be anybody near.

Hard.   'Tis almost time to seek my Eily's cot
At Muckross Head; your boat of course you've got;
You will be ready?

Dan.   Master's but to say
The word, and his fond Danny must obey.
He's but to say 'to Muckross,' and he'll see
My boat will take him *uckross* speedilee.

Hard.   (*bringing* DANNY *down*)
                 It's strange, considering the awful lickings,
                 And the unlimited supply of kickings;
                 The terrible head punchings, and the blows
                 You have received from me upon the nose,
                 That you should love me!

Dan.   Ah! and when a boy
                 You did my graceful figure quite destroy;
                 You flung me off a rock—a dreadful thing—
                 But you were young, and *youth will have its fling.*
                 I, with the chuck, fell like a lump of lead did,
                 And, ever since, have been quite chuckle 'eaded.
                 After you struck me from the rock so neatly,
                 I felt that I was 'off it' most completely.
                 I fell in a ravine, with just one crack,
                 And rose up quite a *ra-vine* maniac.

Hard.   *I* was the maniac, 'twas—more's the pity,
                 One of my *many acts* of stupid*itty.*

Dan.   (*points to his forehead*)
                 Here is the place where the hot blow I got, see,
                 The which did cause my present idi-*otsy.*

Hard.   Your nut was in the way.

Dan.   It *was* I feel;
                 Since which I've been an *utter* imbecile.
                 My back was bent, too, by the fall profound,
                 But, as you see, at last we both *came round.*
                 To keep me in this wicked world afloat
                 You kindly set me up, sir, in a boat.
                 Having no head, you bought me two fine skulls;
                 And though, at first, I 'caught crabs' and made mulls,
                 The ferry—patronised by such a swell—
                 Succeeded, and I now row *ferry* well.

Hard.   That's right. Then presently we'll row to Eily,
                 Although my friends would look upon her shyly,
                 Her education being, so to speak,
                 Unfinished. Get your boat within the creek;

This lover would to his fond mistress go,
So, to my lovely *Juliet, Row me oh!*

Duet.— 'Judy Callaghan.'

Hark, my most faithful of men,
  If my protection you care about;
See your boat's ready at ten,
  Make me aware of your whereabouts.
Eily, vilely I—
  Lately have neglected quite;
Let a week pass by,
  Though each day expected quite
Don't say no, alarming Danny Mann again.

Repeat Ensemble.   Don't say no, &c.

                              Exit DANNY, L.U.E.

Music, 'The Grecian Statues.'—Enter MRS. CREGAN *from house, L., a Tragedy Queen Matron,*[2] *with her hair in curl papers.*[3]

Mrs. C. (L).   This is nice conduct, Hardress, catterwauling
                When, as the poet says, 'the dew is falling;'
                An apt quotation, which reminds me, too,
                That we've a something else that's falling due;
                Corrigan's bill—of which we've none at present,
                Your prospects are remarkably unpleasant;
                Come, look me in the face, my dear boy, quite full,
                And say if they're not dreadful.

Hard.   (R., *looking into his mother's face*) Yes, ma, frightful!

Mrs. C.   Ann Chute's your only chance—she is an heiress;
           She was brought up, as you're aware in Paris.

Hard.   Out of the question, mother, that affair is;
         For me, Ann Chute Ann Chute must ever be.

---

[2] *Tragedy Queen Matron* Eighteenth-century term for a legitimate actress, exemplified by Sarah Siddons, who specialized in playing tragic heroines of regal stature. In the nineteenth century, this theatrical stereotype was mocked in both melodrama and burlesque.

[3] *curl papers* Paper rollers placed overnight in a woman's hair to make it curl.

Mrs. C.	Don't you attempt to teach *and chuter me*. She has a *purse an' all* have liked that knew her.
Hard.	I have a *personal* aversion to her, Besides, Kyrle Daly is engaged to wed her.
Mrs. C.	They've had a row, and don't now row togedder; She—like my hairdresser, who's turned away Because he hinted I was getting gray, And hadn't now the locks of a young girl— No longer is engaged to that *ere Kyrle*.[4]
Hard.	Mother; she of my love, can't be the object So let us talk upon some other subject.
Mrs. C.	*Some other*; Why, with rage I shall *s-m-other*; (*in his ear*) I know it is because you love another. A little bird has told me of a lark That you are carrying on, boy, after dark: Confess—come, come, this love, when did begin it?
Hard.	'Tis but a little *lark*, with little *in it*. Of people fond of smoking on the premises, There's them as isn't, mother, and there's them as is; And so, my 'negrohead' I nightly whiff[5] With Danny, in his most convenient skiff.
Mrs. C.	Pah! Negrohead! It's Muckross Head you mean, Where dwelleth Eily, that poor pale Colleen; That's why you cross the water of a night— Excursions daily to the *Eily white*.[6] Think of Ann Chute, and our ancestral tree, Or up one quite as tall we soon shall be; Knock on the head, at once, this boyish passion.

---

[4] *ere Kyrle* Pun on 'hair curl', relying on the Cockney dropped 'h' in 'hair' to make the rhyme.

[5] *negrohead* Sweetened pipe tobacco.

[6] *Eily white* Pun on the Isle of Wight.

Hard.	Why, though I must confess, ma', me 'twas rash on, And I am very well aware I shouldn't,— I've married her.
Mrs. C.	Oh, marry! Come up, you couldn't. Trample upon your parent, Hardress, go it. (*in deep grief*) What! me a ma-in-law, and not to know it.

Duet.—*Kitty Tyrrell.*

Hard.	I'm married to Eily O'Connor; You'll like her exceedingly.
Mrs. C.	Pooh!
Hard.	Oh, please to look kindly upon her; I'll bring her to see you,
Mrs. C.	Yes, do!
Hard.	Oh, mamma, she's extremely good looking, And virtue is stamped in her face; And then she's so first rate at cooking—
Mrs. C.	Then why don't she take a cook's place.
Hard.	Oh, mother!
Mrs. C.	Oh, bother; your family, boy, you'd disgrace.

(*to the symphony,* MRS. CREGAN *sets to the door and dances in*)

Hard.	Oh! Eily, Eily, wherefore art thou Eily?

Exit, R.U.E.

Enter ANNE CHUTE, L., *followed by* KYRLE DALY.

Anne.	Pooh, sir, you're going on extremely slyly; Well, well, of course you're like all other fellows.
Kyrle.	Ann Chute, what makes you so extremely jealous? Anne, to divine the cause I am not able; I am the mildest youth imaginable;

Indeed, my character's so weak, my charmer,
That I don't see I'm wanted in the drama.[7]

Anne.   Abroad, extremely bad reports are spread;
Where do you go to every night?

Kyrle.   To bed.
And dream that down life's path, as poets sing,
Me an' my Anne are both *me-an-dering.*
If you could see the future as I view it—

Anne.   You want my 'and to ring, but you don't do it.
                                   (*crosses to* L.)
I hate thin folks as very oft I've stated.

Kyrle.   Thin! Recollect how I'm *in-fat-u-ated*;
I'm an anomaly, though I'm encased
Most loosely, yet you see I've *run to waist.*
My groans and tears of anguish don't despise—
And don't make light thus of my heavy sighs.

Anne.   Your sighs though heavy have no weight with *me!*

Kyrle.   Say you'll the wife of poor Kyrle Daly be;
My proper sleep for thought of you, miss, railly,
I misses nightly, then be *Mrs. Daly.*

                    Duet.—*Ring the Banjo*

Anne.   I've done with you, Kyrle Daly,
                        Your conduct's very bad;
            At once I thought you railly
                        Some slight affection had.

Kyrle.   Into a state you throw me,
                        Of downright mise-*ree*;
            Anne Chute, you really blow me
                        Up con-tin-u-al-*lee.*
            Ring, ring, my Anne Chute,

---

[7] *I don't see I'm wanted in the drama* A sly form of dramatic criticism, hinting that the thinly-written character is superfluous in Boucicault's original play. See also n. 46, below.

A wedding ring let be;
A climax to our squabbling—let's
Embrace mat-rim-o-nee.

(ANNE *crosses to* R. *disdainfully*)

Anne. Ring, ring, you Anne Chute,
A wedding ring shan't be;
The climax to our squabbling—let's
Be parted instantly.

Exeunt ANNE, R.—KYRLE, L.

(*as* KYRLE *is rushing off he meets* CORRIGAN, *who is entering, and treads heavily on his feet*)

Corri. Gracious! my favourite corn he's ground to flour!
Of an attorney they shall feel the power;
Ha, ha! now comes a day of retribution;
If they can't pay, I'll pop an execution
Into the house, remorseless my character's,
And sell up all the sticks—I mean the actors.[8]
Here comes the widow, down, compunction, down.

Enter MRS. CREGAN, L., *starts on beholding* CORRIGAN, *and turns from him in contempt.*

Corri. Your servant, lady—nay, don't coldly frown;
I've come to pay you my respects, and you
Will also, in return, mum, pay what's due;
Don't think me bold, that I presumed to call
My little bill's eight thousand pounds—that's all!
(*producing it*)

Mrs. C. A 'trifle light as air!' (*aside*) With fear I stifle.

Corri. I'm very glad you call that *ere* a trifle;
Your son and *heir*, I hope, is pretty bobbish.[9]

---

[8] *stick* Theatrical slang for an incompetent person; i.e., someone who is woodenheaded.
[9] *bobbish* Moneyed.

Mrs. C.   Sir! This familiarity is snobbish.[10]
                 Do not presume—

Corri.   He—hem! Beware, proud beauty;
                 Don't force me to a most unpleasant duty:
                 Could you oblige me?

Mrs. C. (L.)   Sir, I cannot pay.

Corri. (R.)   Oh, then I must oblige *you*, in a way!

Mrs. C.   Mercy!

Corri. (*suddenly kneeling*)   I love you.

Mrs. C.   Rage!

Corri. (*taking her hand*)   I will be truthful.

Enter HARDRESS *at back*, R., *observes them, and comes down behind*
   CORRIGAN.

                 And though I'm not particularly youthful,
                 You are yourself, remember, not a chicken.
                 (*receives a tremendous kick in the back from* HARDRESS.
                    He remains without turning round or rising)
                 It strikes me forcibly that someone's kicking.
                          (*with the air of a martyr*)
                 No matter—I can bear it! Now I've got
                 This chance, I'll strike while yet the iron's hot;
                 On this poor Irishman, so dull and flat,
                 Have *pity*—how my heart beats—*pity Pat*.

Hard.   Pr'aps you'll oblige me, sir, by taking *that*.
                 (*crushes his hat over his eyes, and knocks him
                    on his face*)

Corri.   (R., *sits up*) Young man, you have than pancake beaten flatter
                 My hat.

---

[10] *snobbish* Vulgar; 'snob' was university slang for a townsman (as opposed to a gownsman), with the implication of coarse manners. The word did not then imply pretensions to gentility.

Hard.	(C.)	Your head too will I beat to batter.

Corri.   He—hem! you'd *batter* not.

Mrs. C. (L.)   Try not the latter, he
Would bring an action for assault and *battery*.
We're in the power of this vile solicitor.
          (CORRIGAN *rises, pulls out a note book, and dips*
            his pen in an ink bottle, hanging from his coat)
He is remorseless, boy, as an inquisitor.

Corri.   Pen and *ink wisitor*, as you perceive;[11]
I'll take the inventory, with your leave. (*goes up*)

Mrs. C.   What's to be done? He'll sell us up, that's sure!

              DANNY *runs on from back*, L.U.E.

Dan.   Now, master, dear!

Mrs. C. (*intercepting him*)   Hush! you ill-mannered boor.
          (*melodramatic music, very piano, till end of dialogue*)
          (*bringing him down tragically*)
Come here!
          (*in the manner of tragedians in 'King John'*)[12]
               I had a thing to say!

Dan.   (L., *aside, alarmed*) She looks like that old party in the play.

Mrs. C. (R.)   I've paid you liberal wages, Danny, dear;
Given you Christmas boxes—

Dan.   On the *ear*!

Mrs. C.   That's neither *ere* nor there. Hem! by-the-bye
Just have the kindness, please, to throw thine eye
On yon young girl.   (DANNY *looks about confused*)
                        No, no, she isn't here!

---

[11] *ink wisitor* Pun on inquisitor, with the pronunciation of 'v' as 'w' common in Cockney Jewish dialect.

[12]*King John* Mrs. Charles Selby, who played Mrs. Cregan in the original production, imitated 'King John addressing Hubert' (*Era* 1 December 1861).

I don't know if I make myself quite clear;
On Eily!   (*chord in orchestra*)

Dan.   Oh!

Mrs. C.   She must be put aside;
Your master's anxious for another bride;
Into the water he would have you spill her.

Dan.   (*after a struggle with his feelings*)
I'll be remorseless, ma'am, as the *gorilla*! (*crosses to* R.)

Mrs. C.   Gorilla! Good! The simile's refined,
And that the water's not *too shallow*, mind.

Dan.   If Master Hardress sends his glove to say
He wishes Eily put out of the way,
Because she's in the way of Miss Anne Chute.
'Twill be a dreadful dooty—but I'll do't!

Mrs. C. (*handing a glove to* DANNY)
Behold his glove, my very worthy friend.
                        (DANNY *clutches it in horror*)
(*aside*) He gave it me ten minutes back to mend.
(*to* CORRIGAN) Oh, Mr. Corrigan!

Corri.   (*advancing*, L.)   Ma'am, I attend.

Mrs. C.   As I've a friend, who will the money lend,
Your matrimonial hopes are at an end.

Corri.   I'll bring an action, then, which you'll defend!
(*to* HARDRESS) Yes, if a thousand pounds o'er it I spend.

Hard.   That way your steps be good enough to wend.

Dan.   (*aside to* MRS. CREEGAN, *taking her, aside to* R.)
One dip shall end her, ma'am, on me dip-end.

Quartette.—*Skidamalink*.[13]

Hard.   (L.C., *aside*) Eily, I think a noodle am I, to show this hesitation,
For all my love for you is based upon a wrong foundation,
Why should I shrink at such a misdeed—a mother's a relation;
One ought to save at any risk, one trifling palpitation.

Mrs. C. (R.C., *to* DANNY) Eily's a link, to break it we'll try, and in her situation,
We'll pop Anne Chute, who is a girl high in my estimation.

Dan.   (R., *to* Mrs. C.) A nod, as a wink, to horse that is blind, has the same valuation,
I must imbibe to brace me for this terrible occasion.

Corr. (L.)   Blow this ere ink, it's perfectly dry. Permit me one observation,
If I'm not paid, and shortly too, you'll feel my indignation;
All of the chink: you've raised upon my frame, sir, an abrasion,
I really feel the symptoms of incipient inflammation.

(DANNY, R., *and* CORRIGAN, L., *dance in opposite corners.*—
HARDRESS, L.C., *and his* MOTHER, R.C., *dance up the stage
hand in hand, then down C.*—*Picture formed at the end by
the four in imitation of the celebrated Pas de Quatre.*—
Closed in.)[14]

SCENE SECOND.—*A Landscape.*

MILES NA COPPALEEN *heard singing 'Charley Mount' without, then enters,
L.E., with a small keg of whiskey and a shillelagh.*

---

[13]*Skidamalink* Also 'skilamalink', meaning secret or shady. It was a nonsense word popularized in the 1850s by Frederick Robson at the Olympic Theatre.
[14] *Pas de Quatre* Dance for four ballerinas, choreographed by Jules Perrot to music by Cesare Pugini. It was first performed at Her Majesty's Theatre in 1845. The original star performers in this Romantic ballet were Marie Taglioni, Carlotta Grisi, Fanny Cerrito, and Lucile Grahn.

Song.—Air, 'Charley Mount.'

Oh, Charley Mount is a pretty place as you'd ever wish to see,
But not half so dedaar as my water cave is that pleasant place to me;
It's so cool and so convanient for the making of whis-key,
For lending it its greatest charm is my *small distilleree.*

Miles.   Behold in me that happy, ragged rogue,
                 The stock stage Irishman—without the brogue.
                 To manufacture which, this will you'll see
                 Turn out a never failing recipe.
                 He must have lightish hair, extremely curly,
                 His teeth must be particularly pearly,
                 Because he shows them all whene'er he grins;
                 Dilapidated hose must veil his shins;
                 Not having shaved, he must be blackish muzzled,
                 And this must be his attitude when puzzled.
                       (*striking the stock attitude of the puzzled stage
                         Paddy, with his right hand in his hair*)[15]
                 This he at stated intervals must do
                 Accompanied of course with an 'Huroo'.
                       (*hits his shillelagh on the stage and jumps*)
                 On symptoms of a row the most remote,
                 He must insist on taking off his coat.
                 The stock remark of a dramatic Pat
                 Must be when vexed at all—'Get out of that!'
                 Though 'Arrah' must of all his observations
                 The *arra* root be of his conversations.[16]
                 Now, having caught your Irish hare, with fun
                 He must be highly seasoned, and then done
                 By a brisk rapid fire of jokes—the taste
                 Depend will on the nature of the *baste;*[17]
                 The very sharpest sauce lay on him thickly,
                 Garnish him well with writs, and 'serve him' quickly.
                 Alas! upon this heart Fate's hung its hatchment,
                 I'm prey to an unfortunate attachment.

---

[15] *stage Paddy* Stage Irishman; see the introduction to the play.

[16] *'arra' root* Pun on arrowroot, a medicinal plant. 'Arrah' is Gaelic for the exclamations 'oh' or 'ah'.

[17] *baste* Pun on Irish pronunciation of beast.

Song.—'Billy Patterson.'

Now kind folks, listen to the song
    Of poor Miles na Coppaleen,
I'll soon get it over, and not detain you long.
    She did sell me, she did sell me;
Eily, such conduct on your part was wrong,
    To poor Miles na Coppaleen;
    Unless indeed you've been,
    To Miles na Coppaleen;
    I really think that I
    Will go and do a die;
And having left my goods to Eily in my will,
Go blow myself to atoms, with my old whiskey still.

(*places the keg, C., and walks around it in the manner of clog dancers—sits, C.*)[18]

Music.—CORRIGAN *rushes on in a rage*, R. 1 E.

Corri.   Foiled! Swindled! Beaten! Trampled on, by *Jove*!
            My threats derided, and likewise my *love*;
            Oh; I could punch my head.

Miles.   (*seated on keg, up* L.C.)   Allow *me*,

Corri.   Miles!
            Behold, sir, that most elegant of tiles[19]
            Crushed; at the same time all my young affections.
            Oh! Oh! In short, all sorts of interjections,
            I was knocked over on the ground quite flat.

Miles.   Gracious! Who could *lay down the law like that?*

Corri.   Young Cregan. But he shall repent the blow.
            (*observing the barrel*)

---

[18] *clog dancers* Folk dancers, whether Irish, English, or American, who perform in wooden shoes ('clogs'). Clog dancers are usually solo performers who carry on a tradition of step dancing which, in the twentieth century, evolved into tap dancing. 'Clog' derives from the Gaelic word for time. The clog dancer steps in time to the music, with the shoe's heel keeping the rhythm.

[19] *tiles* Dress hats.

What's in that keg, you've there, sir?—let me know;
Come, sir, reply. I'll tap it, if I'm goaded.

Miles.   (*grinning*) You'd best take care—that single barrel's loaded.

Corri.   Loaded with lawless liquor, I'll maintain.

Miles.   It's only some *illicit*-still champagne.

Corri.   (*aside*) I fear from him I shan't *elicit* much;
(*brings* MILES *down*)
It strikes me, Miles, that you don't often touch
That very filthy dross, termed *lucre*—say.

Miles.   Now, do I *look as* if I did, sir, eh?

Corri.   Now, Pat, if you'd earn all that's there—you shall.

Miles.   You're a *pat-ern-al* individual;
Good as a father to me—the conditions?

Corri.   Well, then, the fact is, I have my suspicions—

Miles.   (*aside*) And very many other people's, too.

Corri.   That Master Hardress Cregan means to do
An act, to say the least, which isn't *Cummy
Fo*;[20] I suspect, *by gum*, he means *bigummy*!
That's if he's married to this Eily.
                    (MILES *fiercely seizes him by the throat*)

Miles.   What?
I'll shake the teeth down your vile throat—the lot;
And if they kill you, that is, stop your breath,
The verdict will be acci-*dental* death.
You're used to lie, so try another lay;
                    (*throws him down flat*)

Corri.   (*sitting up*) I'm altogether in luck's way to-day;
My plan's upset, together with myself, (*rises*)
However, if you should require the pelf,[21]

---

[20] *Cummy Fo* Corruption of *comme il faut* (proper; as it should be).

There's my address. (*gives card—coaxingly*) Come,
    Miles, before you go,
My purse, if you will tell me all you know.

Miles.   A lawyer's purse. Oh, terrible temptation!
    (*takes him by the arm as if about to communicate
    something important*)
Open your ears.

Corri. (*aside, delighted*)   *Now*, for some information!

     Song.— 'The Young Man from the Country.'

Miles.   No doubt you, Mr. Corrigan,
    Imagine that you see
    A mere provincial idiot,
        A poor sill*ee* bill*ee.*
    But been to the metropolis,
        Has Miles na Coppaleen;
    Though this song's sung at Evans's,[22]
        I am no Paddy-*green.*
    I'm a young man from the country,
    But you'll find I'm all serene.

    No doubt you'd like to hear about
        The beautiful Eilee;
    But I, sir, cannot gratify—
        Your curiosity.
    If you go out to Muckross Head,
        You'll see what you shall see;
    I'm a poor lad from the country,
        But you don't get over me.

Miles.   You're not the first one, Sir, by many who
    Have found that same most difficult to do;
    Most travellers tire with crossroads, gates, and stiles
    In trying to 'get over' Irish Miles.
    Comic Music Exeunt MILES, L., *and* CORRIGAN, R.

---

[21] *pelf* Fortune or treasure.
[22] *Evans's* Evans's Supper Rooms, a popular song-and-supper establishment in Covent Garden Piazza. 'Paddy' Green was the popular *maitre'd.*

SCENE THIRD.—*Interior of the Cottage at Muckross Head, arranged as nearly as possible like the Adelphi Scene.*[23] *Large fireplace, R., with transparent log fire, table, two chairs, long settle, R., red cloak and bonnet, coarse bib apron hung up. Music.*—EILY *discovered watching for* HARDRESS *at back.*

Eily.

> I cannot see my spouse, my love, my life!
> This is a bright 'look-out' for a young wife;
> He's past his usual hour, he was the last time;
> It's plain that he looks on me as his—*past-time.*
> Indeed, I've noticed lately gradu-ally,
> He's getting to think me of little valley;
> When first he vowed he loved me he did say,
> I was the sort of girl quite in his way,
> But now so anxious he's our bond to sever,
> I feel I'm much more in his way than ever.
> Once on a time he worshipped my bright tresses,
> When Hardress first did pay me his *hard-dresses*;
> Then he declared he loved my eyes of blue,
> And that my hair was just his favourite hue.
> But now his admiration for it ceases;
> He's changed his *key*, and *picks my locks to pieces*,
> Nothing I ever do remotely pleases him,
> He seldom comes to tea because I teases him;
> He says my grammar's faulty, and declares
> I drops about my H.'s everywheres.
> He comes—and when with happy hours before us,
> I murmur 'Shades of evening close not o'er us,'
> My hint and neat quotation doesn't tell,
> For he says 'Eily, beauty, fare thee well.'

> *Song.*—*'Pretty Girl Milking her Cow.'*

> He liked once, he said, my society,
>> My grammar, he noticed not then,
> But I hear the expression—variety,
>> Is oft in the mouths of young men.
> P'raps he found that I grew melanchol-y too,
>> And regrets his absurd marriage vow,
> And prefers to see one who looks jolly to
>> A pretty girl wrinkling her brow.

---

[23] *Adelphi* London theatre where *The Colleen Bawn* opened in 1860.

Song.—*'Rosalie the Prairie Flower.'*
> Once he said he loved me,
>> Dearer than his life,
> I wish I'd never known the hour;
>> He said, 'Dear, we'll exist in
> (When we're man and wife),
>> So cozilee, a fairy bower,
> Milking of cows, and
>> Churning's my trade,
> Cheeses a thousand,
>> At least I've made,
> Rivals knit their brows, and
>> Called I'm by each blade,
> That Rose Eily the dairy flower.

Enter HARDRESS, C., *from* L.

Hard.   (L.)   My dear *Colleen*. (*aside*) So dirty, I've never seen her.
(*aloud*) You certainly might keep yourself *col-leaner*.

Eily.   (R.)   I have to scrub the floor, to wash the plates,
To dust the furniture, black lead the grates,[24]
Clean all the boots, the numerous errands run,
And I'm so knocked up when my day's work done,
That love, my appetite's not what it might be,
And I must necessarily a sight be.
This overwork is why, my dearest hubby,
I'm a *small eater* and a *little grubby*.

Hard.   My wife scrub floors, upon all fours so flat,
Gracious, to think she should come down to that!

Eily.   Sometimes my knees so tired are, it's no sin
To wish I had *my knees within mine inn*.
(*singing, out of tune*) Oh, Min-knee, dear Min-knee!

Hard.   Oh, pray do not howl out of tune like that.

Eily.   I'm a great fool!!

Hard.   Yes, and a little flat.

---

[24] [to] *black lead the grates* To polish the iron grates of a fireplace with blacklead.

Eily.	Well, if I *am* a great fool, let me mention—

Eily.   Well, if I *am* a great fool, let me mention—

Hard.   You should be *grate-fool* for my condescension.
Pray think how I've demeaned myself, Colleen!

Eily.   How you've *demeaned* yourself! Why, what *de-mean*?
What is the reason—

Hard.   Don't continue teazin,
You are the excessively *plain* reason.

Eily.   I see it all, you wish to leave me?

Hard.   Yes!
I wish to leave you Eily, I confess.

Eily.   Though my poor heart it pierces like a shot,
Why die and leave me—*everything you've got!*
(*with real self-sacrifice*)
You then shall never hear a murmur more.

Hard.   It's strange I never thought of that before;
Exactly—die, and leave you all I've got;
Yet, on the whole, perhaps, it's scarcely what
'Twas my intention to convey—you see
I made a *mésalliance*.

Eily.   Ah! who's he?

Hard.   (*aside*)   Her ignorance is irritating; well
I'm what is commonly now termed a 'swell.'

Eily.   Yes, and though Eily you've of late neglected
Each day you are as *swell as is expected.*

Hard.   Gracious, what grammar! why, my dear, your friends
Are very low, and you scarce make amends
For *relatives*, who all so fond are drink of,
And *antecedents* it don't do to think of.

Eily.   You never for a moment, sure, expected,
Eily O'Connor was *ighly (O) Connnor-ected.*

Hard.   I really don't know, Eily, who you are,
       (*aside*) Don't know her father—*Je ne Connor pa*!
       (*aloud*) Anne Chute, who loves me to distraction, wears
       Hibernian *graces*—sings Italian *airs*,
       And like *Carlotta Grisi* dances—

Eily.   Easy
       Oh, I've no doubt you thin*k a lot o' Grisi.*
         (*going towards* MR. TULLY *in the Orchestra,*
          threateningly)
       If in Italian I am such a dunce,
       Oh, let me go to *hit Tully* at once.
       My heart's so *heavy*, don't be an obstructor,
       It would be so *lightning*, to strike that *conductor*.

Hard.   Pray don't give way, but pity my condition,
       I'm a beggar, list to my petition.

   Medley.—Concerted Piece.— 'I should like to marry.'

Hard.   I should like to marry,
          That is, if I can,
       A superb young lady,
          Which her name is Anne.
       With feeling, and with fancy
          She sings—can likewise play,

Eily.   (*with concentrated rage*) 'I wish I was with Nancy,'
          As little street boys say.
       Oh, boy, you play Old Harry
          With my feelings—can
       You wish Anne Chute to marry?
          Oh, you bad young man!

       Air.— 'Over the Sea.'

Hard.   Hand—Over to me,
          Over to me,
       Your marriage lines, love, immediately. (*pause*)

Eily.   No! 'twould be
                                            Felo de se,[25]
                                 This female don't see it. Go 'long!

Hard.   Then they'll march, march, march
                                       Me to a jail sure as a
                                       Gun: rat I'm poor as a,
                                       Parch, parch, parch,
                                       My throat does with thoughts—Heigho!
Eily.   (*agonizedly*) Oh, dear *me*,
                 (*producing her certificate*) No, no, Eil-*ee*
                                 Loves you—you'll see,
                                 Here is our marriage certifica-*te*.
                                       Off will I flee
                                       To Ameri-*kee*,
                                 Kamschatka, or else to Hongkong.

As HARDRESS *snatches the certificate,* MILES *enters,* L.C., *and comes
slowly down.*

Air.—'The Tank.'

Miles. (C.)   Stop now! Drop now
                                 That marriage certificate.

Eily. (R.)   Gracious me! A dreadful row I think there'll be.

Miles. (C.)   Or, sir—floor, sir,
                                 You I must, and spiflicate[26]
                                 Every feature in your physiognomy.

Hard. (R.)   (*with great scorn*) That rhyme's imperfect.

Miles.   But you'll find the reasoning
                                 Striking and convincing,
                                 You'll be wincing, for you'll see
                                 Your coat, though spicy, is tasteless to the seasoning,
                                 'Twill now get: you're a mess in
                                 Which confessin' soon you'll be.

---

[25] *Felo de se* Suicide or one who commits suicide; literally, a felon of himself.
[26] *spiflicate* To thrash, crush, or destroy.

Omnes.   Stop now—drop now, &c., &c., &c.

                    (MILES *taking* EILY'S *hand and bringing her round*)

                    Air.— 'Cruiskeen Lawn.'

Miles.   Now, I'd bet a thousand pounds
                        That your house and pleasure grounds;
                    You'd gladly sell at once, and pawn
                        All your rich old family plate,
                        For to obsquatulate[27]
                    With this smiling little Colleen Bawn;
                        Oh, grammachree ma cushla,
                        Slanta gal, mavourneen,[28]
                    Though its meaning isn't clear as dawn.
                        Nevertheless for us to sing
                        It's the proper sort of thing
                    To this smiling little Colleen Bawn.
All.   Oh, grammachree ma cushla, &c., &c.

Eily.   Oh, it's very hard indeed,
                        That because I cannot read,
                    My heart in two should thus be sawn;
                        And also thus be chizzeled,
                        All your fond affection's mizzled;[29]
                    I'm a sadly treated Colleen Bawn.
                        Bad grammar Cre-gan shouldn't
                        Supplant a gal—it wouldn't,
                    And I never should have been left forlorn
                        Despite my education
                        If in elevated station
                    Had been this wretched Colleen *Bawn*.
All.   Oh, grammachree, &c. &c.

---

[27] *obsquatulate* Variant of 'absquatulate', a mock-Latin expression of American origin meaning to abscond or to hurry away; literally, to squat away from.

[28] *grammachree...mavourneen* Love of my heart, my darling, bright health of my darling.

[29] *mizzled* Gone away.

Hard.   Enough! I quite perceive that I'm *de trop*,
                 So I shall leave. (*going*)

Eily.   This is a pretty *go*.

Miles. (*loftily*)   Go, sir, this roof though humble, shelters virtue.

Hard.   Dog!

Miles.   Don't repeat that phrase or I might hurt you.
                 The harsh term 'dog' your wife and I forgive;
                 Supported by my *bark* no doubt she'll live.
                         (EILY *weeps on* MILES's *shoulder*)
                 Don't hang your head—come, come, don't be absurd;
                 Keep up your pecker—'cheer up,' like a bird.

Eily.   (*in schoolgirl tones to* HARDRESS *over* MILES'S *shoulder*)
                 Go, to your gay and festive scenes, your halls of dazzling
                         light;
                 Eat, drink, your fill—may good digestion wait on appetite;
                 Go, go, and join the mazy throng—most sumptuously fare it,
                 And as my constitution's strong, I'll try to grin and bear it.

Miles.   (*half crying*) Fol-de-rol-de-dol-de-riddle-dol.
                 Fol-de-rol-de-dol-de-day.

Eily.   And mister Cregan—that is all
                   As I have got to say.

Hard. (*after struggling with his feelings*)   Farewell!
                                   (*rushing out*, L.C.)

Eily.   (*bursting frantically from* MILES)
                 He's gone! He's gone! Ha, ha! he's gone! he's gone!
                     (*sinks on a chair*, R., *on which she has left a stocking*
                     in process of mending)
                 Oh! agony! What's this I'm sitting on?
                         (*clutching the work*)
                 This is a pretty piece of work, Miles, this is!
                 Hardress to go and leave his lawful missus.

Duet.—'Lucia.'

Eily.	What, Hardress left! Oh, I'm bereft Of all my hope and joy; My heart in twain by this is cleft,— He is a heartless boy!
Miles.	I'll go and punch his noble nob, I'll stretch him on the floor! Why did the villain go and rob Poor Miles of Miss Con-nor?

EILY *sinks on chair,* R.C.—MILES *rushes off at opening,* L.C.—*Change of Music*—DANNY MANN *enters,* L.C., *rather drunk from street.*

Air.—DANNY MANN,—*'So early in the Morning.'*

I've had a drop of something short,
And quite feel as I didn't ought,
Like those who, with unsteady pin,
The matert*i*nal milk go in
   With—early in the morning,
   So early in the morning,
   Before the break of day.

Dan. (*aside*)	My heart sinks when I think I've got to drown her, And make of her a subject for the *Crowner*.[30] I've tried to drown remorse in *alcohol, I* Find I'm—the more I drink—more melan*choly.* (*aloud*) Eily! I've got a message from your spouse.
Eily. (*rising*)	After our worst of matrimonial rows.
Dan. (L.)	He says, as his remarks were very 'low,' He hopes that you'll *look over* 'em you know; And also, that you'll not refuse to come And meet him—
Eily.	Where?

---

[30] *a subject for the Crowner* Reference to the Coroner's inquest held after a death.

Dan.   Just down the river, mum.
                    Where with white-bait, and over claret cup,
                    He trusts that you and he may make it up.

Eily.   White-bait! I love 'em; claret cup, I'll come!

Dan. (*aside*)   I feel my limbs all numb.

Eily.   Oh! num! num! num!
                    Let's go at once.

Dan. (*hesitating*)   Why—why—w—

Eily.   Come, don't stutter.
                    Oh! for the lemon, and brown bread and butter;
                    The snowy table cloth, the dapper waiters,
                    Smart as the rightful heirs 'at the *theaytres*;'
                    The broad bow windows, and the steamers passing,
                    Champagne continually pour'd your glass in;
                    The effervescent, or delicious still,
                    The calm—the coffee—
                         (EILY *goes up, and puts on her red cloak and bonnet*)

Dan.   And the little bill.

                    Duet.—'*Garryowen.*'

Dan.   Come along, my dear Eily,
                         Or else we'll be late;
Eily.   I'm devoted to Hardress,
                         Allow me to state.
Dan.   And you're not blind,
                         My dear, to the charms of white-bait,
Eily.   And a snug little dinner
                         Alone, tête-a-tête.
                    I never will be angry more,
                    Of course, my grammar is a bore;
                    Why did he not say so, before
                    He married poor Eily O'Connor.
                    (*dance to symphony—closed in—change of Scene*)

SCENE FOURTH.—*Exterior of Miles's Illicit Distillery—Cottage,* 1st *wing,* R.[31]

Enter MILES, L., *who sings in imitation of Mr. Boucicault.*[32]

Miles.　　　Well, here's my bachelor's unpleasant quarters,
Over against the river's placid waters.
The people round about say that they hear
Strange noises, and they're frightened, it sounds queer
But that which doth with apprehension fill,
The folks is not the *noise*—no it's the *still*.
Secure in there (*pointing to cottage*) I keep my kegs of whiskey;
To open the front portal I use *this* key,
The other entrance, down there by the river,
No one has ever managed to diskiver.
Besides, it don't require a lock and key,
Because the river's full of *Chub's*, you see.[33]

Song.—Air. 'Peter Gray.'

I'm an unfortunate young man,
　　I think I'm getting grey,
My love is blind, my figure in
　　My best in vain I array.
　　　　My best, &c.
I repeat, I
　　Am becoming grey,
This luckless rural laddie, oh,
　　Has truly had his day.

Air.—'Aunt Sally.'

I seek my old haunts sadly,
　　My life's without an aim,
For Eily's used me badly,

---

[31] Miles's monologue and two songs represent a 'carpenter's scene' which, because it is played downstage, allows most of the stage to be masked while an elaborate and lengthy scene change takes place. This scene, which also appears in *The Colleen Bawn* for the same pragmatic purpose, is not essential to either the plot or the action.

[32] In the original manuscript Miles sings 'Charley Mount' upon entering this scene. In the acting edition, however, he sings the song on his first appearance in scene two.

[33] *Chub* Pun on the Chubb Lock and Safe Company founded in the early nineteenth century by the brothers Charles and Jeremiah Chubb.

                    She of my love makes game;
            I've took to whiskey brewin'
                    And drinking it al-so,
            I'm going to my ruin
                    As fast as I can go.
                            Heigho, hi! what a rollicking lad am I,
                                To every move upon the board,
                        This Irish Miles is fly.[34]
            I think I'll go to Londin,
                    Yes, take a foreign tour,
            See Leotard and Blondin,[35]
                    Likewise the Perfect Cure;[36]
            Also the great Gorilla[37]
                    From foreign climates borne,
            That flash noble *man-killer*
                    That now is so much worn.
                            Heigho, hi! what a rollicking, &c.
                                        Exit into cottage, R.

SCENE FIFTH.—*The Water Cave.*

Music.—MILES *appears on rock,* R.

Miles.   Here, in cool grot, where no one e'er doth peer in,
                    I feel I'm out of Ireland, and of *Erin*;
                    To cross to my abode, a hint I take
                    From Leotard—and of a rope and stake
                    Have manufactured a trapeze; I'll wager
                    A trifle this would puzzle any guager.
                        (*seizes the rope and crosses the water, à la
                            Leotard to rock,* L.)[38]

---

[34] *fly* Knowing, shrewd.

[35] *Leotard and Blondin* Jules Léotard (1830-70) and Charles Blondin (1824-97), French acrobats. Léotard invented the flying trapeze. Blondin, in 1859, crossed Niagara Falls on a tightrope.

[36] *Perfect Cure* Song-and-dance routine performed by J.H. Stead in London music halls in the early 1860s. Much of the dancing in his eccentric performance consisted of jumps and gyrations.

[37] *great Gorilla* Discovered only in 1847, a gorilla in captivity was still a sensational novelty.

There! What was that? An otter, p'raps. Holloa!
A voice? Imagination, may be—no
Ripple doth stir the water—all is quiet;
I wish there was an otter to let fly at.
Whene'er I catch one, I think it no sin
To take it from its kith, and sell its *skin*.
Holloa, out there! Is anybody nigh?
Not a rip-ple—I pause for a ripple-*y*,
Now to go down to my secure distillery,
And look after my il-licit artillery;
When I approach my home, I can't help feeling
Love for the 'still—so gently o'er me stealing'.

> (*Music.*—MILES *retires from rock,* R.—*a boat from*
> R.2 E., *with* DANNY *rowing, and* EILY, *pale, and in*
> *a state of alarm, comes on—when the boat comes to the*
> *centre, it bumps against a rock and nearly jerks* EILY
> *out*)

Eily.　　　　What is this place? Speak—it looks very gloomy;
Where are we? Pray speak *to me*—ain't it *tomby*?

Dan. (*wildly*)　Ha, ha!

Eily.　　　　　　　　　　Don't laugh like Mr. N.T. Hicks[39]
When he's about to have a fight with six;
This is no place for white bait, one can see
It isn't capable of shrimps and tea.

Dan.　　　　You mind your steering.

Eily.　　　　　　　　　　　Steering? What's the use,
If you don't pull your skulls, you silly goose?
I shall leave off the river, calm and clear in
So I shall sadly weep, and drop *this steer in*. (*howls*)

Dan.　　　　Don't make a great cry about a little wool,
I'm pulling.

---

[38] *Leotard* See n. 35, above. Instead of swinging on a tree branch, as in *The Colleen Bawn*, burlesque Myles flies across the stage on a trapeze.

[39] *N.T. Hicks* Popular contemporary actor in melodramas performed at London's minor theatres.

Eily.
                              P'raps—but 'I don't see the pull;'
You're what I call a 'bad egg'—and gainst me
You're hatching some most foul conspiracy.

Dan.
        Fowl? I can't *pull it*—miserable wight!
(*fiercely*) Come, no 'eggsauce,' for I'm *eggsausted* quite.

Eily.
        Beneath the flood, it seems to me, you try
To *wash us*, for you hold your *skull awry*.

Dan.
        Wash us—and skull-ry.

Eily.
                            You deserve a switching;
Mind, or from blows, you'll soon find your *back-itching*;
Mind where you're going Danny, gracious—why
You used to have a most unerring eye.

Dan.
        It is un-erring still—but then you know
That this is an excessively *hard-row*;
And talking of *hard-roes* reminds me—

Eily.
                                         Yes.

Dan.
        That I've on business come, from young *Hard-ress*;
That you may better bear this bitter shock,
Suppose you step upon this *bit o'*rock. (*gets on rock,* C.)
Come from the boat, my dear,—

Eily.
                                 I shan't—that's flat.

Dan.
        Now, literally girl, 'Come out of that.'

Eily.
        Mind, I'm not weak.

Dan.
                     Now, Eily come along;

Eily.
        And when I *do* come out, I come out strong.
        (DANNY*hands her on to the rock,* C.—*the boat goes off
          of its own accord,* R.)

Dan.
        Oh, honour;

Eily.
                      Ah, well, I must own I doubt you.

Dan.	(*insinuatingly*) Pray, have you got your marriage lines about you?

Eily.	Rather.

Dan.

(*severely*)   List, girl! No one can hear you if you roar,
That *two-oar'd* skiff floats off *to-wards* the shore;
Hem! Your certificate I'm anxious for:
Scream not, or else the water drowns your din,
Don't put me out, or I must put you in.

Eily.

(*after a pause, shrieks*) Police! I know a member of the corps,
A One![40]

Dan.

        Ha! ha! you should have called B Four.
Your marriage lines!

Eily.

(*falling on her knees*) No, no, your words repeal!

Dan.

I only said the *lines*—don't want *a kneel*;

Eily.

(*rising fiercely*) A kneel! in brogue it would be pronounced a *nail*,
Of which I've ten, and never known 'em fail;
In me you'll find you've come across your match,
You'll soon discover that your wig's a scratch.
Your face, my friend, you'll see—(it's an Old Bailey'un)[41]
That although I'm a native, I'm a *naily 'un*.
Your features when in play I'll run seem o'er
Will be composer I shall provide the score.

Dan.

Away compunctions, all this trifling cease;
Go in.

Eily.

    As I observed before—Police! (*sinks*)

Dan.

Gracious, it's over without any din,
How very smoothly the poor gal went in;
To make a pun, which should be groaned at vilely,

---

[40] *A One* Also 'A1'; excellent or first-class.

[41] *Old Bailey* Street in the City of London where the Central Criminal Court is located. The Court itself, London's principal criminal court, is commonly known as 'The Old Bailey'.

<pre>
                    She slipped in smoothly, p'raps because she's *iley*.
                    I didn't think at all that she'd give way so.

Eily.   (*rising*) I say—you know—if you're in fun, just say so;
                    I'm not one of those fortunate young women,
                    Who've been instructed in the art of swimming;
                    Hardress could never mean to take my life;—
                    A nice way to 'throw over' a young wife.

Dan.   He set his life upon a cast,

Eily.   And *I*
                    Shall have to 'stand the hazard of the *die*';
                    If it's a joke—a hapless wife to drown,
                    I don't think it's a joke that should

Dan.   Go down!
                                        (*pushes her into the water*)
                    Once more she's sunk like any lump of lead!

Eily.   (*rising*) There's such a cold a cubbing in by head.

Dan.   (*wildly*) Away! (*pushes her off again into the water*)
                                            I am the wretchedest of men;
                    But now it's over.

Eily.   (*rising—provokingly, in the manner of a clown*)
                                            Here we go again!

                         Duet.—'Sally, come up.'

Eily.   When Hardress comes the news to hear,
                    He will avenge me, never fear,
                    For giving me this wat'ry bier.
                    I'm sinking gradu-ally.
                              No—no. Othel-
                              Lo e'er so mel-
                              Ancholy could be
                              As Hardress you see
                    Will become when he thinks on my wally.[42]
</pre>

---

[42] *wally* Cockney slang for cucumber pickled in brine.

Dan.   Eily! come up!
                                       Eily! go down!

Eily.   Well, if I do I'm safe to drown. (*sinks*)

Dan.   She's done for now, I'll lay a crown.

(*report and flash of gun*, L; DANNY *stands transfixed—pause*)

Some one's shot me right through the middle.
                                  (*falls into the water*)

MILES *appears on rock,* L.

Miles.   Whatever that was—I shot him, or shot her.
                       I rather fancy that I hit a hotter.
                       (*seizes rope, and re-crosses the water, as before to* R.)
                       (*on rock,* R.) Upon that stone, with summer heat opprest,
                       The otters, to get cooler, sit and rest.
                       (*feeling in the water from rock,* R.) My! it's the biggest
                                  one I ever shot.
                       Murder in Irish! Why, what's this I've got?
                       This ain't an *otther*! Gracious, it's a gal!
                       That's quite *an other* kind of ani*mal*.
                       (*raises* EILY *from the water*) What, Eily! ope your eyes—
                                  how came you here?
                       Open your *eyelid, dear*—my *Eily dear*!
                          (EILY *opens one eye, and sneezes violently*—
                          MILES *lets her go—she sinks*)
                       Oh, philliloo! She's sunk beneath the wave.
                       And what a cold she's got!—Oh, well, to save
                       That sweet *divinity's* dear life to-day,
                       Why a *dive in it is* the only way;
                       Though, if she lives, I ne'er can hope to wed her,
                       Still I can take the grand sensation 'header'.
                                      (*dives down*)

Duet.—The Cure.[43]

(*during this* EILY *and* MILES *appear through the water,
bobbing up and down, as if in the attempt to see each other*

---

[43] *The Cure* See n. 36, above.

—They dive down to symphony, and re-appear in
different parts of the Scene)[44]

Miles. (C. *trap*)	Good gracious, dear,
	Where are you?
Eily. (R. *trap*)	Here!
Miles.	I think I can get *to* her.
Eily.	You best of men—(*sinks*)
Miles.	She's 'down again;'
	Myself I will immure. (*dives*)
Eily. (C. *trap*)	Where *has* he gone?
	I reckoned on
	My being saved as sure.
	Of proverbs fust
	Is 'man don't trust'—
	There never was a truer. (*sinks*)
Miles. (*rising* C. *trap*)	Her I don't see;
	Good gracious me!
	Is this illusion pure?
	She sinks from view
	Like syrens, who
	Young men used to allure.

(EILY *rises close to* MILES—*he clutches her in his arms*)
     She's saved at last,
     I've got her fast
Some warm 'potheen' I'll brew her;
     For whiskey hot
     I *know* is what
Will work a perfect cure.

                 (*Picture closed in by*)

SCENE SIXTH—(*Same as Scene Fourth.*)

Music.—CORRIGAN *rushes on from* L.—SERGEANT O'TOORALOORAL—'*an*
active and intelligent Officer' *with his* POLICEMEN, *all hideous*
fellows.

Corri.	This *is* a slice of luck—to think that I
	Stopping at Danny's cottage just to dry

---

[44] *dive down to symphony* (stage direction) The characters dive under the water—that is,
disappear beneath the scenery—in time to the orchestral music.

Myself, should hear the vagabond's confession:
Won't we astonish the entire procession!
Sergeant O'Too-ra-loo-ral!

Serg.   Sir!

Corri.   Be wary,
Say—Can we trust you, bold constabu-lary?

Serg.   *Trust*, noble sir? Can you discern the traces
Of aught dishonest in those open faces?
Behold their flashing eyes, their eager looks,
Forgetting, for the time, their favourite cooks;
Behold! Ambition swells each bosom's lord,
With thoughts of glory, and of the reward!
None there'd disgrace his uniform and button;
The charms of the proverbial leg of mutton—
Even the blandishments of beer or beauty
Would fail to tempt *my* peelers from their duty!
In fact, the mere suspicion raises here—
Perhaps, sir, you'll excuse a manly tear.
                                        (*wipes away a tear*)

Corri.   Don't weep, my Tooralooral—dry your eyes!
Think of the prize, sir, and the great sur-prize
That we've in store, for, as before I said,
I have placed twenty pounds upon his head!

Serg.   But twenty pounds upon his head—what's that?
I only wish you had to wear this hat.

               Duet.—'West Country Ditty.'

Corri.   Sergeant O'Tooral
                    Ooral, follow me,
                    With all your rural
                    Con-stab-u-laree,
        We will astonish this matrimonial fête, oh,
        Drop down upon them just like a hot potato.
Serg.   Count on each arm and truncheon!
                    All there are prime at punchin'

	Heads; we'll pop in to luncheon
	Unexpectedlee.
Corri.	Quick, me your leader, foller
	And be prepared to collar
	Young Cre-gan
Serg.	'Never holler,'
	Leave it all to me.

CORRIGAN *and* SERGEANT *go off,* R., *mysteriously to piano symphony—all the* POLICEMEN *with the exception of one who has fallen asleep, follow stepping to the time of the music—the one* POLICEMAN *being left alone, wakes up with a loud note on the trombone, and rushes off on the wrong side.*

SCENE LAST.—*Castle Chute—the Reception Hall, brilliantly lighted—entrance from raised platform, and steps,* C.

Music.—Enter the BRIDESMAIDS L. 1 E., *with their right arms extended after the manner of the Opera chorus.*

Chorus.

Ladies.	Joy, joy, joy! happy day, happy day! oh, joy!

Enter the GENTLEMEN, R. 1 E., *with their left arms extended in the same manner.*

Gent.	Joy, joy, joy! happy day, happy day! oh, joy!

(*the Operatic Chorus turns into an Irish jig, which the guests dance, at the conclusion, drawing back into two lines; down the avenue thus formed* MRS. CREGAN *enters,* C., *grandly dressed, marching (to the Wedding March) with tragedy-queen strides, then* ANNE CHUTE *and* HARDRESS *follow, and* KYRLE DALY, *with his eyes red with weeping, comes last.*)

Hard. (*to* ANNE)	Oh, happy day! as sings the Opera Chorus,
	Let's hope we've many such, my dear, before us.
	(*aside*) Heigho!

Anne. (*aside*)	Heigho!

Kyrle. (*aside*)	Heigho!

Mrs. C. (*aside*) The groom and bride,
And groomsman, too, they all three sighed aside.
(*to* HARDRESS) In this way don't heigho, absurd young man,
Remember what I *howe* to Corrigan.

Anne. (*to* KYRLE) What are you crying at?

Kyrle. The tears will flow,
To think that you're a going for to go,
To marry Hardress Cregan—oh, oh, oh!
Of tears within this miserable head
I have a *little store*, and little shed.

Anne. Go up to 'Muckross Head,' and see your *Eily*;
Kyrle Daly, I have done with you *enti-ly*.

The NOTARY—*an operatic version of the Magistrate here advances.*

Notary. Now then, now then my merry lads and lasses
The tempus fugits that is—the time passes.
Remember, too, 'the wine is ruby bright'
If of my love for poesy I might
Another pleasing specimen afford;
Likewise 'the glasses sparkle on the board'.
Behold my very wealthy friends in me
What at the Opera's termed the Notaree.
I generally come on at the end,
My presence and authority to lend
At signing marriage contracts and consigning
The villain to his punishment, then joining
The virtuous peasants—all as brave as Rollas—
With hearts as open as are their shirt collars,
In the finale just to give variety.
The Notary is quite a Notoriety.

Mrs. C. (*to* HARDRESS) Now, sir, your signature.
(*going to table,* L.)

Hard. (*signing*) There's mine. (*handing pen to* ANNE)

Notary. The Nib's
Quite worthy Miss, a lady of your 'Dibbs'.

Kyrle. (*to* ANNE *as she goes*) Think what you do!

Anne. (*with pen in hand*)   I fear that I shall drop.

Mrs. C. (*aside*) She signs—we're saved!

Hard. (*aside*)   She thinks about it.

(CORRIGAN *has entered from* C. *unperceived—now seizes the paper*)

Corri.   Stop!

(*consternation and chord, all get to places*—KYRLE, ANNE, HARDRESS, R.—MRS. CREEGAN, C.—CORRIGAN, LADIES, *table*, L.)

Corri.   This marriage don't proceed!

Mrs. C.   What do you mean?

Corri.   Of course you've heard what's come to the Colleen.

(MRS. CREGAN *is strongly agitated, and leans against* HARDRESS)

Anne. (*speaking at* KYRLE) At last we shall your perfidy discover.

Corri.   She's been chucked in the river by her lover!

All.   Oh!

Corri.   Though not found drowned *herself*, some clothes we've got
        Of hers which were *found round* about the spot.

Anne. (R., *pushing* KYRLE *forward*) Seize him! Oh, after all your vows and
                letters;
        How I could comb your hair! (*to* SERG.) produce your fetters;
        Your heaviest—he's strong as are some lions.

Kyrle.   Fetters! You wouldn't see your *Kyrle in irons*?
                                            (*weeps*)

Corri.   Lions! Ha, ha!

Serg.   He howls as if in pain.
                    This lion is a turning on the *main*.
                    He's not the prisoner at all.

Kyrle.   Oh, joy!

Mrs. C.   Who is the guilty party, then?

Corri. (*maliciously*)   Your boy.

            (ANNE *falls against* KYRLE—MRS. C. *against* HARDRESS.)
Hard.   I drown the Colleen Bawn!—my wife!

Anne. (*reviving*)   Holloa!
                    I think you said your *wife*.
Corri. (L.)   Precisely so.
            (*to* HARDRESS) If drowned, this conduct *small of you* must be
                    And if she's living why it's *big o' me*.

Mrs. C.   My Hardress commit bigamy! Oh jigger me,
                    Polygamy! Oh horror!

Kyrle. (R.)   Dash the wig o' me.
                    Idiot—to thus decline 'wife' in the plural.

Corri.   Your duty do, Sergeant O'Tooralooral;
                    Behold your prisoner!—handcuff him.

                    (SERGEANT *comes down with handcuffs*, L.)

Mrs. C. (*standing before* HARDRESS)   Do!
                    I may be bold, but I'll warm *h*-and cuff you.

Hard.   Fortune has showered on me her rebuffs;
                    'Stead of Anne *Chute*, I've only got *'and-cuffs*.

Corri.   Away with him! upon the villain seize.

Notary.   Oh, let's not be operatic if you please.

Anne. (*stepping forward*, R.) Ladies, if you've one spark of courage left—

Of Irish pluck, if you're not quite bereft,
Protect young Cregan from these hounds.

1st. Lady.   Our hands
And nails likewise are yours, speak your commands.

2nd Lady.   Tell us to scratch his face and we'll obey
Oh, this is something like a wedding day.

Anne.   Form Crinoline! (*the* LADIES *stand in a row*)
Dress! Good!—surround that youth—
(*they form a sort of square*, R.C., *kneeling, with their fans*
open—HARDRESS *stands in the middle—Picture.*)

Corri.   I'm getting rather nervous, that's the truth.
(*aloud*) I'll dash, my friend, your Matrimonial Cup.
Sergeant O'Tooralooral back me up.

(*As he advances*, MRS. CREGAN *seizes and thumps him.*)

Mrs. C.   There! there! and there!

Corri.   Ha! ha! a blow!
Sergeant, you witnessed that assault, you know.
War to the knife.

Notary.   War: all this wrangling cease;
Let me suggest a grand concerted piece.

(*When the air of 'The Cure' is heard, piano, all the*
characters stand in attitude of great surprise)[45]

Concerted Piece.— 'The Cure.'

Hard. (*dancing*) What sounds are those that break upon mine ears in tones so wild?
Mrs. C. (*dancing*) Oh! something tells me that I shan't be parted from my child.
(*a* FOOTMAN *dances on to* C. *from* L.)
Footman. (*dancing*) Oh! if you please, there is a gent and lady at the door.
Hard.   Then go and show them in at once—that man's a perfect boor.
All. (*jumping*)   A boor! a boor! a boor! &c. &c. &c.
Exit, FOOTMAN, L.—*jumping.*

---

[45] *attitude* A static, but richly expressive pose held by a performer during the climax of a
scene.

Enter MILES, *dancing from* L., *and down* C.

Miles.	A kind good morrow, ladies all,
	    And gentlemen as well;
	To aid the wedding peal, I've brought
	    Another marriage belle.
	Oh, please look on her kindly,
	    For she's virtuous, though poor.

Hard.	Good gracious me—who can it be?

Enter EILY—*dancing from* L., *and down* C.

Eily   Why, Eily, to be sure!

All. (*dancing*)   Oh sure! oh sure! oh sure! &c. &c. &c.
                         (*stop dancing*)

Hard. (R.C.)   Returned?

Mrs. C. (L.C.)   Like a bad shilling—very strange.

Eily. (C.)   I love you still—bad shillings never change!

Miles. (L. *of* EILY) What, Eily a bad shilling, no such thing;
            She's good—and you may know that *by the ring.*
    (*to* HARDRESS) Oh, take her to your arms, and don't be shy;
            Don't be at all uneasy—she's quite dry.

Corri. (L.)   Two wives you'll have, thanks to this new arrival;
            Well, this is a most wonderful *revival.*

                  (HARDRESS *and* EILY embrace)

Kyrle. (R.)   Oh, Anne, pray say that you forgive me too.

Anne. (L. *of* KYRLE) Well, as you've not done anything—I do.[46]
                    (*they embrace*)

Corri.   This seems to be such fine embracing weather
            Sergeant! suppose we do a hug together.

---

[46] *you've not done anything* Refers both to Kyrle's innocence and to his irrelevance in terms of the plot structure: he hasn't 'done anything' wrong and he hasn't 'done anything' to assist the play. See also n. 7, above.

(CORRIGAN *and* SERGEANT *embrace, L., corner*)

Music.—DANNY MAN *appears at C., from L., and comes down—appears
very mouldy, his nose red, and made up generally to appear influenza-ish.*

Miles. (L.C.) Why, how have you turned up?

Dan. (L. *of* MILES)   I don't know whether
　　　　　　　　I oughtn't to be 'turned up' altogether.
　　　　　　　　What with my taking cold in that there *watter*,
　　　　　　　　And being shot, and taken for a hotter;
　　　　　　　　You thought you shot an otter, but you shot a man,
　　　　　　　　A Turkish bath in fact you gave this *otter-man.*
　　　　　　　　But I survived sufficiently, my hearty,
　　　　　　　　To join the chorus and the wedding party;
　　　　　　　　For most extremely anxious to be on,
　　　　　　　　Was Danny Man, at this her *Danny-mong.*[47]

Corri. (L.)　　　I've got you in my power, and I'll show it;
　　　　　　　　About my bill—you *owe it*—oh—*bill-ow it!*
　　　　　　　　I've never seen the colour of your metal.

Miles.　　　　　We've something much more pressing first to settle.
　　　　　　　　(*to the Audience*) Some critics may be found to rail
　　　　　　　　　　　　　in fury,
　　　　　　　　At rhyme and rubbish on the stage of Drury;[48]
　　　　　　　　But surely no particular harm's done,
　　　　　　　　If for the foggy nights we get some fun,
　　　　　　　　Without the works of genius ridiculing,
　　　　　　　　Or vexing great men's ghosts with our tom-fooling;
　　　　　　　　Our object's but an hour away to while
　　　　　　　　In mirth, we simply seek to raise a smile
　　　　　　　　At nobody's expense—save those who pay,
　　　　　　　　To come and see our merry little play:
　　　　　　　　Then pray accept the dish we've set before ye,
　　　　　　　　Applaud our wild per-version of the story,
　　　　　　　　And welcome Miss O'Connor—*con-a-more.*[49]

---

[47] *Danny-mong* Corruption of 'denouement'.

[48] *Drury* Drury Lane Theatre, where *Miss Eily O'Connor* was first performed in 1861.

[49] *con amore* With affection; also, a pun on Connamore, a city in the County of Cork, Ireland.

Finale.— '*Rosalie, the Prairie Flower.*'

Hard.	Smile on the endeavour
	We have made to-night,
Dan.	We've tried the utmost of our power,
Hard.	Though by no means clever,
	Say we give you slight
Dan.	Amusement for an idle hour.
Miles.	We can't be always weeping—
	Tears in winter time
	Are apt to freeze, so keep in
	Good temper at our rime,
	Tell your friends to peep in
	Ere the pantomime
Eily.	On Rose Eilee, the Dairy Flower.

CURTAIN

1863; OR,
THE SENSATIONS OF THE PAST SEASON

H.J.BYRON
(1863)

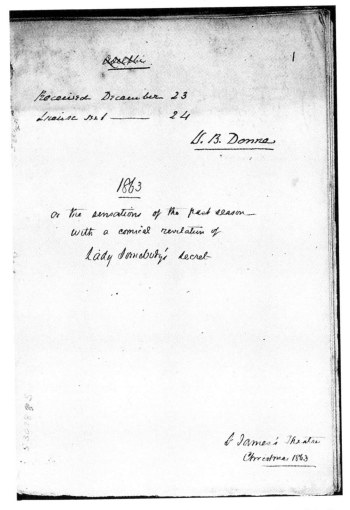

9 Title page of the original manuscript of *1863; or, the Sensations of the Past Season*
(British Library Add Ms 53,028 S)

Editor's Introduction

1863; or, The Sensations of the Past Season

H.J. Byron's *1863; or, The Sensations of the Past Season*, which premiered at the St. James's Theatre on Boxing Day in 1863, is part revue and part burlesque. The first half of this disjointed, but amusing play—a survey of the 1863 London theatre season—recalls Planché's similarly topical revues *Success; or, a Hit if You Like* (Adelphi 1825), *The Drama at Home; or, An Evening with Puff* (Haymarket 1844), *The Camp at the Olympic* (Olympic 1853), and *The New Haymarket Spring Meeting* (Haymarket 1855).[1]   The usual conceit for this type of performance is that an actor-manager, playing himself, seeks the advice of a magical sprite or allegorical figure to help him decide which play his theatre should produce first.   Much of the performance consists of speeches by personifications of the principal dramatic genres (tragedy, comedy, melodrama, farce, pantomime, and burlesque), allusions to recent theatrical productions, and even parodic recreations of memorable scenes from those productions.   In *1863*, Byron directs much of his satire at the Adelphi Theatre and its productions of such sensational melodramas as *Aurora Floyd*, *The Haunted Man and the Ghost's Bargain*, *Lady Audley's Secret*, and *Leah, the Jewish Maiden*.

Like Planché before him, Byron uses burlesque not only to satirize contemporary performances but also to declare the legitimacy of the seemingly illegitimate genre of burlesque.   Through the character of the Author—perhaps a stand-in for the comic dramatist himself—Byron defends the burlesque's traditional claim to elevate the standards of dramatic literature through its constructive ridicule:

> Burlesque is like the winnowing machine:
> It simply blows away the husks, you know,
> The goodly corn is not moved by the blow.
> What arrant rubbish of the clap-trap school
> Has vanished—thanks to pungent ridicule;
> What stock stage customs, nigh to bursting goaded,
> With so much blowing up have now exploded.

In asserting the critical value of burlesque, Byron dramatizes theatrical ghosts who demand revenge for having been ill-treated by 'legitimate' actor-managers.   To be sure, stage ghosts were something of a cliché even in the Victorian theatre.   Earlier that year, Tom Taylor had employed the same strategy in *An Awful Rise in Spirits*.   Byron, for his part, invokes ghostly characters from *The Haunted Man*,

The Corsican Brothers, *Macbeth*, and *Hamlet*.   In a felicitous example of theatrical parody, Banquo's ghost complains that 'Archaeologists' have dismissed his traditional stage costume as 'improper'.   The allusion here is to the historically accurate sets, costumes, and properties featured in contemporary Shakespearean revivals.   By 1863, burlesque Banquo's anachronistic tartan kilt, yellow stockings, and beribboned bonnet would have offended the sensibilities of historically conscious theatregoers.   Yet the vogue for theatrical historicism is not the only threat facing Byron's venerable stage spectre.   The ghost fears that he is about to be cast aside in favour of 'Pepper's Ghost', a popular magic trick which produces convincing stage apparitions through the manipulation of '[l]imelight and glass'.   In short, Banquo's ghost is besieged on all sides.   High-minded theatrical antiquarians dress him in borrowed robes while sensationalizing producers want to replace him with a magic trick.

       The second half of *1863* is a straightforward burlesque of George Roberts' melodrama *Lady Audley's Secret*, the 'sanction[ed]' stage version of Mary Elizabeth Braddon's extremely popular sensation novel published a year earlier.[2] The St. James's Theatre was, in this instance, burlesquing itself since it had produced Roberts' play the previous season.   The 'legitimate' production of *Lady Audley's Secret*, whose cast included the actor-manager Frank Mathews, remained on the nightly bill at the St. James's for several months.   Like other sensation melodramas, the plot consisted primarily of astonishing coincidences, contrivances, and revelations.   George Talboys, a young soldier, has abandoned his wife and infant son to seek his fortune in Australia.   His impoverished wife Helen, leaving their son in her father's care, reinvents herself as Lucy Graham and becomes a governess in a respectable household in the English countryside. Shortly thereafter, she meets—and soon marries—Sir Robert Audley, a wealthy widower.   Sir Robert, unaware of his wife's true identity, does not realize that he has entered into a bigamous marriage.   The play begins when Talboys, now a wealthy man, returns from Australia.   Believing his wife dead, Talboys seeks solace in the company of his friend Robert Audley, Sir Michael's nephew.   Robert suggests a visit to Audley Court, his uncle's estate.   Little does Talboys expect to discover that his wife not only is alive but that she has become Lady Audley.   The first act culminates in Talboys' fatal confrontation with his estranged wife, who, not wanting to be exposed as a bigamist, pushes him down a well.[3]   In the second act, Lady Audley's guilt is exposed and Talboys miraculously reappears, having been secretly rescued by the gamekeeper Luke Marks.   Lady Audley, overwhelmed by the events her deception set in motion, collapses in a fit of madness.[4]

       In *1863*, the young J.L. Toole starred as burlesque Lady Audley, Fanny Josephs played the 'trouser' role of Robert Audley, and the corpulent Paul Bedford (then more famous than Toole) appeared as   'George Tall (or Paul) Boys'. Byron's parodic sketch drastically abbreviates Roberts' melodrama, which itself necessarily abbreviates Braddon's original novel.   What Byron has written, then, is an absurdly compressed narrative which is acutely conscious of its own gaps and omissions.   Only ten minutes after Tallboys' disappearance Robert Audley confidently concludes that his friend has been murdered.   Toward the end of the play, Lady Audley concedes that 'it's much too late' for her to do 'all sorts of things [she] ought to do;/According to the story'.   And in the final moment, when Tallboys emerges from the well, a 'fog' descends upon the stage, emblematizing the murkiness of the unresolved dramatic narrative. Fancy, expediting matters, insists that 'long explanations would be rather slow' and that everyone would be better off simply by singing the finale. The ensemble does just that, pushing the performance into a hasty and forced conclusion.

The text of *1863* is taken from Lacy's acting edition, collated with the British Library manuscript (Add Ms 53,028 S) and an original promptbook in the Frank Pettingell Collection at the University of Kent at Canterbury.[5] As a comparison between the manuscript and the promptbook reveals, almost the entire final scene was written at the last minute—that is, after the script had been sent to the Lord Chamberlain's Office for licensing. Since plays were usually licensed only a day or two before they opened, Byron would not have had much time for revision. So we should not be surprised that the new scene was written on loose sheets of paper simply inserted at the back of the promptbook. Initially, the play had only four scenes and ended with Fancy's injunction to '[s]ing a finale'. In the revised version, however, scene four concludes with Lady Audley fainting as Tallboys climbs out of the well, singing 'I'm all alive, oh!/I did survive, oh!'. At the beginning of the new (fifth) scene, Lady Audley paces the stage, wondering how to handle her '[t]wo husbands'. She has a brief scene with Robert Audley, who threatens to send for the police. Their exchange concludes with a song and dance to the tune 'Hop light, Loo'. The play then continues with dialogue written for the original scene four, with fog descending and Fancy introducing three 'transformation' scenes: 'The Land of the Thistle' (Scotland), 'The Land of the Shamrock' (Ireland), and 'The Land of the Roses' (England).

Why did Byron write a new scene practically the day before his play opened? One clue provided by the promptbook is that the new scene was performed as a 'front scene'—that is, a scene played far downstage in front of a backdrop which masked an intricate scene change. What most likely happened is that the stagehands needed more time to put the three transformation scenes in place. Yet the only way to get more time was for Byron to write a new scene, ideally one which included songs that could be encored if yet further time were needed to change the set. This is exactly what happened on opening night. The excruciatingly slow changeover compelled Fancy to keep on singing, and the 'gods' in the gallery grew impatient with the delay. As the *Era* observed, the repeated songs 'drew down ominous sounds from the upper portions of the house'.[6] Byron's last-minute revisions vividly attest that the burlesque script was essentially a function of the performance—and not the other way around.

For biographical information on H.J. Byron, see the introduction to *Miss Eily O'Connor*.

Notes

[1] For a brief discussion of *The Camp at the Olympic*, see the introduction to this volume.

[2] Playbill, St. James's Theatre, London, 16 March 1863, Harvard Theatre Collection, The Houghton Library. The other principal stage version, by Colin Hazelwood, premiered at the working-class Victoria Theatre (now the 'Old Vic'), also in 1863.

[3] In Roberts' play, the final, murderous act occurs off-stage and is narrated for the audience by Luke Marks, who sees it from a distance. The burlesque puts the action at centre stage. The novel, by contrast, does not include the scene at all.

[4] Braddon's novel is much more a detective story than any of its stage adaptations. George Talboys disappears fairly early on, and most of the story is about Robert Audley's obsessive drive to identify—and then hunt down—his friend's killer.

[5] The promptbook is unhelpfully indexed under the mangled sub-title *Lady Somebury's Secret*.

[6] *Era* 3 January 1864.

1863; or, The Sensations of the Past Season

First performed at the Theatre Royal, St. James's, (under the management of Mr. Benjamin Webster,) on Saturday, the 26th of December, 1863.

The Highly Successful Comical Conglomerative Absurdity, entitled

1863;
OR, THE SENSATIONS OF THE PAST SEASON, WITH A SHAMEFUL REVELATION OF LADY SOMEBODY'S SECRET![1]

Programme of Scenery, Characters, &c.

Scene 1. THE AUTHOR'S CHAMBERS.

Fancy (*only Fancy*)...Miss Adeline Cottrell
An Author (*who is supposed to supply the Management with
    a Piece, but doesn't*)................................Miss Fanny Josephs
Mrs. Brown (*by permission of Arthur Sketchley—his
    Housekeeper*)...Mr. J.L. Toole
The Haunted Man..............{ 'Black Spirits }......................''..........
Our Dear Friend, Banquo......{ and White,   } ....''..........
Hamlet's Father.................{ Red Spirits }......................''..........
A Corsican Brother.............{ and Grey,' }.....................''............

Scene 2. A HOARDING IN LONDON

A French Gentleman from the Lyceum......................….......Mr. J. L. Toole
A Misanthropic Gentleman from Drury Lane.....…...….......''.............
An Alluring Lady from the Adelphi...........................…......Miss Percival

THE NOVEL DETERMINATION AND THE DUET.

---

[1] The promptbook in the Frank Pettingell Collection, University of Kent at Canterbury, gives another sub-title: 'Comical Revelation of Lady Somebody's Secret'.

Scene 3. ROBERT AUDLEY'S CHAMBERS.

Robert Audley (*a young Barrister, who does not find that Life
        is Brief*)...Miss Fanny Josephs
George Tall (or Paul) Boys (*who finding himself short at home
        has been long abroad*)................................Mr. Paul Bedford

TO AUDLEY COURT, AWAY!

Scene 4. THE GOTHIC CHAMBER AND THE LIME-TREE WALK!

Lady Audley (*can't describe her—see her*).....................Mr. J.L. Toole
Sir Michael (*who proves that all's Fish that comes to the
        Baro-net*)..Mr. Chamberlain
Luke Marks (*bad marks decidedly*).....................Mr. James Johnstone
Phoebe (*a Damsel who hasn't much to do
        and does it*)...Miss Dalton

The Meeting! The Crime! All's well that ends swell—several exciting
    incidents, leading to a Decided Fog—and eventually to a charming
                        closing Scene, illustrative of the
    Land of Thistles, Land of Shamrocks, and the Land of the Roses!

Eventually combining in the FINAL SCENE of

THE HERALDIC HOLIDAY.

SCENE FIRST.—*Study of the* AUTHOR—*a handsome apartment, comfortably
furnished. Bookshelves—table covered with papers, pens, ink, &c; door* R. *and*
L.; *mysterious music.*

Enter from L. *door, the* AUTHOR, *he is smoking a cigar—he walks up and down
the room for some moments—pauses and hits his forehead.*

Author.   I've got it! No, I haven't—wish I had.
               Hum! my position's really rather sad;
               I am an author—pity if you can,
               I need it more than any *author* man.
               T'wards winter time the agonies increase
               Of those, who like me have to find a piece
               For Christmas, and I can't a subject get;—
               I haven't got the smallest piece as yet.
               I've had the *fee*; my brain will *addled* be

E're I've the piece done for the *Addle-fee*.[2]
I've worked most certainly, but I must say
At present it's been all work and no play.
             (*goes to table and sits*)
The mighty Molière, I have heard it said,
To his old housekeeper his dramas read.
Her critical remarks determined what
Slight alteration in the words and plot
Would make them more effective. I, (*rises*) like him,
Will from her lonely kitchen deep and dim,
Call Mrs. Brown, my housekeeper, she may
Give me a hint perhaps for my Christmas play.

    (*Ballet Music—the* AUTHOR *goes through pantomime*
        business and rings bell—he then comes down
        to front)

Enter MRS. BROWN, R., *door, a Gampish elderly female*.[3]

    Come, Mrs. Brown, ma'am, your advice is needed.

Mrs. B.   Which when the bell was rung and frighten me it did,
            For nerves had always been with me through life
            A drawback—going through me like a knife—
            I was a sittin' down to—I declare—
            As nice a hand of pork as ever were,
            Which is not my habit, beyond question,
            To suppers eat, because of indigestion,
            Which troubled with I've been, I must admit,
            Since a mere infant, 'but a little bit,'
            Says Mrs. Mivins, sir, a friend of mine
            She is, and lives at number thirty-nine
            Little Godolphin street, just past the baker's,
            And almost opposite the undertaker's.
            'A little bit,' she says, says she, 'won't do
            No harm to me, mum—no—nor yet to you,
            Which little 'appiness you ever get.'
            And there, upon the instant, off she set
            Together *with* a basin *and* a saucer,
            Which the biled pork till nine from half-past four, sir,
            Is, as a body might say, 'laid on;' which,
            A simmering for hours, it gets that rich,
            Not to say juicy, as makes party's feel

---

[2] *Addle-fee* Pun on the Adelphi Theatre, where the original *Lady Audley's Secret* was performed.
[3] *Gampish* Gossipy.

That 'ungry, which it's an unwholesome meal
Of that I am aware, but werry nice,
And if I might suggest an 'umble slice—
If not, you won't consider me too bold,
But pork's a nasty knack of gittin cold.

Author.   Bother. Shut up. Hem! Pauca verba. Stop it.

Mrs. B.   A small bit on a hot plate I'll just pop it,
A piece of nice peas pudding too and—

Author.   Cease.
I wish to speak about another piece—
A Christmas one. I don't know what to do.
Can't you suggest a subject, something new?

Mrs. B.   Which at suggestions I'm by no means happy,
Ain't there no news at present on the tappy?

(*Music. Vampire*)

FANCY *enters suddenly through the panelling,* C.,
MRS. BROWN *shrieks.*

Fancy. (C.)   Don't be alarmed. I'm Fancy—only Fancy!

Mrs. B. (R.)   Which I must say I wish I was with Nancy.

Author.   You're Fancy are you? It appears to me
That most decidedly you're Fancy free.

Fancy.   Now don't be personal or I retort.
I've come to aid you.

Author. (L., *aside*)   Which are things *is* short.

Fancy.   You want a subject—very good. Let's see.
How about D'Anois?[4]

Author.   Done to death.

Fancy.   May be,
But still—

_____

[4] *D'Anois* Marie-Catherine, Countess d'Anois (1650-1705), author of fairy tales and nursery stories, including the original *Goldilocks* (*Belle aux Cheaveaux d'Or*). Many of her stories were turned into stage extravaganzas during the nineteenth century (see n. 5, below).

Author.	A brilliant graceful pen you know Has worked that golden mine out long ago.[5]
Fancy.	The classics?
Author.	Done, both jovially and neatly.
Fancy.	The Arabian Nights?
Author.	. Used up.
Fancy.	What all?
Author.	Completely.
Mrs. B.	Might I suggest Will Watch, or more amusing, Jonathan Bradford, sir, or Black Eyed Susing.[6] Though I must say one really didn't ought For to see reticule on either brought.

Medley Trio.—'Wanted, a Governess.'

Author.	Wanted a subject that's suited to fill The front of the house and the manager's till, A powerful name for the holiday bill; There's ever a way when you've once got the will, When you've once got the will. One that with fun and with pun's sure to kill.

'I'm not Guilty.'—La Sonnambula.

Fancy.	Italian opera With choruses tra la la la, Have been done to death And punn'd to death, Over and over again.

---

[5] *brilliant graceful pen* Reference to the playwright J.R. Planché (1796-1880), who wrote numerous extravaganzas based upon stories by the Countess d'Anois. Among them are *The Fair One with the Golden Locks* (1844), *Fortunio and his Seven Gifted Servants* (1843), *The Golden Branch* (1848), *The Island of Jewels* (1849), and *The King of the Peacocks* (1848). Following in Planché's footsteps, Byron himself later wrote extravaganzas based on the Countess's stories, including *The Orange Tree and the Humble Bee* (1871) and *Princess Spring-Time* (1864).

[6] *Jonathan Bradford* (1833) Melodrama by Edward Fitzball (1792-1873); *Black Eyed Sus[an]* (1820), a nautical melodrama by Douglas Jerrold (1803-57). See F.C. Burnand's burlesque *The Very Latest Edition of Black-Eyed Susan* (1866) in this volume.

> Ballets popular,
> Mazurka and the Corsair
> Have been both extravaganza'd
> And have answered very well.[7]

'Polly Perkins.'

Mrs. B.   Oh, ain't there no song as is going about,
           Which is set to the horgins, and little boys shout;[8]
           There's a ditty as is poppylar, if the subject's conven-
           Ient, called Pretty Polly Perkins of Paddington Green.
All.   There's a ditty, &c.

Fancy.   Is there no serious drama now the go
           That's capable of comic treatment?

Author.   No.

Fancy.   Can't anything be done about Tom King,
           British endurance, and that sort of thing?[9]
Author.   That's a mere episode, besides it's low,
           I want a *subject*, not a King, you know.

Fancy.   A bright idea's struck me; wait a bit.

Author.   Well, if it *struck* you, it must be a *hit*.
           What is it?

Fancy.   Well, suppose instead of one
           Subject, at which to poke one's Christmas fun,
           We go through the sensations of the season,
           With rhyme, in which may lurk a little reason;
           A retrospective glance take of the past;
           And with a comprehensive vision vast,
           At the sensations take a sight, you see,
           Of bygone Eighteen hundred sixty-three.

---

[7] Opera and ballet were frequently burlesqued in such plays as Leicester Buckingham's *La Traviata; or, the Lady Chameleon* (1857) and Charles Selby's *The Judgment of Paris; or, the Pas de Pippins* (1846).

[8] *horgins* Transcription of the Cockney pronunciation of 'organs'; a reference to itinerant organ-grinders and other street musicians.

[9] *Tom King* A reference to W.E. Suter's play *Dick Turpin & Tom King* (1861). Turpin and King were both eighteenth-century highwaymen who worked together to rob travellers along the road from London to Oxford.

Then when we've done, 'twill be for you to choose
The one most calculated to amuse.

Author.   Your hand upon't—a first-rate notion.

Fancy.   Well;
At once, I'd best commence to weave my spell.
The lights a little down, please—take your post,
While I first summon the Adelphi Ghost.
               (*lights lowered—tremulous music*)
      From your distant spirit can,
      Dircks and Pepper's Haunted Man;[10]
      Or from out your box where you
      Kept are till the lights burn blue;
      By the run you had of late,
      By the ashes of the grate,
      By the spectral music weird,
      Which they played when you appeared;
      By the shiver in the pit,
      When you laughed at Redlaw's hit,[11]
      By the folks who places sought,
      By the lots of tin you brought,
      By the hearts in dread which beat,
      By the length of your 'poor feet,'
      By the stage, the wings, the flies,
      By plum puddings and mince pies,
      I command thee to arise.

(*incantation music from 'Robert the Devil,'* and the ADELPHI
GHOST OF HAUNTED MAN *rises C-more miserable, if
possible, than ever*)[12]

---

[10] *Dircks and Pepper's Haunted Man* The magician John Henry Pepper and his partner Henry Dircks created an ingenious mechanism whereby a stage 'ghost' could appear to materialize in front of an audience. In Pepper's trick, popularized at the Royal Polytechnic, the image of a person standing beneath the stage floor was projected through a series of mirrors onto a large sheet of glass slotted into the stage floor and held up by imperceptible wires. From the audience's perspective the resulting projection appeared to be an incorporeal presence. Because 'Pepper's Ghost' was only a reflection a stage actor could seem to pierce it with a knife or even to walk through it. When the gas lamps beneath the stage were turned on and off, the stage ghost seemed to materialize and to vanish.

[11] The promptbook reads 'When you didn't mind the hit'.

[12] *Adelphi Ghost of Haunted Man* A highlight of the Adelphi's 1862-3 season was its production of *The Haunted Man and the Ghost's Bargain*, Mark Lemon's dramatic adaptation of the 1848 story by Charles Dickens. The popular Adelphi production, which ran for eighty-five nights, included several tableaux in which ghosts appeared. The novel performance, starring J.L. Toole, copied the technique of Pepper's Ghost.

Author.   Is this the Ghost? He seems in sad condition.

Ghost of H.M.   Oh, I'm a very wretched Pepper-ition!

Mrs. B.   Which, *ap*parition, I suppose, is meant.

Ghost of H.M.   You recollect how very well I went;
                     Well, hosts of copies rose around about—
                     The speculation paying past a doubt.
                     But my ghost, like a knife at the theayters,
                     Cut out the specs of all the imi*taters*.
                     Still, Pepper said I should protected be;
                     He's now, like Horniman's, a *patent-tea*.[13]
                     The Chancellor did grant it—it's a bore
                     To those who rather dread the *chance o' law*.
                     The others are *ex*-spectres now, you see,
                     Which they did not of course *expecter* be.

                     (*Music of a Caledonian nature, at the last
                            note Banquo comes up trap* L. *quickly*)

Fancy.   Hah! by the itching of my thumbs
                     There's something Scottish this way comes.[14]
                     'Tis Banquo's Ghost. We'll have 'em all, and see
                     Which is the best one for our travestie.

Author.   He came up sharp enough, too, from below.

Fancy.   The Scotch do rise uncommon quick, you know.

Mrs. B.   The trap which hoists a Scot with sudden pop
                     Must have been purchased at a *Scott's hoister* shop.

Ghost of Banquo (*shaking*). A weel, weel, weel, weel. (*pause*)

Fancy.   Proceed, I pray.
                     You might go on with *four wheels*, I should say.

The *Observer* praised the 'vividness of the illusions' but complained that the ghosts did not serve a 'better dramatic purpose' (22 June 1863).

[13] *Horniman's, a patent-tea* A popular brand of tea in the Victorian era, manufactured by the merchant John Horniman; also a pun on 'patentee', the name for a theatrical proprietor who owned an exclusive right—a royal patent—to produce spoken theatre in London. The patent oligopoly, dating from the Restoration, was abolished when the Theatres Regulation Act was passed in 1843. In this instance, 'patentee' is used in the looser sense of a producer who has leased a theatre.

[14] Cf. Second Witch, 'By the pricking of my thumbs,/Something wicked this way comes' (*Macbeth* 4.1.44-5).

Ghost of Banquo. I dinna ken the joke. Well, Mistress Fancy,
        I answer to the call of necromancy.
        I've left my native clime, and here I've come.

Mrs. B.   He won't be a Scotch *missed* there, will he, mum?

Ghost of Banquo. Alas! the times are changed. Some years ago
        I wore—

Mrs. B.   A wreath of roses?

Fancy.   Silence!

Ghost of Banquo.   No;
        But cross-barred stockings, kilt pouch, large Scotch bonnet,
        My neck a broad gash of rose pink had on it;
        My arms and legs did yellow fleshings wear,
        And looked, excepting wrinkles, really bare.
        But Archaeologists clapped on a stopper,
        Declaring that my costume was improper.[15]

Mrs. B.   Which they was right. I've often said to Brown,
        'How them Scotch gents can walk about the town,
        Especially in such cold weather—'

Ghost of Banquo.   So,
        They changed my dress; but heavier far the blow
        I'm to endure. The Ghost of Pepper means
        To take my place at future banquet scenes.
        Limelight and glass contrive to overthrow[16]
        The flesh and blood ghost of defunct Banquo.
        This for the drama's an unlucky age,
        When thus they *cast reflections* on the stage.

Fancy.   We must march with the times, my friend; but stay,
        Another ghost had better step this way.
        The Ghost of Hamlet's father.

Mrs. B.   Which I were
        Took quite aback by him at Greenwich Fair.

---

[15] On parodies of historically correct costumes, see the introduction to this play.

[16] *contrive* The promptbook reads 'combine'.

> Which Hamlet, Susan Hopley, and a ballet,[17]
> Was played in ten minnits exactually.

The GHOST OF HAMLET'S FATHER *enters through trap in the bookcase,* C.

Author.   Right through the book! Let's see, which volume—where?
                     The works of Martin Tupper, I declare![18]
                     In eighteen volumes—see—two lengthy rows;

Mrs. B.   He was a clever ghost to *get through* those.

Ghost of H.F.   You talk of your disgrace, indeed; it's small
                     Compared to mine at Canterbury Hall;[19]
                     Exhibited—but not allowed to speak—
                     For—but I can't say what I got a week.
                     It's driven me to drink; for when I think
                     Of what I was, despondently I sink;
                     And recollection of before my fall,
                     I in the full de-*canter bury all.*
                     Frown not, my son; I don't your anger merit—
                     I'm never drunk, though I'm thy father's *spirit!*

Fancy.   Another still—one of the noted pair
                     Of twins!
                               (*the 'Ghost Melody' from 'The Corsican Brothers'*)
                     I feel he comes from that Kean air![20]

The GHOST OF THE CORSICAN BROTHER *rises,* R.

---

[17] George Dibdin Pitt's *Susan Hopley; or, the Vicissitudes of a Servant Girl* (1841) was a melodramatic 'thriller' first produced at the Victoria Theatre but later performed elsewhere, including the Adelphi. The play was adapted from Catherine Crowe's novel *The Adventures of Susan Hopley* (1841).

[18] Martin Farquhar Tupper (1810-89), Victorian moralist and author of the best-selling *Proverbial Philosophy* (1838). Tupper, nicknamed 'The People's Poet Laureate', was a frequent object of ridicule.

[19] *Canterbury Hall* One of the first London music halls, built in Lambeth, south London, in the 1850s. Music halls were not licensed to perform scripted drama, hence the Ghost's complaint that he could not speak. The subsequent reference to 'drink' alludes to the music halls' licence to serve alcohol. Managers of West End theatres grew increasingly frustrated that music halls could reap greater profits than 'legitimate' theatres simply because of their ability to sell liquor.

[20] *Kean air* Pun on the actor-manager Charles Kean, who first produced Dion Boucicault's melodrama *The Corsican Brothers* at the Princess's Theatre, London, in 1852. See H.J. Byron's *The Corsican 'Bothers'* in this volume. As the only child of the legendary tragedian Edmund Kean, he was indeed a 'Kean air [heir]'.

Ghost of C.B.   What's this? the ghost of Fabian dei Franchi[21]
Give way to Dircks and Pepper's hankey pankey?
I, who in distant forest was laid low,
With one artistic fatal *Fontaine blow*.[22]
The instant that I met with my mishap,
Upon the spot I jumped into a *trap*;[23]
And did appear, although it's rather far,
In course o' time, over in Corsica.
A ghost who does such things shall ne'er be stooper
To the lime-light reflection of a super
Thrown on a sheet of plate glass—it's a shame!
No wonder I'm in such a wretched frame.
I seldom let a friend untreated pass;
But in this case I will *not* 'stand a glass'.[24]

Mrs. B.   I don't feel altogether easy; and
If a lone party might—

Fancy. (*to* GHOSTS)   You understand!
You may retire upon your wretched missions;

Mrs. B.   Which I must say, they seem *un*happy-ritions.
Hope they'll go soon!

Author.   Of that there's little fear;
My spirits always go soon when you're here.

Mrs. B.   Don't let's dispute about such parties, please;
Because tain't often as we disagrees;
Which Brown observed—he seldom spoke at random—
De *ghost*ibus not est disputandem.[25]

---

[21] *Fabian dei Franchi* One of the eponymous Corsican brothers in Boucicault's play. After being murdered in France, his ghost appears to his brother Louis in Corsica. See the introduction to *The Corsican 'Bothers'* in this volume.

[22] *Fontaine blow* Fabien dei Franchi is killed in a duel in the forest of Fontainbleau, outside Paris.

[23] *trap* The 'Corsican Trap'. See the introduction to *The Corsican 'Bothers'* in this volume.

[24] *stand a glass* Pun meaning both to buy someone a drink and to tolerate Pepper's Ghost. See n. 10, above.

[25] *De* ghost*ibus not est disputandem* Pun on *de gustibus non est disputandem* (there's no arguing with someone's taste).

Concerted Piece.—'The Ghost Gallop.'—By F. Musgrave.

Fancy.   Now you down below,
                                    Everyone must toddle,
                          To this pleasant gallop,
                                    Which is called the Ghost.
Mrs. B.   Morning air, you know,
                                    Doesn't suit your noddle.
Author.   You can only stand it for ten minutes at the most.
Ghost of H.M.   I must pop off to the Strand!
Ghost of Banquo.   I must go to Scotland!
Ghost of C.B.   I'm off to Australia to join my brother there![26]
Ghost of H.F.   I must go to what I must denominate a hot land!
Fancy.   Very much obliged to you, pray of yourselves take care.

To the dance finale each GHOST *does a walk round characteristic of his nature—All dance off,* L. 1 E.[27]

SCENE SECOND.—*A large Street Hoarding covered with large advertising Posters of 'Leah,' 'Bel Demonio,' 'Manfred,' &c.*[28]

Enter FANCY *and* AUTHOR, L. 1 E .

Fancy.   A street in London as was lately seen:
                 In advertising now, one can't be mean;
                 If you would catch the capital at all,
                 You must have capitals upon the wall.

Author.   The weakest go unto the wall, they say.[29]

Fancy.   Once, but it's not so in the present day,
                 These railroad times, if you don't mind you'll find
                 Though *right* before, you'll soon be *left* behind.
                 Don't try to save in printing and engraving.

---

[26] *Australia* Reference to Charles Kean's Australian tour.

[27] *walk round* Staging convention borrowed from minstrel shows in which each performer paraded around the stage at the end of a scene, engaging in a dance or movement uniquely identified with his or her character.

[28] *Leah, Bel Demonio, Manfred* Plays performed at London theatres in 1863. Augustin Daly's drama *Leah, the Jewish Maiden* was produced at the Adelphi. It was a phenomenal success, running for over two hundred nights. Lord Byron's dramatic poem *Manfred* (1817) was revived at Drury Lane, and John Brougham's *Bel Demonio*, adapted from a story by Paul Féval, played at the Lyceum.

[29] Cf. Gregory in *Romeo and Juliet*, 'the weakest go to the wall' (1.1.13-14).

Author.   There's much more there of *hoarding* than of saving.

Fancy.   Now keep your eye upon that corner, well,
            Whilst I commence to weave my magic spell. (*Music*)
            Brave Bel Demonio, brigand, lover true,
            Who four long acts and one thick wall gets through;
            Who makes love in a way insinuating,
            Setting all female hearts a palpitating;
            Who, soon as a few tender words are spoken,
            Shows that his English, like his heart, is broken;—
            Fancy commands him to appear. Appear! (*Music*)

(*portion of scene opens and* BEL DEMONIO *appears*, R.)[30]

Bel.   Where is my Lena? Lena isn't here.

Fancy.   You see he's quite agreeable and chatty.

Bel.   My Lena! Oh! I *had a Lena.*

Author.   Patti?

Bel.   She was about to be a nun, I stopped it;
            There was a guard who interfered—I whopped it;
            I put my wife upon my breast and flew;
            But there were fifty at the least to two.
            They took her back—a sleeping draught they gave her,
            And upon stone, the rascals did engrave her;
            But through a buttress thick I slided slap;
            I always was a *buttery* sort of chap;
            I went down, saw my Lena sleeping there,
            So young, so innocent, so passing fair—
            The very beetles stopped to have a stare.
            I shake her once—twice;—Ha, ha, ha, she wakes!
            See! she's reviving in a brace of shakes.
            Angelo! Lena! Ha, my wife! My hubby!
            She recognizes me, though rather grubby.
            A shriek—embrace. Enter the people, headed
            By the old Cardinal, who says we're wedded.
            Convulsive grief distends her father's thorax,
            And mutual forgiveness ends the four acts.

Author.   My gallant foreigner. (*crossing to him*)
                              I'm glad to know you,[31]

---

[30] Toole played the burlesque Bel Demonio as a parody of the Anglo-French actor
Charles Fechter, who played the original role at the Lyceum.

And I admit we really much do owe you,
Our stage did alterations greatly need,
Though the French carpenters did *not* succeed.

Trio.—Air, 'C'est moi qui suis le petit clerc.'

Fancy.   Brave Bel Demonio, pray take care,
                                    And don't give away too much, mon cher,
                                        To this sensation,
                                        And situation;
Author.   But on your dialogues as well,
                                    Bestow your educated taste;
Bel.   But show and bustle always tell,[32]
                                    And money spent on paint's no waste.
                                        And this correction—
Fancy.   We've no objection,
                                        To what you do,
                                        But say to you,
All.   Brave Bel Demonio, pray take care,
                                    And give your patrons solid fare.

Exit BEL DEMONIO *through scene,* R.

Fancy.   Well, there's a subject for you!

Author.   No, it isn't;
                Some things in it if joked would not be pleasant.

Fancy.   The subject though could surely not offend,—
                A strong French melo-drama.

Author.   No, my friend!
                But still I'd rather not.

Fancy.   What would you take?
                Not a grand subject foolery to make?
                Don't drag down works of genius!

Author.   Oh dear, no;
                But, pray, don't turned so very thick-skinned though.
                Though some may scout it, it's as oft's been seen,
                Burlesque is like the winnowing machine:
                It simply blows away the husks, you know,
                The goodly corn is not moved by the blow.

---

[31] *glad* The promptbook reads 'proud'.
[32] *tell* Theatrical jargon for succeeding at the box-office.

What arrant rubbish of the clap-trap school
Has vanished thanks to pungent ridicule;
What stock stage customs, nigh to bursting goaded,
With so much blowing up have now exploded.
Had our light writers done no good save this,
Their doggerel efforts scarce had been amiss.
That's a big poster, and what letters!

Fancy.   Yes,
How they *can* post such letters I can't guess.
Let us invoke him—He's the public well hit.
There, you can *read* the poster while I *spell it*. (*Music*)
Manfred from Drury—gloomy, sombre, pray
Oblige us please by coming round this way.

Author.   He doesn't come.

Fancy.   Have patience, don't you know
Without his scenery he's rather *slow*.

The scene flaps over, discovering Manfred on the rock.[33]

Behold him there upon the rocky brink,
Of misanthropic heroes quite the pink.
Felo de se it seems a case of quite,[34]
A *fellow does see* him through, and holds him tight.
A chamois hunter, and they struggle, but
The chamois hunter's very sure of fut
And saves him. Stay! he speaks.

Manfred.   Oh, fickle town
Who can say what will or won't go down?
Conceived in poet's brain, not to be acted,
It's most extraordinary I attracted.[35]
Remorse at heart, dark fancies in my skull,
Could I be anything but very dull?
My long soliloquies though seldom tired
The crowded audience listened and perspired.
Though 'twas two hours full e'er I'd talking done,

---

[33] A parody of the scene in Lord Byron's play when Manfred, standing on the cliffs of the Jungfrau, is saved by the chamois hunter from committing suicide. As burlesque Manfred, Toole imitated the tragedian Samuel Phelps who had played the role earlier that year at Drury Lane.

[34] *felo de se* Suicide or one who commits suicide; literally, a felon of himself.

[35] *not to be acted* Refers generally to Romantic 'closet' dramas, which were never intended for performance.

I still had breath for a tremendous *run*.
My scenery drew, too, which the fact denotes,
The public must be *canvassed* for their votes.
When you've a good play do all that you can for it.
Say, am I right—or any other Man-fred?

Author.   Manfred won't do to joke, you may retire.[36]

Fancy.   Quite right, good morning.

                                    (*flap closes up*)

Author.   Those overtopping letters look unsteady,
                 As if they'd been imbibing something heady.

Fancy.   Success you know's intoxicating. Leah
                 Has drawn and still draws folks from far and near.
                 A *Jewish* maiden. What! *you wish* to see her?
                 Leah, appear!

                 Music—Enter LEAH *through scene*, L.

                 *Song.—*FANCY*—'Lord Bateman.'*

                 Lord Bateman was a noble lord,
                         A noble lord of high degree,
                 But he was nothing, take my word,
                         To Miss Bateman of the Adelphee.[37]

Leah.   I came across the seas from distant land,
                 And settled safely on a friendly strand.[38]
                 Adelphi, in the Greek, doth brothers mean;
                 Brothers and sisters have the public been.
                 No petty jealousy, no selfish smart
                 Have warped their sense of justice and of art;

---

[36] Possibly a reference to the burlesque *Mad-Fred* performed at the Surrey Theatre in 1863.

[37] *Miss Bateman of the Adelphi* Kate Josephine Bateman (Mrs. George Crowe), an American-born actress who appeared at the Adelphi between 1863 and 1865. Her most famous part was the title role in *Leah*. In James Joyce's *Ulysses*, Leopold Bloom recalls that his father waited for hours outside the Adelphi to obtain a ticket to see Bateman as Ophelia. Her father, Colonel Bateman, was for many years manager of the Lyceum.

And the Old Country has with ardour true
Welcomed this importation from the New.

Author.   Like winking, all are rushing off to see her.

Fancy.   Yes, it's like *winking*, perhaps, 'cos it's a *leer.*

Author.   Leah won't do to touch. You may retire
                                                  Exit LEAH, L.

Fancy.   Good gracious, man, what is it you require?
              The Nile's discovery:—Come, Grant and Speke:[39]
              The great fact of the year.

Author.   The year? It's *weak.*

Fancy.   I see a song to open with, bedad!

Author.   What's that?

Fancy.   Why, 'whistle *a Nile* come to you, my lad.'
              Then at the end cheers from the front to wring,
              Make them all finish with *an 'ile*and fling.

Author.   Nothing could come from it, no, not a bit,
              You know the motto, 'ex nilo nil fit'.[40]

Fancy.   You'v got *an ill fit* of the blues, dear me!
              Nothing will suit you for a play: let's see.
              Oh! there's the Emperor's Congress.[41]

Author.   Prythee cease;
              I wish that congress could but make a *piece.*
              Are there no novels of the season?

Fancy.   Well,
              Some might raise laughter.

---

[38] *friendly strand* Pun on The Strand, the London thoroughfare where the Adelphi
Theatre was located.

[39] *The Nile's discovery* In 1863, John Hanning Speke and Capt. James Augustus Grant
identified Lake Victoria as the source of the Nile River. Speke published his account of
the expedition in his *Journal of the Discovery of the Source of the Nile* (1863).

[40] *ex nilo nil fit* Corruption of *ex nihilo nihil fit*—nothing comes from nothing.

[41] *Emperor's Congress* In 1863 Emperor Franz Joseph of Austria presided over a
congress of German princes held in Frankfurt.

Author.   Yes, they're made to sell.
            Isn't there one would make a screamer?[42]

Fancy.   True,
            There's something Floyd.

Author.   A *roarer*—that'll do. [43]

Fancy.   Take its companion Lady Audley.

Author.   Not so bad—hear, hear!
            That was the literary rage last year;
            The thinnest skinned can't quarrel at our taking it,
            And into a short piece of nonsense making it.

Fancy.   The book's too capital a novel much
            To suffer from the comic writer's touch.
            Don't vulgarise; be droll, but don't deride;
            Most serious subjects have their funny side.
            Let's see together if we can't increase
            The season's laughter with a Christmas piece.

                    Duet.—Bolero (Arditi).

Fancy.   We will then at once set about
            Our duties so pleasant, our duties so pleasant.

Author.   Yes we will, and instanter the secret to fun turn.
                    When we've a good story,
                    As good as Aurory
                    Floyd, parley no more.   *Exit*, R. 1 E.

Fancy.   And now while they're setting the scenery there,[44]
            I'll sing the Bolero, to prom'naders dear,
                    As Jul-li-ens, where

---

[42] *screamer* Theatrical slang for resoundingly popular comic plays which made audiences 'scream' with laughter. The Adelphi produced so many of these plays in the nineteenth century that it gave its name to the theatrical genre 'Adelphi screamers'.

[43] *Floyd. A roarer* Corruption of Braddon's novel *Aurora Floyd* (1863) which, like *Lady Audley's Secret*, deals with bigamy and murder. The novel was quickly melodramatized in several versions, including one by George Roberts, with productions at the Adelphi, the Effingham, the Princess's, and the Queen's Theatre that same year.

[44] *setting the scene* A reference to the stage carpenters putting in place the set for the next scene—that is, for the parody of *Lady Audley's Secret*. The scene between Fancy and the Author is played close to the audience so that as much of the stage as possible can be given over to the set for the remaining scenes.

> Their shouts rend the air,
> And all round you hear brava!
> Like flute, oh! it's as sweet, oh!
> And frisky, frisky also is.
> In fact it's the very thing
> To fill up the gap now
> Sorry to, sorry to, sorry to
> P'raps impede, oh! but you see,
> Whilst they are setting
> The scene there, the scene there, the scene there,
> I'm solely the party that's left here in front.
> And so indeed, oh! and so indeed, oh!
> I am obliged thus to sing.
> And yes indeed, oh! ah, yes indeed, oh!
> Ah, si mi piace brillar,
> Mi piace brillar, brillar!   *Exit*, R. 1 E.

SCENE THIRD.—*The Chambers of Robert Audley, in the Temple; pictures of horses, dancers, &c.*[45]

Enter ROBERT AUDLEY, R. 1 E., *smoking, with book, which he throws on table.*

Robert.   That last French novel's duller than the law.
               Pish! Tush! and Bother! Rubbish! also Pshaw!
               The story's actually rather moral,
               It's strongest feature's a domestic quarrel.
               The husband doesn't once your feelings shock,
               And doesn't give his wife (*knock at door*) a single knock;
               It's not a client gave that door a stout hit,
               At least, I'm very much in *client* to doubt it.
               Come in.   (*door opens*, R.)

     Enter GEORGE TALLBOYS, L., *covered with travelling wrappers,
          furs, &c.*

George. (*starting melodramatically*) Ha, ha,—'Tis he, if I don't err!

Robert. (*aside—noticing his fur cloak*) And who is this distinguished
               furry-ner?

George.   What, don't you recollect George Tall—

---

[45] *Temple* Legal district of London which includes the Inns of Court, Lincoln's Inn, and the Inner and Middle Temples.

Robert. (*excitedly*)   Boys! Bless me!
                    Is it my boyhood's friend that doth address me?
                    Embrace me. (*they embrace*) Come now, tell us all about it.

George.   I was a villain, Robert!

Robert.   I don't doubt it.

George.   I loved my wife: we had a beauteous boy!
                    His mother's hope, likewise his father's joy.
                    I'd an allowance from my father, small.

Robert.   Your father?

George.   The allowance. Not at all
                    What you'd expect. Therefore, it wasn't funny
                    It should grow very short.

Robert.   The boy?

George.   The money.
                    I had a ring—our infant, food to bring—
                    I pawned it.

Robert.   What, the infant?

George.   No; the ring.
                    That fed us for a week; the furniture, then
                    Went, stick by stick, our dinners to procure then.
                    Then we'd to live upon our wits—don't grin—
                    The consequence was we grew rather thin.
                    Disgusted with the world, I went gold digging,
                    And a most wonderful large nugget twigging,[46]
                    I got it soon out of its earthy bed—
                    A golden opportunity, I said.
                    I shall, I uttered, as out forth I dug it,
                    Embrace it.

Robert.   Yes, precisely, take *an'ug it.*

George.   The diggings that I took turned out good sorts,
                    They's first rate p'ints, and also splendid quartz.

Robert.   Then, you've come back with money?

---

[46] *twigging* Perceiving, catching sight of.

George.   Money—lorts!

Robert.   Rich! Let's embrace again.

George.   With all my heart.
                                                                    (*they embrace*)

Robert.   While you've a penny, George, we'll never part.

George.   I long to see my wife; she little knows
                    That I've come back.

Robert.   You've written, I suppose.

George.   Not lately, though I must admit I ought.
                                                        (*takes up the paper and sits*)

Robert.   Well, I was going down to Audley Court,
                    To see my uncle's young new wife. (*seeing* GEORGE *start*)
                    Hulloa!

George. (*struck with something in the paper*) Gone—gone! good gracious!
                    what a dreadful go!

Robert.   Has something bit you, George?

George.   Why did I marry?
                    O, *bit you, George*—see the *o-bit-u-arry*!

Robert. (*reading from paper*) Hum! Mrs. Tallboys.—Bear up like a man.

George.   Well, I can't promise—I'll do what I can.
                    Though we occasionally p'rhaps had rows,
                    I'd always great affection for my spouse.
                    My Lucy, Lucy, oh, come back again!
                    My *Lucy*—

Robert.   Come on; we shall *lose se* train.
                                                        (*pulls him off with a jerk*, L.)

SCENE FOURTH.—*Double Scene. On* L., *of stage, a Handsome Apartment; on*
R. *of stage, exterior, showing the Lime-tree Walk; a practicable Well.*

SIR MICHAEL AUDLEY *seated reading in the room,* L.; PHOEBE, *a tall, Pre-
Raphaelite female, in sober grey dress, plain braided hair, and pale face,
standing by the well, by which is seated* MARKS, *whittling a stick—Picture.*

Sir M. (*throwing aside his book, and coming down*) I must admit I
　　　　　　　feel uncommon lonely;
　　　　　Though I've been married just a few months only,
　　　　　I feel as if her ladyship was part
　　　　　Of my existence. When a tough old heart
　　　　　Grows tender once again, the passion's more
　　　　　Absorbing than when one is twenty-four!
　　　　　Where is my Lucy! (*goes up*)

Marks.　　　　　　　　　　Don't you talk to me;
　　　　　Your *mister-ess* has got a *mister-ee*!
　　　　　But tain't no mystery to us; cos, why?
　　　　　We knows it—

Phoebe. (*in alarm*)　　Luke, dear, would you have me die?

Marks.　　No, not afore we're married! Get more tin from her;
　　　　　You haven't had the walley of a pin from her.
　　　　　Say you're aware her husband has forsook her.

Phoebe.　　Oh, Luke, dear Luke, you are so fond of *loocre*.

Marks.　　I wants a public house; I've seen one too,
　　　　　Up at Mount Stanning, as I think'll do.

Phoebe.　　Don't whittle in that savage way—take care!

Marks.　　I wants to be a *licensed wittler* there.
　　　　　I ain't a hurting you now, am I—eh?

Phoebe.　　Well, cut your stick; but in another way.[47]

Marks.　　Her ladyship's beneath our pair of thumbs!

　　　　　(*they go up and off*)

Sir M.　　I hear her fairy footstep; here she comes!

　　　　　(*Music.* LADY AUDLEY *bounds in the room with a
　　　　　little hat on, which she removes and shakes out
　　　　　her hair which is very abundant, and arranged in
　　　　　a profusion of little feathery curls*)

　　　　　My charming Lucy—you I do adore!
　　　　　I hope, my pet, you've never loved before.

---

[47] *cut your stick* Slang for 'go away'.

Lady A. (*aside, with a spasmodic smothered shriek*) Oh, oh! now do I look as
                    if I had?

Sir M.   You know I'm old enough to be your dad!

Lady A.   'Tis true, my hair is golden, thick, and frizzly;
                 Whilst yours, what there is of it's rather grizzly.
                 'Tis true, my eyes are bright as silver—Nicolls'—
                 Whilst yours cannot see well without spec*tickles*!
                 'Tis true, my manners on the queenly border;
                 Whilst yours are rather of the Cobbler order;
                 But what are such disparities as these?
                 What, though you're somewhat shaky in the knees;
                 Take snuff at meals; tell anecdotes which bore;
                 And after dinner drop asleep and snore?
                 You are my husband, and I love you dearly;
                 Look at the pin-money you give me yearly—
                 The pretty books you bring me down from town;
                 The purchases in vertu so extensive;
                 Just as if nothing, love, *ver-too* expensive.
                 The carriages—the horses—oh, such spankers!
                 My own account, at Mopus's, the bankers;
                 My pet dogs, parrots, love birds, cockatoos,
                 Squirrels, canaries; lots to me amuse.
                 Oh, how she loves you, you dear nice old swell, you
                 Poor Lady Audley; she can *audley* tell you!

Sir M.   Yet when I first proposed, my petsy wetsy—

Lady A.   I said, 'Oh, go along with your barrow-netcy.'
                 I though you didn't mean my hand to win!
                 (*aside*) Besides, I wasn't sure about the tin!

Sir M.   My nephew, Bob, is coming down to-day;
                 He's bringing an old friend, he writes to say;
                 One Mr. Tallboys—

Lady A. (*with a shriek*)   No—unsay the word!
                 Impossible! Ridiculous! Absurd!
                 It can't be—shan't be. Madness and despair!

Sir M.   Good gracious! Mind, you're damaging your hair.
                 Police! (*rings bell*)

                    Enter PHOEBE, L.

Phoebe.   My lady.

Sir M.   Water—quick—make haste!
                    Exit PHOEBE, L.

Lady A.   It's nothing—I'm a little tightly laced.
                    There's not the *laced* cause for alarm—I'm better:
                    (*aside*) If fortune wishes to defy me, let her.
                    When things come to their worst they're sure to mend.

                    Enter SERVANT, L.

Servant.   Hem—Mr. Robert Haudley.

Sir M.   Hah!

Servant.   And friend.

                    Enter ROBERT *and* TALLBOYS, L.

Sir M.   Dear Bob—your aunt. (*they bow*)

Lady A. (*curtseys*)   I'm proud to know you.

Robert.   Thankee.

Lady A.   But where is your acquaintance, Mr. Lanky?

Robert.   Hem—Mr. Tallboys.

Lady A.   Well, it's all the same;
                    As Shakespeare says, you know, 'What's in a name?'
                    ''Twas mine,' ''tis his,' 'to be or not to be.'

Robert.   Tallboys, allow me—Lady Audley.

George.   Oh!

                    (LADY AUDLEY *staggers and falls in* SIR MICHAEL'S
                    arms—all crowd round her—GEORGE *staggers out at back*)

Lady A.   It's nothing—nothing—nothing. Oh, dear, no!

                    LUKE *and* PHOEBE *re-enter,* R.

                    (*aside*) He lives; he recognises me—his sposa!
                    One look's enough: he *eyes* her, and he *nose* her.
                    I thought he'd died out at the diggings yonder—
                    Oh, why the diggings didn't he, I wonder.
                    He might have died, and let his wife forget him;

But no, his nasty temper wouldn't let him.

                         (*turning round sharply*)

Leave me; I wish to be alone—yet stay—

A chorus, p'rhaps, before you go away.

Concerted Piece, Soldier's Chorus from Blanche de Nevers.

        Oh! what is the cause, I wonder do,

             Of that sudden outbreak, rare?

        There is no clue to help us to

             A solu—a solu-tion of all that 'ere;

        It's no very—very trifling thing,

             But it's something wrong,

             Yes, it's something wrong;

        Very—very irri-ta-ta-ting.

             Oh! what is the cause, &c.

(LUKE *and* PHOEBE *run off, behind the well, R.—*
SIR MICHAEL, ROBERT AUDLEY, *and*
TALLBOYS L., *leaving* LADY AUDLEY *alone,* C.)

Lady A.	Two stars keep not their motion in one sphere.
	If Tallboys stops in England, it's quite clear
	I can't; one of us must depart, you see;
	And something tells me that it won't be me.
	I'll cool my fevered brain out in the grounds.

                  (*goes through door into Lime-tree Walk, turns to
                       shut door—*TALLBOYS *has entered on the
                       garden side*)

George.   My wife! my wife, for twenty thousand pounds?

              Falsehood, thy name is woman.

Lady A.   George. (*turn and stand gazing at each other*)

George.   Yes, Lucy.

        Your tones are icy.

Lady A.   *I see*; what do *you* see?

George.   I see my wife.

Lady A.   As was.

George.   As was—don't quiz.

Lady A.	I am not now so much your wife *as 'tis*.

Lady A. I am not now so much your wife *as 'is*.
You left me.

George.   Left? well, perhaps that wasn't right.
I certainly did take a trip one night
As far as the Antipodes; but then
I meant, of course, to soon return again.

Lady A. How could I know what had of you become?

George. You surely got my letters?

Lady A.   Only some.
The *only sum* you sent me, by-the-bye.
There I sat piping of my widowed eye
In a most fearful state of poverty.
As on my schooling pa'd paid some amount,
My talents then I soon turned to account.

George. Turned to *account*. I can't the fact forget
That you turned also to a *baronet*.

Lady A. I went out as a governess—a spinster,
Clever, petite, and nothing known against her.
Sir Michael married me, I know 'twas wrong,
You'd gone a long way though.

George.   Oh, go along!

Lady A. Pity your little Lucy. Oh, don't blame me.

George. My *little Lucy*? Pooh! It was *big-Amy*.
Your marriage with Sir Michael's null and void,
His happiness must be at once destroyed.
                    (*going to pass her—she intercepts him*)

Lady A. What would you do? He's old and shaky very
And not allowed more than a glass of Sherry.
'Twould break his heart.

George.   You never thought of mine
When in the *Times* you put that cruel line,
And married this Sir Michael for his wealth.

Lady A. But really in a shocking state of health.
Oh! leave me to my misery.

George.   I go—(*turn R., up to well*)

Lady A.	Thankee, I'm much obliged.

George.   To let folks know
That Lady Audley's—

Lady A.   What?

George.   A swindler—there!

Lady A.   George Tallboys, mark me, mark me—if you dare!
You know my temper when it's roused is horrid;
I feel that I'm becoming very florid,
My temples throb and burn with heat that's torrid,
And every vein's a swelling in my forrid.
My 'ma and 'pa were both a little mad,
And latent lunacy's in *me*, my lad.
I feel I'm going cranky with my grief,
And I've come out without a handkerchief.
(*singing*) To-morrow it is St. Valentine's day,
                 And nobody's coming to woo;
And all the words that he could say
                 Was hoop de dooden doo.

George.   All's thrown away. I'll have no pity, none;
I'll smoke a mild cigar here till you've done.
                                        (*sits by well and smokes*)

Lucy. (*aside*)   I don't like his manner
Your poor wife hates the smell of your Havana.

George.   Oh do, pray, cease, you clacker.

Lucy.   Go off router—

George.   Front her—I but take *to back her*.
You'd really better not appear so riled
But follow my example (*smokes*) draw it mild.
Well, it don't draw well, though I'm seated by one;
I beg your pardon, Lucy, you try one.

Lady A.   What, will I try one? Ah, you little think,
How much *you* try one—

George.   Anything to drink?

Lady A.   Yes; down the well there's water.

George.   Just so *low*
        To make a rather venerable Joe;
        Talking of trying you, you little fury—
        You will be tried by—

Lady A.   What?

George.   A British jury.

Lady A. (*starting violently—clutching her hair*) What—brought up to a Court?

George.   Precisely so,
        You were not *brought up to a Court*, you know,
        And Audley Court is not your station.

Lady A.   Eh?
        What is my station?

George. (*comes down*)   *Bow-street*, I should say.[48]

Lady A. (*coquettishly*) How can you threaten Bow-street—what's the use?
        Oh, don't say *Bow* to such a little *goose*!
              (*putting her arm around him*)
        Can you to Lucy such unkind words say?

George. (*removing her arm*) Thank you; you don't get round me in that way.

Lady A.   Then do your worst.

Song.—LADY A.

You mark my words, George Tallboys, you'll be sorry
        that you spoke;
The situation forces me to make an aged joke;
To go away and leave your wife, to scamper off to sea,
That act was very *small of you*, while mine was *big o' me*.
           Fol de rol, &c.
You should remember you'd a wife at home across the sea.
And tip her now and then a line from the *an-tip-her*-des.
But no—you left me here to starve, until I got so thin,
There was nothing intervening 'twixt the bones and outer skin.
           Fol de rol, &c.
A baronet he came and flopped upon his gouty knee,
Says he 'My home's at your disposal if you'll marry me;

---

[48] *Bow-street* Site of the Magistrates Court in central London, opposite Covent Garden Theatre.

My rheumatiz is not at my command—there are no cures,
But though it's not at mine, my drawing *room it is* at yours.'
           Fol de rol, &c.
Well, what was I to do, you know? I felt bewildered quite.
Now there you needn't call me wrong.—I married him outright.
And Audley Court is mine. Now tell me why I'm like—
        you ought—
A halfpenny publication? 'Cos I'm the *Mistress of the Court.*
           Fol de rol, &c.

George.   Good-bye. (*going up*)

Lady A.   One word.

George.   Beg pardon, did you call?
(*pauses and leans against the windlass of the well*)[49]

Lady A. (*sidling up to him*) I simply mean to say—

George.   Well,

Lady A.   *Well*, that's all.
(*she pulls out the spindle suddenly, and TALLBOYS vanishes*
      down the well)
Ha—ha! my tortures, from this moment, end—
That's the best way, I know, to drop a friend.
Truth lies, they say, at bottom of a well,
(Though by the way, truth lying seems a sell)
And in that well my truthful history'll keep.
George always bragged of being very deep;
All's still! Like codfish when one buys a pound,
In this case there's decidedly no *sound.*
He's kicked the bucket in the well, it's clear.
           (*she is leaning down, listening*)

       Enter ROBERT AUDLEY *suddenly*, L.U.E.

Robert.   Huh, Lady Audley, pray what do you here?

Lady A. (*innocently*) I don't hear anything at all.

Robert.   I mean
What are you doing here? (*aside*) Her looks surprise me.

---

[49] *windlass* Rope pulley.

Lady A. (*aside*) How very hard young Mr. Audley eyes me.
              Can he suspect?

(*crosses L., and pulls out a sketch book, commences painting*)

Robert. (*sitting on a camp stool,* R.) My friend has vanished.

Lady A.   Vanished! Take a seat.
              I'll paint you.

Robert.   Paint! He's *varnished* I repeat.

Lady A.   What's that to do with me? Look pleasant, try.
              Now shut your mouth—that's it—now mind your eye.

Robert.   Mind yours!

Lady A. (*starting*)   Ha, ha!

Robert.   I've sought him high and low;
              He's gone without observing that he'd go.
              He has been absent now—

Lady A. (*aside*)   With fear I'm thrilled.

Robert.   Ten minutes—very odd—I think he's killed.

Lady A.   Isn't that jumping to conclusions, eh?

Robert.   I am accustomed evidence to weigh;
              There's something in your manner—

Lady A. (*rising and eyeing him malevolently*) Robert Audley,
              You'll find you'll come to grief, sir, very *shordly*,
              If you attempt your legal tricks with me;
              For *any hints* on your *hints any-tee*[50]
              Will lock you up. My feelings don't you rile 'em,
              Or in an *ace I'll* send to an *a-sy-lum*,
              And have two doctors, who, whilst thus your bent is,
              Are safe to settle you're non compos mentis.[51]

Robert.   If that *meant is* for threatening, I'm your man.

Lady A.   Then who can prove I'm guilty?

---

[50] *hints any-tee* Punning transcription of the Cockney pronunciation of 'insanity'.
[51] *non compos mentis* Not of sound mind.

Enter suddenly LUKE MARKS *and* PHOEBE, R.U.E.

Luke.   Why, I can.
I seen you pitch him down.

Lady A.   What could be richer?
You can—ha, ha!—you *can*!

Luke.   Ha, ha, you *pitcher*!

Lady A.   What, Luke?

Luke.   Just so, I was a *look*ing on.

Lady A.   Away—get out—absquatulate—begone![52]

Robert.   Call out Sir Michael.

Lady A. (*shrieking and falling on her knees*) No!

Luke.   Yes, do; he ought
To larn what rigs is played in Audley Court.[53]

(*pantomime rally*—ROBERT, LADY AUDLEY, LUKE, *and*
PHOEBE)[54]

Enter SIR MICHAEL, R.U.E. *They pause.*

Sir M.   What's this—what's this?

Robert.   My aunt—my aunt!

Sir M.   Aunt what?

Robert.   She arn't my aunt.

Sir M.   She are.

Lady A.   Am.

Luke.   Air!

---

[52] *absquatulate* Mock-Latin expression of American origin meaning to abscond or to hurry away; literally, to squat away from.

[53] *rigs* Tricks or swindles.

[54] *pantomime rally* The finale of the 'harlequinade' part of a Victorian pantomime in which all the characters rushed onstage and threw objects, usually vegetables.

Phoebe.   Is!

Robert.   *Not!*
    Prepare yourself Sir Michael, for a blow.
    She were!

Lady A.   Was!

Luke.   Is.

Robert.   A married woman.

Sir M.   *No!*

    I won't—I shan't!

Lady A.   Can't!

Robert.   Aunt!

Luke.   Darn't!

Sir M.   Believe it—there!
    Lucy, elucidate—you are—?

Lady A.   *I air.*

Sir M.   This English is confusing—wait a bit.
    By gum! I—

Lady A.   Yes, *Bi-gum-my*, that's just it.

Concerted Piece, 'The Kermesse Scene from Faust.'

Robert.   That there young woman, sir's, taken you in.
Sir M.   Gracious me, what do I hear? What do I hear?
Lady A.   Whilst I'd a husband, sir, I married agin.
Luke.   Phoebe, lass, ever hear the likes of that theer?

Lady A.   What a situation,
                        This narration,
                There's no doubt is very true;
                        But be lenient
                        If convenient,
                I'll be as penitent as any two.

Sir M.   Here's a go. Oh! yes, here's a go.
                With rage expire I shall.

A man at my time of life ought to know
Better than to marry a bit of a gal.

Waltz, 'Faust.'

Robert.   It serves you right, sir,
                     Oh! yes, quite, sir,
                     For you might sir,
                     Well have known, sir,
                     Wealth alone, sir,
                     Could have tempted this beauteous damsel.
Lady A.   Tra, la, la &c.
        (*waltzing solemnly round—stop at last note—pause*)

GEORGE TALLBOYS *heard in the well singing the Choral March.*
                     I'm all alive, oh!
                     I did survive, oh!
                     And I've climbed from below.

TALLBOYS *rises on the last note.*

All.   Oh, gracious! oh, lawks! oh, gracious! oh gracious!

        (LADY AUDLEY *falls into* SIR MICHAEL'S *arms—tableau—scene
        closed in*)

SCENE FIFTH.—*Front Scene, A Woody Landscape*

        Enter LADY AUDLEY, L., *paces the stage.*

Lady A.   Two husbands, two, and at the same time too!
             There are all sorts of things I ought to do;
             According to the story—Marks's Inn
             Burnt to the ground, by this hand, should have *bin*.[55]
             But now it's much too late, to have things righted,
             Or I should be delighted for to light it.

        Enter ROBERT AUDLEY, R. 1 E.

---

[55] In Roberts' play, Lady Audley, hoping to kill Luke Marks, sets fire to the Chequers
Inn by leaving a lit candle on the staircase. Marks survives the fire, however, and
denounces Lady Audley in the final scene. The passage also alludes to actions
depicted in the legitimate stage version which had to be omitted in the even more
accelerated burlesque.

Robert, me of my liberty don't rob;
I'm very miserable, so help me Bob!

Robert.   You'd better ask your help mates to do that,
                I've sent for the police,
Lady A.   Mind what you're at.
                With misery, which luckless fate doth deal her,
                This belle's wrung hard, so don't send for a peeler.[56]

Duet—'Hop light, Loo.'

Robert.   You'll a pair of handcuffs have upon your wrists
                Which won't permit them to get loose, whichever way they
                        twists.
Lady A.   Live on bread and water, that's miserable fare,
                Which bigamy is not the proper thing, I am aware.
Robert.   *No light you*'ll have within your cell,
                No company but spiders.
Lady A.   Oh determination fell!
Robert.   And when the people come to look, the turnkeys all will
                        tell,
                'That's Lady Audley, she as popped her husband down the well.'
Both.   No light you'll, &c.

Enter FANCY, R. 1 E.

Fancy.   There's not the slightest doubt it was a wicked thing to do,
                But isn't it delightful the whole thing isn't true;
                It's all a piece of fancy, and acquitted, ma'am, are *you.*
Lady A. (*with a caper*) Oh, flip up in de skid a ma jink, and hoop-de-doo-den-
                        doo,
                Oh, hoop-de-doo-den-doo, and fol-de-rol-de-*ray.*
Robert.   Fol de rol de riddle ol,
Fancy.   And too-ra-loo-ra-*lay*;
                And now we put a climax to our little bit of play,
Lady A.   With my bootle 'ee umpty, doodle 'ee umpty, boodle 'ee
                        umpty day.
All.   Oh, hoop-de-doo-den-doo, &c.

                        (*at end of chorus each dances round, during which
                                fog scene rises*)[57]

Lady A.   What's to be done now?

---

[56] *peeler* Policeman, named after Sir Robert Peel, founder and commissioner of London's first organized police force in 1829. Also, a pun on the 'peal' of a bell.
[57] *rises* Raising a scenic backdrop from beneath the stage floor.

Fancy.   Well, my magic aid
                Will have to help you out, I'm much afraid.
                Now that George Tallboys is restored, you know,
                Long explanations would be rather slow.
                Sing a finale—not to be thought mean,
                I'll back you up with a bright Christmas scene.

Author.   Well, but the piece we talked of—

Fancy. (*to audience*)   Kindly say,
                If you'll, instead of the stock Christmas play,
                Accept what we have done—and if you will,
                Why, then, we'll keep it on our Christmas bill;
                Which bill for your acceptance then we proffer,
                And if you'll kindly smile upon the offer,
                Our only wish to please you will be gained,
                If your good word we have to-night obtained.

Robert.   Stay though, what's this?

Fancy.   A fog, it can't offend,
                Pieces are often foggy at the end;
                And it enables them to sit behind
                The pretty closing scene, which you will find
                To be worth waiting for. (*fog scene sinks*)[58]
                                              The fog disperses!
                Now for the climax with appropriate verses.

        Enter LUKE, PHOEBE, *and* TALLBOYS, R.1 E., SIR MICHAEL,
        L.1 E,—*scene changes to Land of Thistles.*

                The Land of Thistles, Scotland, staunch and true,
                Oh! this, the Land of Thistle—

Lady A.   *This'll do.*

                (*scene changes to Land of Shamrocks*)

Fancy.   Ireland, that green isle where the shamrocks grow.

Lady A.   They *pique* themselves on their *sham rocks*, you know.

                (*scene changes to Land of Roses*)[59]

---

[58] *sinks* Lowering a scenic backdrop beneath the stage floor.
[59] At the back of 'The Land of Roses' were medallion portraits of the Prince and Princess of Wales adorned by coloured, revolving stars. The royal couple had married

Robert.   The Land of Roses, our own sunny clime,
                     A welcome sight this chilly Christmas time.

                     Finale.—Crown Diamonds.

Lady A.   For now in fear
                                 Behold us here,
                     Entreating you won't be severe;
                                 But make us glad,
                                 And say we add
                                 A trifle to your Christmas cheer.

Fancy.   Frown not on our efforts, pray,
                                 If you think our merit's slight;
                     Come again another day,
                                 Don't condemn us here to-night.

All.   For now in fear, &c.

                           CURTAIN

on 10 March 1863. The promptbook refers to the starts as 'whirligigs'. The *Era* wearily observed that an image of the royal couple was 'not a very new design' (3 January 1864).

THE VERY LATEST EDITION OF BLACK-EYED SUSAN

F.C. BURNAND
(1866)

10 Title page of the original manuscript of *The Very Latest Edition of Black-Eyed Susan* (British Library Add Ms 53,055 O)

Editor's Introduction

The Very Latest Edition of Black-Eyed Susan

The Very Latest Edition of Black-Eyed Susan was F.C. Burnand's burlesque of Douglas Jerrold's famed nautical melodrama *Black-Ey'd Susan* (Surrey Theatre 1829).[1] Flourishing in the decades following the Napoleonic Wars, nautical melodramas celebrated Britain's naval prowess and expanding imperial dominion. Their hero was always the 'Jolly Jack Tarr', a popular icon of British courage and national pride. T.P. Cooke, the original William in *Black-Ey'd Susan*, was the most celebrated performer in nautical melodramas. He was closely identified with the Surrey Theatre in south London, whose working-class audience, J.S. Bratton argues, found itself 'interpellated as sailor heroes by the discourse of imperialism over many generations'.[2]

The plot of Jerrold's melodrama is well-known. William goes out to sea, leaving his faithful wife Susan at the mercy of poverty and predators. She is beset upon by suitors who try to convince her that William is dead. Her uncle, Doggrass, threatens to evict her from her modest dwelling. William returns home and quickly sets matters aright. Yet just as he is about to set sail, a drunken Captain Crosstree insults Susan. Defending his wife's honour, William strikes his own superior officer. For this offence he is tried, convicted, and sentenced to die. At the last minute he is reprieved when a repentant Crosstree reveals that William had already been discharged when the altercation occurred. Since William was no longer the 'king's sailor' when he struck Crosstree, he could not be prosecuted under naval regulations. Once more a free man, William is restored to the arms of his beloved Susan.

In 1866, when nautical melodramas were nearly forty years out of date—and thus ripe for burlesque treatment—Burnand wrote his ironically titled parody, *The Very Latest Edition of Black-Eyed Susan*. He offered the piece first to the Surrey, presuming that an audience long familiar with Jerrold's original play· would be the ideal one to appreciate a burlesque version. Burnand could not have been more wrong. As the Surrey's manager explained, his audience wanted to see only the 'genuine article' and not a burlesque (Burnand, *Records and Reminiscences*, II, p. 25). This particular audience, then, was likely to regard *The Very Latest Edition of Black-Eyed Susan* as an inferior version of a much-loved play. Indeed, a working-class audience might well have objected to a parody of its own ideal of patriotic heroism. For the eventual West End audience—which included few members of the working class—the burlesque's desecration of William and Susan was not likely to be perceived as threatening. If anything, the reverse could be true. For some spectators the pleasured afforded by a burlesque of *Black-Ey'd Susan* was precisely its ridicule of the iconic Jolly Jack Tarr.

   The Very Latest Edition of Black-Eyed Susan found a home at the New Royalty Theatre, Soho, hardly a distinguished West End venue. As Burnand recalled, the theatre in Dean Street was carved out of a 'dingy old house' and boasted an 'up-late-last-night' appearance.[3] Makeshift dressing rooms were set up in the basement and kitchen, while the stage door, accessible only on foot, was through the former stable. The production triumphed over its unsightly surroundings, however, and played to enthusiastic audiences. Patty Oliver memorably starred as Susan, Rosina Ranoe took the 'trouser' role of William, Edward Danvers played the 'skirt' role of Dame Hatley, and the future Sir Charles Wyndham (whose London theatre still bears his name) acted the smuggler Hatchett. The *Athenaeum* praised Danvers' performance as Dame Hatley for being 'remarkably grotesque'.[4] Raker, Gnatbrain and Shaun O'Ploughshare were all played by young women. Clad in white shirts and blue satin trousers which displayed their 'symmetry of figure to the best advantage', the ladies of the *corps de ballet* impersonated stalwart British sailors.[5] Burnand's account of the quintet 'Pretty Seeusan' vividly captures the frenzied energy and vitality of consummate burlesque artists. Led by Oliver, the leading performers

> all danc[ed] the while, and never for an instant quiet any
> one of them, except for the second, when all had to listen to
> Patty Oliver's nightingale trill, which, leading from the
> verse to the refrain, literally brought down the house in
> thunders of applause. Then the dancing and chorus were
> resumed, the steps became more and more varied, the
> movement faster and faster, until Danvers as Dame Hatley,
> after bounding about like an irresponsible indiarubber rag
> doll, or a puppet in a fantoccini show, and after responding
> to some half a dozen encores, which roused the quintette to
> fresh exertions, sank exhausted; whereupon Patty Oliver,
> gasping and smiling, and looking prettier than ever,
> curtsied in acknowledgment of the compliment paid to her
> and her companions.
> (Burnand, *Records and Reminiscences*, II, p. 35)[6]

   The author's congratulatory account of the performance should not blind us to the complaints lodged against the play. The *Era* dismissed the plot as 'trifling' (2 December 1866). In a more sustained criticism, Percy Fitzgerald argued that there was no true burlesque humour in having the sailor William acted by a 'young girl in blue satin trousers' who dances 'breakdowns' and sings 'comic songs'.[7] Though churlish, Fitzgerald's view does contain some insight. A better burlesque of *Black-Ey'd Susan*, he maintained, would have ridiculed William's 'heroic sentiments' and incongruously elevated diction. Even so, Fitzgerald was in the minority, and the critical response to Burnand's burlesque was generally positive. The popular response was even more enthusiastic, and the burlesque ran for over four hundred performances—an unbelievably long run for a theatrical genre which prided itself on novelty. In 1884, nearly twenty years after its premiere, *The Very Latest Edition of Black-Eyed Susan* was successfully revived at the Alhambra Music Hall in London, an establishment not generally associated with burlesque. Burnand himself revised the script and lyrics to accommodate a more spectacular production which included the sailors—again played by female dancers—performing a routine with broadswords.[8]

The play's most ingenious topical reference occurs in the prologue, appropriately set in the Atlantic Ocean. The comic allusion is to the then recent completion of the first transatlantic telegraph cable by the Anglo-American Telegraph Company. The submerged cable stretched from Ireland to Trinity Bay, Newfoundland. It was carried on the ship *Great Eastern*, which left Ireland on 13 July 1866 and landed in Newfoundland fourteen days later. For the first time a telegraph message could be sent between North America and the United Kingdom. A parallel cable, using the remnants of an unsuccessful attempt a year earlier, was put in place two months later. In Burnand's prologue, the personified Atlantic Cable (Wireno) addresses Neptune from above: that is, as if the cable were being lowered onto the ocean floor. The parallel cable is dubbed Wirena, the feminine counterpart to Wireno. Neptune, the mythological monarch of the sea, takes offence at his realm being invaded by new technology.

Though not indicated in the published script, the burlesque's concluding scene is a 'Telegraphical, Atlantical, and Allegorical' tableau which occurs after William's aborted court-martial on the H.M.S. 'Polly Phemus' (*Era* 2 December 1866). To be sure, the finale complements the equally 'telegraphical' prologue. More importantly, however, both the prologue and the final scene allow the burlesque to stage its own version of the spectacular transformation scenes which occurred the end of pantomimes. Since the burlesque opened in late November (and no one then imagined that it would enjoy a long run) its immediate competition would have been the pantomimes which would open a few weeks later at nearly all London theatres. In order to remain viable, then, the Royalty's burlesque had to provide audiences with something to rival the spectacle which they had come to associate with performances at Christmas and New Year.

Apart from its topical prologue and concluding tableau, *The Very Latest Edition of Black-Eyed Susan* largely follows the narrative of Jerrold's original melodrama. The burlesque critiques the conventions of melodrama in the court-martial scene. The original *Black-Ey'd Susan*, like other plays of its kind, upholds an ultimately conservative morality. Because William escapes death on a mere technicality (the date on which his naval commission ended) the ideological structures which secured his unjust conviction remain unchallenged. Indeed, they are reaffirmed: if William *had* been a sailor when he attacked Captain Crosstree then he would have deserved to die. The politics of nineteenth-century melodramas are now seen as questionable. But they seemed questionable to Burnand as well, since the only aspect of the original plot which he alters is William's trial. In the burlesque, Crosstree explains that he fell over not because William struck him but because he was drunk. The Lord High Admiral, refusing to listen, maintains that '[t]here is no flaw/In the indictment'. Hatchett then produces a letter which testifies to William's innocence. Without any reading of the letter—or, indeed, any explanation of its contents—the sailor's innocence is automatically presumed just as his guilt had been only moments before. In this deliberately preposterous course of events Burnand calls into doubt the legitimacy of all melodramatic resolutions (which, in fact, are no resolutions at all) and the imperialist ideology which those resolutions perpetuate.

The text for *The Very Latest Edition of Black-Eyed Susan* is taken from Lacy's Acting Edition, collated with the British Library manuscript (Add Ms 53,055 O). The manuscript bears the traces of multiple revisions. It is also distinctive for including several sketches to illustrate intricate stage business, including fights and dances.

F.C. BURNAND (1836-1917), the son of a London stockbroker, studied at Eton and Trinity College, Cambridge, where he founded the Amateur Dramatic Club (the 'A.D.C.'). A convert to Roman Catholicism, he first prepared for the priesthood. But as Burnand later explained to a shocked Cardinal Manning, he discovered that his true—and only—vocation was for the stage. One of the most industrious playwrights of the nineteenth century, Burnand wrote more than two hundred burlesques, comedies, and adaptations of French plays. In addition to *The Very Latest Edition of Black-Eyed Susan*, his most successful burlesques were *Ixion* (1863), *Diplunacy* (1878), *Stage Dora* (1883), and *Paw Clawdian* (1884). His long association with the comic magazine *Punch* began in 1863. He succeeded Tom Taylor as editor in 1880, and held that post for twenty-six years. A longtime friend of Edward VII, Burnand was knighted in 1902. His autobiographical works include *Records and Reminiscences* (1904) and *The 'A.D.C.'* (1880).

Notes

[1] Other burlesque versions include Frederick Fox Cooper's *Black-Eyed Sukey* (Olympic 1829), Francis Talfourd's *Harlequin Black-Eyed Susan* (Strand 1855), the anonymous *The Ups and Downs of Deal and Black-Eyed Susan* (Marylebone 1867), and Horace Lehnard and Oscar Barrett's *Too Lovely Black-Eyed Susan* (Crystal Palace 1888).
[2] J.S. Bratton, 'British Heroism and the Structure of Melodrama', *Acts of Supremacy: The British Empire and the Stage, 1790-1830*, ed. J.S. Bratton *et al.* (Manchester and New York: Manchester University Press, 1991), p. 34.
[3] F.C. Burnand, 'Reminiscences of the Royalty', *The Theatre* 1 January 1896.
[4] *Athenaeum* 8 December 1866.
[5] *Era* 2 December 1866.
[6] 'How they cheered and encored', Clement Scott recalled in *The Drama of Yesterday and To-day*, when 'Patty Oliver, with her fascinating trill, sang till she was nearly exhausted "Pretty See-usan don't say No!" How they roared at Dewar's "Captain Crosstree is my name," and his assertive shirt collars! How they marvelled at the dancing of Danvers as Dame Hatley, for he seemed to be on wires or made of gutta percha!' Clement Scott, *The Drama of Yesterday and To-day* 2 vols (London: Macmillan and Co., Ltd., 1899), I, p. 231.
[7] Percy Fitzgerald, *The Principles of Comic and Dramatic Effect* (London: Tinsley Brothers, 1870), p. 166.
[8] Michael Slater, 'The Transformations of Susan', *Theatre Notebook* 50.3 (1996), p. 174 n. 37.

The Very Latest Edition of Black-Eyed Susan; or, The Little Bill That was Taken Up

First produced at the New Royalty Theatre, (under the Management of Miss Oliver) on Nov. 29, 1866.

PROLOGUE

Neptune	Mr. Gemmer
Wireno	Miss Severn
Wirena	Miss Carew

THE DRAMA

Lord High Admiral	Mr. D. Fairfield
Captain Crosstree, R.N.	Mr. F. Dewar
William	Miss Rosina Ranoe
Hatchett (*a Deal Smuggler*)	Mr. C. Wyndham
Raker (*an I-deal Smuggler*)	Miss Ada Taylor
Doggrass (*Susan's Uncle*)	Mr. J. Russell
Gnatbrain	Miss Heath
Admiral of the Red	Mr. Hollis
Admiral of the Blue	Mr. Gemmer
Admiral of the Yellow	Mr. Abbott
Admiral of the White	Mr. Smith
Admiral of the Black	Mr. Granville
Shaun O'Ploughshare	Miss Annie Bourke
Telegraph Clerk	Master White
Susan	Miss M. Oliver
Dolly Mayflower	Miss N. Bromley
Dame Hatley	Mr. E. Danvers

Ocean Nymphs. Sailors. Marines. Lasses.

PROLOGUE[1]

SCENE.—*The Ocean's Bed.* OCEAN NYMPHS *discovered. Their dance is suddenly interrupted by the descent of an enormous grapnel—in terror they run up to where* NEPTUNE *is reposing.*[2]

Nept.

Sleep, gentle sleep, I cannot stand this number
Of people interfering with my slumber;
Uneasy lies the head that wears a crown[3]—(*sees grapnel*)
Good gracious me, what's this that's coming down?
Where are my glasses? let me have a look—
Ah! I have got my *eye* upon a *hook*,
Catch it, it's gone; again to bed I'll go,
And try to sleep.

Atlantic Cable. (*above*)   Hullo! look out below.[4]

Nept.

Look out below! this is a sort of thing
I do not like—they can't know I'm a king.

Cable. (*above*)   Now look out for'ard. (*grapnel*)

Nept.

                                    This is too absurd,
(*gets R., another grapnel catches his dress behind.*)
'Hem, look out for'ard wasn't quite the word—

Enter WIRENO, L.U.E., *with broken piece of cable.*

Wireno. (L.)   Unhook me, girls, that is if you are able.

Nept. (R.)   And who are you?

Wireno.

                                    I'm the Atlantic Cable
Of sixty-six, just come down from above,

---

[1] The Prologue seems to have been an afterthought. In the original manuscript, the title and list of characters appear on the same page as the beginning of Scene One (fol. 7). The Prologue was thus affixed to what was already a completed script.

[2] *grapnel* Anchor; in this instance, used to hold the submerged cable in place.

[3] Cf. Henry IV, 'Uneasy lies the head that wears a crown' *2 Henry IV* (3.1.31).

[4] *Atlantic Cable* See the introduction to the play.

To find Wirena, my last year's lost love![5]
Say, gentle shepherd, have you seen—

Nept.   Not seen her;
And I don't know her if I did.

Wireno.   Wirena!
She fell, and then I thought I heard her squeals,
She's taken p'raps to her *electric eels*.
My hair stood up on end, sir, lock by lock,
My wig resembled an *electric shock*.

Nept.   Or to adapt an old Shakesperian line,
Like quills upon th'*electric* porcupine.[6]

Wireno.   Don't jest, but think upon the ruinous cost,
If after all poor sixty-five is lost;
I am all right, but still the whole affair
Is not complete until we can repair
The past.

Nept.   Says Mrs. Glass 'first catch your hare'.

Wireno.   That saying now-a-days my friend won't pass
Muster with us, but *à propos* of Glass
We the old saw have thus re-set entire,
As *Mister* Glass does say, first catch your wire.

Enter WIRENA, R.1 E., *and crosses to* C. embrace.

Nept. (*here gets* R.) In each other's arms thus locked
By their electric sympathies, I'm shocked.

Wireno. (L.)   I am so glad to find you here alive,
So fresh—

Nept. (R.)   So young.

Wirena. (C.)   Although I'm sixty-five.

---

[5] *last year's love* A reference to the failed attempt to lay a transatlantic cable in
1865—i.e., one year before the play. The mission ended in failure only 600 miles off
the Newfoundland coast and the incomplete cable was abandoned two-and-a-half miles
under the sea.
[6] Cf. the ghost of Old Hamlet, 'And each particular hair to stand an end/Like quills
upon the fretful porpentine' (*Hamlet* 1.5.19-20).

Nept.   Well, you don't look it; Time don't play his tricks
With you—

Wireno (L.)   Or me, for I am sixty-six.
Your loss gave all our friends much pain,
How glad they'll be to see you once again.
A failure, cried out many a reporter,
We'd more though than one iron in the water—
And here you are.

Wirena. (C.)   Sorry to distress you,

Nept. (*crosses behind* WIRENO *to C. and joins their hands*)
Well, there I join your hands my children, bless you.

Wireno.   Now then for separate maintenance; so nice you
Can go about alone, but first I'll splice you.
          (*Fixes shore end on, then pulls a cracker in
          front of him*)
The electric spark, you see, comes from the link,
What kept you?

Wirena (*getting* R.)   Something wrong, dear, with my *kink*.

Nept. (*down* C.) But now you are all right?

Wireno. (L.)   From coast to coast
Thousands of miles, believe me I don't boast,
In one brief minute, will our hands, yours, mine
Transmit a message, now we've dropped a line;
Old with new country thus communicates,
Making the two of the True United States.

Nept. (C.)   A message in a minute by the cable,
To me it sounds like some Great Eastern fable.[7]
                    (*A shock, they jump.*)

Wirena. (R.)   A message (*chord*)

Wireno. (*second shock*)   Answered.

Nept.   Tell me.

[7] *Great Eastern* Ship that carried the transatlantic cable in the expeditions of 1865 and 1866; see the introduction to the play.

Wireno.	We can't keep one Secret from you, who are the thorough deep one; I'll tell you 'tis from Black-eyed Susan to Her William.
Nept.	What does she want him to do?
Wirena.	Give him the story.
Nept.	While I've leisure, now.
Wireno.	Good, you shall learn why, wherefore, and the how.
Nept.	Lord Howe the Admiral, oh, I recollect:[8]
Wireno.	No, come and see the cause and the effect, So wind up your horn, above they'll *wind the drum*. (NEPTUNE *blows his shell horn and NYMPHS re-assemble*) Up to the surface of the sea we'll come.
Wirena.	There you will show him.
Wireno.	Everything I meant And satisfy him to his *heart's content*.

GRAND TRIO.

Wireno. (R.)	From the bottom of the sea
	    We will rise; 'twill be a lark;
	Susan's story hear from me—
	    I am the electric spark.

Wirena. (L.)	Thus united, go we must
	    To the top and look alive;
	For the cable you may trust,
	    Sixty-six and Sixty-five.

Trio.	Merrily, merrily proceeding.
Wireno.	Come with me, and come with me;
Trio.	Speedily we will set you reading
Wireno.	Our new message
Trio.	From the sea! From the bottom of the sea We will rise; 'twill be a lark;

---

[8] *Lord Howe* Admiral Lord Richard Howe ('Black Dick') (1726-99), commander of the British Navy during the American Revolution. He was made First Lord of the Admiralty in 1783.

Susan's story hear from me—
I am the electric spark.
Thus united, go we must
To the top and look alive;
For the cable you may trust,
Sixty-six and Sixty-five.
Merrily, merrily proceeding.

Wireno.	Come with me, and come with me;
Trio.	Speedily we will set you reading
Wireno.	Our new message
Trio.	From the sea!

STORY.

SCENE FIRST—. *The Downs of Deal, being a view wherein you'll see a deal of the Downs.—Melodramatic music. Enter* HATCHETT *mysteriously* L.2 E., *he beckons off to* RAKER *who enters cautiously,* L.2 E.[9]

Hatch.	Belay you snivelling varmint or you'll catch it.
	(*swings* RAKER *round to* R.)
Raker.	Stop! Don't. I want to ax, to *ax* you Hatchett Why you have brought me here? Is it to make a Fool of me?
Hatch. (L.)	No, *that* can't be done *now*, Raker, hey, Raker?
Raker.	I call a spade a spade and don't like dodges.
Hatch.	You know the cottage where Dame Hatley lodges. (*starts and looks round*)
Raker.	Where Black-eyed Susan dwells?
Hatch.	The very same. Sweet Susan!
Raker.	Oh! is that your little game.
Hatch.	I'm going—
Raker.	Then good bye, don't stay for me.

---

[9] *The Downs of Deal* The hills of Deal, a seaside town in the county of Kent in southern England. In the eighteenth and nineteenth centuries Deal was a frequent haunt of English smugglers.

Hatch.   You albatrosss, avast! I'm going to be—

Raker.   Make haste, my nerves are dreadfully unstrung.

Hatch.   I'm going to *be*—eh! do you guess?

Raker.   Yes: hung.

Hatch. (*starting back,* L.) Broadsides and booms! I'm going to be spliced.

Raker.   Jibs, junks, and capsterns! whom have you enticed?

Hatch.   What should you say if I said Susan?

Raker.   Why
I should observe that you told a lie,
But, I would add, from observation past,
'Tisn't the first and 'twill not be the last.

Hatch.   Aha!

Raker.   Slack your caboose! or I'll instead—(*aside to audience*)
He *has* slacked his caboose as I have said.

Hatch.   I'll gain her hand and two black eyes: oh, fine!

Raker.   Her hand, I'll give you two black eyes with mine.

Hatch.   Aha!

Raker.   Haul in your mizen: for I see
Doggrass, your other rascal.

Enter DOGGRASS, R. 2 E., and gets C. DOGGRASS has his hat in hand, in saluting. HATCHETT gives his red cap in exchange.

Dog. (C., *sweetly*)   Meaning me?

Hatch. (L.)   Stow yarns, and say on what tack are you bent.

Dog.   Well, I am *tacking* for a little rent
Which Mrs. Hatley owes me; poor old soul.

Raker. (R.)   What *all*?

Dog.   I look on *my rent* as a *whole*,
That is my tack as you have quaintly said.

Hatch.   I knew. (*smacks* DOGGRASS *on back.*)

Dog.   You hit the right *tack* on the head.
                    Yes, with my feelings I've had many battles—
                    I'm going to seize poor Susan's goods and chattels.

Hatch.   But if I pay the tin for Black-eyed S.,
                    You won't oppose her marrying me?

Dog.   Oh! yes.

Hatch.   Aha!

Dog. (*crosses* L.)   I mean. Oh, no. (*aside*) That black-eyed belle,
                    This mariner's for marryin' her—well,
                    (*aloud*, L.) Let it be so; but p'raps you think I silly am,
                    Aren't she—

Hatch. (C.)   Eh? What?

Raker. (R.)   He means—the wife of William!

Hatch.   Anchors and maintops! William! I will
                    Pay *you*, and also settle that there *Bill*.

Dog.   But ain't that little Bill soon due on shore?

Hatch.   No: he has got to run two years or more.
                    And even then her Bill she will not meet,
                    For which no one can send her to the Fleet,
                    Because it is as plain as is my fist,
                    The Fleet, as used to was, does not exist,
                    And what is more—

Rake. (*starts*)   What's more?

Hatch.   Why William ain't,
                    He bean't no more. (*crosses to* R.)

Rake.   He bean't, you mean he bain't.

Dog. (L.)   Gone to the shrimps, and lobsters and the rest—
                    Well, everything as is, is for the best.

(*Holds red cap under his eyes, as if to drop a tear.* RAKER *takes it and wipes his eyes, and gives it to* HATCHETT, *who discovers the exchange, throws* DOGGRASS'S *hat over to him and puts on red cap.*)

Rake. (C.)   It happened—

Hatch. (R.)   Nigh twelve months ago: near here—

Dog.   Our lobsters were uncommon fine, last year.

Hatch.   Avast with your salt water! What would you
        Say if I said as what I said warn't true.

Dog.   Not drownded, I should say. Would you, eh?

Rake.   I
        Should say, you'd been and told another lie.

Hatch.   Aha! (DOGGRASS *gets behind* RAKER, L.)

Raker. (L.C.)   Oh dowse your glim.[10]

Dog. (*aside* to RAKER)   You manage *him*.
        I don't know how to make him dowse his glim.

Hatch.   Well?

Raker.   I've a twinge. (*goes up* C.)

Dog. (L, *wheedling*)   The money you will pay.
                (HATCHETT *takes* DOGGRASS *by the hand*)

Raker. (*down* R.) I've gagged the pilot conscience.

Hatch. (*taking* RAKER'S *hand*)   Right. Belay.

                (*All cross hands*)

                TRIO.—Air—*Policeman*, 99 X.

Dog. (L.)   You will go to see
                        With me
                The house of Black-eyed Susan.
Hatch. (C.)   You will go intent
                        On rent
                The which she cannot pay.
Dog.   When I find she is 'behind'
                And payment is 'refusion,'

---

[10] *dowse the glim* Put out the light.

Raker. (*to* HATCHETT) You come down,
                                 With half a crown
                                 Or more: I see the way.

Hatch. (*to* RAKER) You must tell a lie, too.

Raker. (C.)   A resource to fly to
                                 Which—

Dog.   And so have I too,
                     An objection you would say.

Trio.   We must tell a lie, too
                                 A resource to fly to,
                                 Which—well we must try to
                                 Our objections drive away.

Hatch. (*to* RAKER)   You will tell her,
                                 Just to sell her,
                                 That you saw young Billy
                                 Knocked down by a marlin-spike,
                                 Or drownded in the sea.

Raker.   Yes, I understand,
                                 By hand,
                                 I saw him knocked quite silly—
                                 Out of time, and this in rhyme
                                 I'll tell her: trust to me.
                                 Susan doesn't know me,
                                 She'll believe it, blow me!
                                 What a pretty set of ugly villains
                                 We must be.

Trio.   Susan doesn't know him (me) &c.

(*Dance generally characteristic of villainy. Exeunt the three* R.)

Music—to which the British Fleet you see, because it is in sight—a boat leaves the vessel. One Gun. Enter SAILORS L. *and* R.U.E. *A boat containing* WILLIAM *rowing and* CAPTAIN CROSSTREE *steering comes alongside.* WILLIAM *jumps out. The bow of boat goes up and the stern down, so that* CAPTAIN CROSSTREE *almost disappears, except his cocked hat—great cheering—*WILLIAM *then turns round and gives his hand to* CAPTAIN CROSSTREE *who jumps on a* SAILOR'S *back and waves his telescope—Tableau—one cheer—during the next speech the* CAPTAIN *arranges his dress, dusts off his boots, and looks anxiously through his telescope off* R. *and* L., *then* R.U.E. *and* L.U.E., *while* SAILORS *come down.*

Wil. (C.)   Shiver my anchors! bless my marlin-spikes!
                                 If this ain't just the sort o'thing I likes!
                                 Messmates, what cheer? (*they cheer*)
                                        Another! (*they cheer again*)
                                        Reef my spars!
                               Naval and Milit'ry: *sailors* with *Huzzas,*

Let one for Captain Crosstree (*he comes down*)
Wake the dyke (*they cheer*)

Capt. (*down* C.)   *Ah any* thing you like
'All in the Downs'—look sharp—for our ship hoves
In sight of such a lot of downy coves.
Now don't look such uncommon solemn folks
And always laugh, boys, at your Captain's jokes.

(*Music—The* GIRLS *come on* L.—*The* CAPTAIN C. *puts his hand up to stop their going to* SAILORS, R.—SAILORS *on* L. *cross over to* SAILORS *on* R.—WILLIAM *remains* L. *and inspects girls as they pass.*)

Wil. (*aside, down* L.) Susan!

Capt.   Now, in a quiet sort of way,
You boys and girls may all go out and play.

(*Music.—The* GIRLS *mix with the* SAILORS.—WILLIAM *goes from one to another and can't find* SUSAN.)

Capt. (*in front.* GIRLS *and* SAILORS *go off during his speech.*)

'Twas from the maintop gallant that I saw
The fairest damsel standing on the shore,
                    (*first couple,* R. 2 E.)
Where she was wandering, the pretty loiterer,
I brought her near me with my reconnoiterer,
                    (*second couple*, R.U.E.)
So near that I could almost hear her voice
Sighing, give me that Captain for my choice.
                    (*third couple*, L.U.E.)
Yes, there's about me, as the gods all do say,
A *Jenny say quor*, you know, as parleyvoos say.
                    (*fourth couple*, L. 2 E.)
Talking of *ginny* I must get a glass
Of something neat, and then to find this lass.
                    (*fifth couple*, L.)
Down here some fine old fruity I could toss:
But where?—at the Port Admiral's of course.
                    (*Exit* CAPTAIN, R.)

(*The last couple have now gone off and* WILLIAM *comes down.*)

Wil.   Where's Susan? I have raked 'em fore and aft.
No. Is there trickery about my craft?
'Bout her not coming I won't make no rumpus,
But Black-eyed Susan's heart should be her compass.

Her needle, sharp as Horse-marine's gun bag'net,
Hope it ain't been attracted by some magnate.
I'm chicken-hearted! lay me under hatches,
Or in the cockpit.

Enter SHAUN O'PLOUGHSHARE, L. 2 E.

        Ha!—belay! Dispatches!

Shaun. (L.)   Why, wirra, wirra, was I iver born?

Wil. (R.)   Don't look so sheepish.

Shaun.   Sheepish? sure I'm Shaun,
'Tis Shaun-the-Post, in England re-appearing,
But I'm no sheep.

Wil.   Then where to are you *sheering*?
Give us your grappling iron.

Shaun.   If you mane
My fist—I'll give yez that, sorr, nate and clane,
Ye'll tread upon the tail, sorr, of my coat.
    (*crosses to* R.—WILLIAM *catches hold of him.*)
Unhand me, sorr, for William I've a note,
For William who's at sea.

Wil.   'Tis mine.

Shaun.   Bedad!

Wil.   Give it to me.

Shaun.   I'll give it you, my lad.
Horrush! (*whirls his shillelagh about, strikes* WILLIAM
*who suddenly catches the other end of it and raps
him on the head—he falls down in a sitting position as*
DOLLY MAYFLOWER *runs in* L.—*beat on drum as*
SHAUN *falls*)

Dolly. (L.)   It cannot be! you are—

Wil. (C.)   I are!
    (*embraces* DOLLY)

Enter GNATBRAIN, L.

Gnat.   What Dolly Mayflower hugging of a tar:
Your Gnatbrain says ta, ta for ever. Go (*going* L.)

Dolly. (*pulls him back by coat*)   You jealous donkey. Why, it's William.

Gnat.   Oh.
Sweet William (*crossing*)

Wil. (R.C.)   Yes, young gard'ner, I that Billy am.
(*shakes hands with* GNATBRAIN.)

Shaun. (R.)   Gard'ner! I've got a cutting from sweet William.
I ought to recollect your faytures, sure
I never set my eyes on yez befure.

Wil.   And what's the news of Susan?

Shaun.   Oh, bedad.
This letter. (*gives letter to* WILLIAM.)

Wil.   I can't read it. (*gives it to* DOLLY)

Dolly. (*gives letter to* GNATBRAIN)   Well, it's bad.

Wil.   Shiver my timbers!

Shaun.   Shivering his timbers?
That's *his* expression, as I well remembers.

Wil.   And my dear eyes. (DOLLY *talks to him up* C.)

Gnat. (*with letter*)   Yes, that's about the size,
I know him by the expression of his eyes.

Wil. (R.C.)   The dame and Susan scuttled!

Dolly. (L.C.)   Ah, poor souls!

Gnat.   Scuttled! They've not a penny to buy coals.

Shaun.   They'll sell her up, down to an ould tin pail.

Wil. (*down* R.C.) They'll sell her, will they? Then we'll crowd all sail,
Bid for each lot.

Gnat.   We will, *by jingo*.

Wil. (R.C.)   What?
By jingo? no *buy* everything she's got.
If we don't beat the sharks off, that's my fault,
They don't expect *a sailor* and *assault.*
Now, heave ahead! heave on.

Shaun. (R.)   Your wink's a nod.

Dolly. (L.C., *coming down*) The sailors always *heavin'.*

Gnat. (L.)   Ain't it h'*odd.*

QUARTETTE. Air—*Perambulator.*[11]

Wil. (R.C.)   My Susan she has cut for me
                                        Each monkeyfied land lubber,
                               She's in a willage near a wale
                                        And her uncle makes her blubber.
                               I've sailed to east, to west I've been.
                                        Aboard of flag and guardships,
                               While every sort of ship I've seen,
                                        Except my Susan's hardships.
                               She's the girl to make you stare
                               And she wears her own hair,
                                        The lovely locks o' natur,
                               No wife could be
                               More fitter than she
                                        For a British navigator.
Shaun. (R.)   I'm sorry for the wretched state
                                        Of this black-eyed young cratur,
                               For bedad she's not a bit to ate,
                                        Not even a cold potatur.
                               And thim what persecutes a gal
                                        I'd sind to the Ould Bailey,[12]
                               Or give thim instead, some advice on that head,
                                        With a word from my shillelagh.
                               Oh! it puts me in a rage
                               Any fellows I'd engage
                                        Who dare to touch or bate her,
                               Sure I don't care
                               Not even if he were

---

[11] *Perambulator.* The manuscript submitted to the Lord Chamberlain indicates that the quartet sings 'Champagne Charley'.
[12] *Ould Bailey* Street in the City of London where the Central Criminal Court is located. The Court itself, London's principal criminal court, is commonly known as 'The Old Bailey'.

	A Turk or an alligator.
Gnat. (L.)	If Susan's not enough to eat,
	A little treat we'll take her,
	From the top of the hill take a roll we will,
	And say it comes from the baker.
Dolly. (L.C.)	Something to drink she'd like, I think,
	So to my care confide her,
	She'll be beside herself when she
	Sees the tipple, being *be-cider*.
	For she's just about the age
	When one would engage
	Her for a parlour waiter.
	Or as ladies maid.
	Or a nurse well paid
	To drive a perambulator.

Chorus

She's the girl to make you stare,
And she wears her own hair,
　The lovely locks o' natur;
　　No wife could be
　　More fitter than she
　For a British navigator.　　(*Dance and exeunt.*)

SCENE SECOND.—*Interior of Dame Hatley's Cottage.*

Music. Enter DAME HATLEY, *door*, L.

Dame.	It's very hard, and nothing can be harder
	Than for three weeks to have an empty larder;
	I'm in the leaf of life that's sere and yellar[13]
	Requiring little luxuries in the cellar.
	There are no *cellars* such as I requires,
	But there soon will be, when there are some *buyers*.
	Destiny's finger to the work'us points,[14]
	A stern voice whispers 'Time is out of joints'.[15]

---

[13] Cf. Macbeth, 'I have liv'd long enough; my way of life /Is fall'n into the sere, the yellow leaf' (*Macbeth* 5.2.22-3).

[14] *work'us* Workhouse—asylums for the urban poor in the nineteenth century which, in exchange for labour, provided food, shelter, and meagre earnings. The workhouse, a consequence of the New Poor Law (1834), was the last resort for indigent families because they would not be permitted to live together. Much-maligned by contemporary social reformers for their inhumanity, workhouses were instituted as a state alternative to unregulated, individual acts of philanthropy (i.e., the tradition of alms-giving).

[15] Cf. Hamlet, 'The time is out of joint. O cursed spite,/That ever I was born to set it right!' (*Hamlet* 2.1.196-7).

I used to live by washing, now no doubt,
As I can't get it, I must live without—
The turncock turned the water off—dear me!
I showed no quarter—and no more did he.
Thus, with the richer laundress I can't cope.
Being at present badly off for soap.
My son, the comfort of the aged widdy,
Is still a sailor, not yet made a middy,
But sailing far away: it may be *my* son
Is setting somewhere out by the horizon.
He's cruising in the offing, far away,
Would he were here, I very offing say.   (*Music.*)
Susan returns, I see her through the pane,
She's sold our last resource.

Enter SUSAN, *hurriedly*, L., *door—bars door and stands with her back against it.*

Dame. (R.)   Yes!

Susan. (L.)   Sold again!

Dame.   What's sold?

Susan.   A captain with a picket
                   Of marines, who followed me.

Dame.   You've got the ticket?

Susan.   Ticket? what, anything on that you mean?
                   They've done it five times on your crinoline,
                   It had no strength he said, and so I bent on it
                   But broke it, showing nothing could be lent on it.
                   I couldn't press it on him, that's the truth,
                   'Cos it had passed the *spring* time of its youth.
                   His heart's like steel. (*gives* DAME *crinoline and goes to
                                 window.*)

Dame. (*going to door*, L.)   Like that in which I dressed;
                   No, no, for that would '*give*' on being *press'd*,
                   I'll try myself. (*unbars door*) I will get on my bonnet.
                                 (*takes bonnet from peg at door*, L.)

Susan.   Get on your bonnet? *What* can you *get on* it?

DOGGRASS *opens door.* DAME *gets behind it. He knocks his hat off, and
       stands curtseying* L. *when he turns.*

Dog. (C.)   How do you do, dear niece?

Susan. (R.)   Do not dear me, drop it;
                   You are my uncle—

(DAME *hangs bonnet on peg L., but keeps crinoline for future
      business.*)

Dog.   Uncle? Yes, my poppet.
                   I came to have a talk.

Dame. (L.)   Oh, pooh, get out.

Susan. (R.)   As you're my uncle, you can't come to spout.

Dame.   You come to see me, Doggrass.

Dog.   Yes, ma'am, you,
                   For rent and yet for rent I come to *Sue.*
                   So if you can't stump up, good Missis Hatley,
                   You'll both turn out of doors, I'll tell you flatly.

Susan.   Flatly! You needn't speak so sharply though
                   We can pay you part of what we owe;
                   Just half a farthing in the pound.

Dog.   What's that?
                   You took the whole; I don't let out a flat.

Dame.   No, you take precious care to let 'em in
                   For a considerable amount of tin.[16]

Susan.   This is a run up house, and we're done brown.[17]

Dog.   A run up house? Come, don't you run it down.

Susan. (R.)   No wall or window is without a crack.

Dame. (L.)   I've always had rheumatics in the back
                   Since I've been here: each day I'm more rheumaticker.

Dog. (C.)   Are you, indeed!

Susan.   I've suffered from sciatica.

---

[16] *tin* Money.

[17] *done brown* Swindled.

Dame.   And from the draughts, I do not know a *day* go
                   Without a horrid touch of the lumbago.

Susan.   The walls are damp.

Dog.   Then wipe 'em till they're drier.

Dame.   The chimnies smoke.

Dog.   Well, mum, don't light a fire.

Susan.   The windows let the draughts in.

Dog.   I've no doubt—
                   But recollect they also let it out.
                   When I did let you this cottage by the sea,
                   You didn't think that you would have it free.

Susan. (C.)   You were my uncle, and on this occasion
                   Your stinginess proves you a *near* relation.

Dog. (R.)   I am respected in this town of Deal.

Susan.   To those who do not know you, you appeal.

Dog.   I'm a plain dealer, niece.

Dame. (L.)   You are. (SUSAN *calms her.*)

Susan.   True: for
                   I never a much plainer dealer saw.
                   Once, you a pedlar were, and on your back
                   A box—in fact a dealer with a pack.
                   Talking of packs, pack off, we will not kneel
                   To you, you've played your card, now cut for Deal.[18]

Dog.   Without my rent, no, no.

Dame. (*crossing in front of* SUSAN *to* C. SUSAN *holds her back.*)
                              I'd like to shake him.

Dog. (*crossing to* C. *as if going to* L. DAME *gets behind to* R.)
                   With it I'll go to Deal.

---

[18] *to cut* To leave, to depart for, with pun on cutting a pack of cards before dealing them.

Susan.   You will—(*aside*) *Deil* take him.

CONCERTED PIECE.
Air. '*In the Gypsey's Life.*' (*Bohemian Girl.*)

Susan. (C.)	In the landlord's face you read The happy life you're going to lead, Sometimes under roof, and sometimes Sleeping in the open air.
Dame. (R.)	Our wants are few.
Dog.	They will be fewer too. And easy to supply.
Susan (L.)	But what is worse I have no purse.
Dog.	A want you feel as well as I.
Susan.	My heart t'will wring!
Susan and Dame.	My heart t'will wring!
Dog.	That is a thing. That is a thing. Which we don't know in Deal.

TRIO.
In the Landlord's face we read,
The happy life, &c., &c. (*as before.*)

(*Chord—Enter* HATCHETT *and* RAKER *dancing down C. through door,*
both carrying large purses, which they chink while dancing and
singing.)

Air.—*Pretty Jemima.*[19]

Hatch. (L.C.)	We've come right upon a starboard tack.
Raker. (R.C.)	Your tick and our tack, And our tack-tick-tack.
Hatch.	We've got enough money to pay your whack,[20] And you will live rent free.
Raker.	You'll never again have to work, I've brought you a pound of tea!
Susan. (L.)	Oh! what an event! He's paid your rent! And settled the difficul*tee.* Oh!
Hatch.	Pretty Seeusan, what you owe, O you O,

---

[19] *Pretty Jemima* See the introduction to this play for a description of the dance.

[20] *whack* Share or portion.

O heigh O,
Pretty Seeusan, what you owe,
You only owe to me.

Chorus
Pretty Seeusan, what you owe,
O you O,
Ohio!
Pretty Seeusan, what you owe,
I only owe to he!

(*Short dance to symphony.*)

Hatch.	Now I am anxious to know my fate.
Susan.	Know his fate?
	Oh; you must wait.
Hatch.	Say, will you enter the happy state,
	That is, of matrimon*ee*?
Susan.	You do not know,
	But I'll tell you so.
	That to marry I am not free,
	For I've got a spouse,
	At Ryde or Cowes,
	And his name is little Billee.[21]
	Oh!

Pretty Seeusan must say no,
Oh! oh, no, no, no,
Pretty Seeusan must say no,
For she can't married be.

Chorus
Pretty Seeusan, don't say no,
Don't say no.   Ohio.
Pretty Seeusan, don't say no,
Answer we'll married be.

Susan.	Thanks generous stranger, but I must refuse.
Hatch.	Here's William's messmate as he has got some news.
Susan.	His messmate!
Hatch.	That you were, Tom, warn't you.

---

[21] *little Billee* In W.M. Thackeray's eponymous comic ballad, 'Little Billee' is one of three sailors from Bristol lost at sea. When the supply of food runs out, Billee narrowly escapes being eaten by his comrades 'gorging Jack' and 'guzzling Jimmy'.

Rake. (*sulkily*)   Yes.

Hatch.   You found him.

Susan.   Where?

Rake. (C.)   In such a jolly mess.

Dog. (R.)   You saw him last.

Rake.   I didn't.

Susan.   Not so fast.

Dame. (R.C.)   You saw him last?

Rake.   No; 'cos he didn't last.
          We struck; and Bill went down full fathom five,

          Enter WILLIAM, L.D., *gets* C.²²

          I turned and saw—(DAME *starts forward to left,* RAKER
                              starts back to R.)

Susan.   Ah, William! Alive! (*Tableau.*)

Wil.   What, Susan! My dear eyes! You ugly swabs,
          Belay there, mother, while I punch their nobs.
          One of the British navy can wop six
          Of you. I'll soon 'confound your knaveyish tricks,'²³
          So rule *Britannia*: don't let this unman yer,
          While I with this ere small sword *Bright-tan-yer.*
          Clear the decks all of you. Attend to orders.

Dog. (*crossing to* C.) But they're my lodgers.

Wil.   No, they're parlour-*boarders.*

Fight.—WILLIAM, HATCHETT, *and* RAKER. DOGGRASS *and* DAME, R.
HATCHETT *is beaten on one knee,* R.; RAKER, L. WILLIAM *on one knee,* C.,
when at the window appear two marines with guns, pointing them at
HATCHETT *and* RAKER, *and* CAPTAIN CROSSTREE *enters* C. *After fight,*

---

²² *L.D.* Down left: the area closest to the audience on the stage left side.

²³ *'confound your knaveyish tricks'* Punning version of the British national anthem:
'O Lord God arise,/Scatter our enemies,/And make them fall!/Confound their knavish
tricks,/Confuse their politics,/On you our hopes are fixed,/God save the Queen'.

RAKER *sneaks over to* R., *is met by a marine, and is caught by the leg by* DOGGRASS *whom the* DAME *has beaten down and covered with crinoline.* HATCHETT *does the same business.* DOGGRASS *catching him on his* L.

Capt.   Present! don't fire yet upon these strugglers,
                  I needn't tell you that these two are smugglers,
                  Handcuff 'em.

Dame. (L. *corner*)   Let me do it.

Capt. (*gets* L.)   You?

Dame.   Oh! dear—
                  It's on my card sir, 'Ironing done here.'

Capt. (*aside*)   'Tis she! my heart!

Dog. (*crosses to* C.)   Young Will, your uncle means
                  Kindly to both.

Wil.   Tell that to the marines.
              (*crosses and salutes the* CAPTAIN, *then speaks to* DAME.)

Hatch.   He's one of us.

Dog.   I drop these *smugglers* here,
                  And in repentance drop a *private* tear.

Capt. (*aside*)   She shall be mine. (*takes* L.H. *corner*)

Wil.   Now pitch care overboard,
                  Tipple the grog and drink it like a lord—
                  Captain you'll drink, free gratis to all comers,
                  Let's start the rummyest cask, and fill the rummers.
                  Those fellows there, upon whose track we've crept,
                  Know where the very best of liquor's kept
                  That's not paid toll; that's mum, and it's our booty,
                  England expects her sons to 'do' their duty,
                  And England shan't be disappointed—Eh?
                  So pipe all hands for fiddling. Pipe away!

Susan.   Visions of piping times of peace, entrancing!
                  Listen to me, and pipe all legs for dancing.

Capt.   Well, as the changes upon pipes you're ringing,
                  Let us begin with clear all pipes for singing. (*all cough*)

SONG.—Air—*Jenny Riddle.*

Wil.	Let us broach a cask of grog,
	And together let us jog,
	For *I* have found my Susan true, my Black-eyed pretty *gal.*
Susan.	Oh, I can't tell what you mean,
	But the notion is marine,
	And your joy's expressed in manner very nauti*cal.*
Capt. (*aside*)	Oh, she is such a Venus,
	But William's between us.
	She must be, and she shall be too, my pretty turtle dove.
Dame.	We'll have a dinner, and I'll griddle
	A steak, you get a fiddle
	And dance up and down the middle
	With your own true love!
All.	For our dinner she will griddle
	A small steak, &c.
Hatch.	I'm afraid, which isn't pleasant,
	That at this we shan't be present,
	And shan't have a steak or pheasant
	Shall we, eh, my pal?
Rake.	Yes, but if we play our cards
	Werry well before our guards,
	They will give a little ticket to each individual.
Dog.	'Taint likely, I will bet it,
	Though I wish that you may get it,
	But not again with me will you be hand and glove.
Wil.	Now for dinner go and griddle,
[All.]	While we're dancing to a fiddle.
	For no one now will diddle me (him)
	Of my (his) true love.

(*Dance everyone, and off.*)

SCENE THIRD.—*Exterior of the Admiral Benbow Tavern*—SAILORS *and* GIRLS *discovered.* GNATBRAIN R.C., *acting as waiter at the Admiral Benbow.* DOLLY MAYFLOWER *as barmaid,* L. *They are serving the sailors, a sailor attempts to kiss* DOLLY. *Two large tables. Jug on table,* R.

Gnat. (*brings her down; she carries a jug and mug*)	
	Don't you go winking at those sailor fellows,
	Or else you'll go and make your Gnatbrain jealous;
	I've watched you.
Dolly. (R.)	Have you? and I've watched you drinking.
Gnat. (L.C.)	Young woman, you've been going on like-winkin'.

Enter SHAUN O'PLOUGHSHARE, R.U.E., *he comes down* L.

Gnat.   I saw them spooning you; and then one 'ups
               And kisses you.

Dolly.   They're *spoons* when in their *cups*.

Gnat.   I saw him round you *whisk his* arm too frisky.

Shaun. (L.)   Now did I hear tell anything o'whisky?

Dolly. (*crossing* C.) A little drop (*preparing to pour it out*)

Shaun.   Sure, why's that like your waist?
               The littlest drop? bekase it's that that's laste. (*laced*)

                              DOLLY *goes up to sailors*.

Gnat.   This didn't see the Customs, I can do it,

Shaun.   The Customs wouldn't see it, if they knew it.

Enter DOGGRASS, L.U.E. *and down* L., *as he comes down he orders*
     something of DOLLY, *who brings a stone bottle and mugs to table*
     L. GNATBRAIN, R.

Shaun.   My little bottle, if ye plaze, ye'll fill. (*to* GNATBRAIN.)
               Whiskey, with all thy faults, I love thee still. (*drinks.*)

Dog.   (*hitting* SHAUN *on the back while he's drinking*)
               Pat!

Shaun. (*chokes*)   Don't.

Dog.   I was but patting you.

Shaun.   I'm blessed
               If that's a pattern, sorr to set the rest.

Dog. (*motioning him up to* L., GNATBRAIN *up* R. *at back looking after*
     DOLLY) You'll take a glass of Eau de Vie.

Shaun. (*crossing in front of* DOGGRASS *to* L. *of* L. *table*)
                                        That O!
               Sounds like some Irish liquor I don't know. (*sits.*)

Dog. (*sits* R. *of table.* SHAUN *drinks*) I think you've got a letter, Shaun,
     for me.

Shaun. You're very welcome if you like to see.

(DOGGRASS *opens* SHAUN'S *post bag, and takes out lots of letters.*)

Dolly. (*to sailor,* R.) Leave me alone.

Gnat. (L.C. *bringing her down* C.) You wicked flirting crittur!

Shaun. (*looking at heap of letters*) Sure them notes makes a mighty *tidy litter.*

Gnat. (R.C. *with* DOLLY) I saw a sailor kiss you. Oh, if I
Had but been born a giant ten foot high.

Dolly. (R.) Kiss me? You fancy it.

Gnat. Now, that I call
Absurd, for I don't fancy it at all. (*she goes up, and he
after her*)

Shaun. This Odewee is very pleasant tipple,
I'm in Ould Ireland, seeing *Dublin* people.

Dog. Gifts you with second sight: a quaintish whim
(*aside*) But he can't see me *doubling* on him.
(*pockets a letter, and rising.*)
Thank you; don't move: no, I must go away—
As you insist upon it, you shall pay.
(*reads address of letter aside, going* R.)
'To Captain Crosstree,' p'raps a prize worth landin'
If not, at all events, 'twill keep my hand in. (*Exit* R.)

(SHAUN *goes on drinking at table stupidly.* GNATBRAIN *looks
off* R. *at back.* SAILORS *rise.*)

Gnat. (*to* 1st SAILOR) Three cheers for William.

Dolly. (*to* 2nd SAILOR) And Black-eyed Susan.

(SAILORS *cheer and form* R. *and* L. *Enter* WILLIAM *and* SUSAN *from
back, and come down* C.—DAME *follows.*)

Wil. Thanks, messmates, have you got your dancing shoes on?

Susan. Now, mother, you must dance. No doleful dumps.

Dame. I'm a mere wreck.

Wil. A wreck, pooh! Work your pumps.

(WILLIAM *talks to* DOLLY *and* SAILORS. GNATBRAIN R.C.)

Gnat.   She seems 'all in the Downs'.

Susan. (*supporting* DAME.)   She will be when
                        She hears a tune. All in the *Breakdowns* then.[24]

Enter CAPTAIN CROSSTREE *from Public House* R. *with bottle and glass.*
        SUSAN *leaves* DAME, *who sits and drinks* SHAUN'S *liquor.*

Wil (R.)   The captain.

Capt. (C.)   Well, my tight trim sailors, might
                        Your captain ask you not to get too tight,
                        As everyone must be aboard to-night. (*sensation*)
                        The time and tide we can't afford to lose—

Susan.   This is a very *tidy* bit of news. (*turns to* WILLIAM)

Capt. (*starting aside*) Ah! there she is, she's lovely, on my life!
                        Who is she? (*brings* GNATBRAIN *down.*)

Gnat.   Black-eyed Susan—William's wife.

Capt. (*aside*)   His wife! Aha! Perdition catch my soul,
                        But I do love thee! This is far from droll—
                        It's very wrong. Another glass of wine! (*drinks.*)
                        She could—she should—she must—she shall be mine!
                        If William interferes let William tremble.
                        But soft—I am observed; I must dissemble.

Susan.   Your honour!

Capt. (*aside*, L.C.)   She's appealing to my honour.

Susan.   We want to ask—

Capt.   The lovely Black-eyed donna.
                        Donner and blitzen!

Susan.   If, sir, your proclivities
                        Are musical, you'd join in our festivities
                        And sing—
All.   A song.

---

[24] *All in the Breakdowns* Pun on 'All in the Downs', the sub-title of Jerrold's original
play and taken from John Gay's ballad. For a description of a 'breakdown' dance, see
the introduction to this volume, p. xxix.

Capt. (*coughs affectedly*) You hear me cough too often!

Susan. Then why not sing the old song, Long Tom Coffin?

Capt. Worth any lot of notes are those sweet looks!

Dame. (*while* SHAUN *raps the table with his shillelagh*)
Silence! for number Onety in the books.

SONG
Air.—'Champagne Charley is my name.'

Capt. Oh! when I was no higher than
A small powder mon-kee,
I was shipped aboard the Leviathan,
And sent away to sea;
I sat among the mainstay bobs,
As happy as a flea,
And the mermaids came to comb their nobs,
And wink their eyes at me.
Captain Crosstree is my name! (*bis*)
Good for any game to-night, my boy;
Then, brave boys! back again to sea.

Chorus Captain Crosstree, &c.

Wil. I know the little story, 'cos
It's known all over Deal;
It happened when the party was
A-sitting on a keel.
A mermaid came up on the spray,
And he gives her a kiss;
But *Mister* Mermaid said belay!
Your name, sir, and address.
Captain Crosstree, &c.

Chorus Captain Crosstree, &c.

Susan. She said that she should be his wife,
And his wife she'd have been,
If she had left her water life
And worn a crinoline,
Her father cussed the Cap'en from
His head down to his heel,
So one don't know what may happen from

His sitting on a keel.
Captain Crosstree is his name, &c.

Chorus   Captain Crosstree, &c.

Shaun.   Here's the Captain's health—the song's a ripper.

Capt. (*at table*, R.) And I'll propose a dance, as I'm the skipper.

Susan. (L.C.)   You'll want a partner?

Capt. (*down* C.)   Partner (*aside*) I must smother
          My joy.

Wil.   Let me present you to—(SUSAN *leaves him and goes
                        up as* DAME *comes in her place, while the* CAPTAIN
                        is bowing)   My mother.

Capt. (*aside*, R.C.) Dash it! (*aloud*) Perhaps a round dance makes you giddy,
          Or you're engaged. (*as if going.*)

Dame. (L.C. *taking his arm*) Engaged? No, I'm a widdy.

Capt.   Then I shall have the pleasure (*aside*) Hum.

Dame.   You will—
          The mazy waltz, the polka, or quadrille,
          You'll find I am, of exercise, no shirker,
          I'll join you in a shuffle, jig, mazourka.
          (*imitates and crosses to* R.)

Capt. (L.)   I'm yours. (*bows profoundly.*)

Dame.   He is as stately as a Kemble.[25]

Capt. (*offers his arm*) Come (*aside*) as said before I must dissemble. (*goes up* R.)

*Dance.—*WILLIAM *and* SUSAN, GNATBRAIN *playing the fiddle* L. *on table,
and* SHAUN *the pipes, standing* L. *of table.* CAPTAIN CROSSTREE *plays on
his telescope like a trombone and* DAME *plays on the table with spoons as*

---

[25] *as stately as a Kemble* A reference to the distinguished theatrical family headed by John Philip Kemble (1757-1823), which also included his brother Charles (1775-1854) and his sister Sarah Siddons (1755-1831). Unlike more animated actors such as Edmund Kean, John Philip Kemble and Siddons were renowned for their dignified, formal bearing.

drumsticks. WILLIAM *and* SUSAN *do the double hornpipe, and then exeunt*
R.U.E. *Then* CAPTAIN CROSSTREE, DAME, GNATBRAIN, SHAUN *and*
DOLLY *dance an Irish jig,* CROSSTREE *and* DAME *doing it on a door that is
laid down immediately.*[26] WILLIAM *and* SUSAN *have danced off.*
CROSSTREE *and* DAME *are both tired out, having danced each other down,
and are carried off by* SHAUN *and* GNATBRAIN R. *and* L., *followed by*
DOLLY. GNATBRAIN *carries* DAME *off* R. *After this the Sailors and Girls
execute a naval dance with flags, and exeunt dancing. Then enter from Inn*
CAPTAIN CROSSTREE *very intoxicated.*

Capt.	Would that these arms could Black-eyed Sue enfold?
	That which has made me drunk, hath made them bold—[27]
	I don't mean that, I mean that I have been
	Taking too much—and don't know what I mean.
	I think, I thought, I thought, I thank, I thunk,
	Crosstree, my worthy creature, you are drunk.
	Drunk's not the word, I am not very clear
	What is—I fancy though, it's the idea—
	The English language is so, so confoosin'
	There's only one word in it, and that's Susan.

Enter SUSAN *pensively,* R.U.E. *and down* L.

Susan. (C.)	So William's going to leave again, ah, me.
Capt. (R.)	The very person that I want to see,
	Come here, my dear.
Susan. (*aside*)	The truth is on me dawning,
	Yes, it was he who followed me this morning—
	I thought so.
Capt.	Sweetisht!
Susan.	But his speech is thicker,
	I scarcely know him, so disguised in liquor.
Capt. (*approaching, unsteadily*)	I love you to subtraction.[28]

---

[26] The dance is a 'cellar-flap' breakdown since it is performed on a door laid
horizontally.

[27] Cf. Lady Macbeth, 'That which hath made them drunk hath made me bold' (*Macbeth*
2.2.1-2).

[28] *subtraction* A corruption of the stock melodramatic phrase 'I love you to
distraction'.

Susan. (*eludes him and gets behind table,* L.)   If you please
          Do let me go. (*he sprawls on table.*)

Capt. (*steadying himself*)   You are, my dear, the cheese,
          And I've been toasting you! It is my habit.

Susan.   Oh! you've had something stronger than Welch rabbit.[29]

Capt.   I'll a Port Admiral be, one day, my gal.

          (*She passes in front of him to* R. *he seizes her gown.*)

Susan. (L.)   Port Admiral, more like a *Ginny*-ral.

Capt.   Gin a body
                         See a body
                    Walking all awry,
                         If a body
                         Kiss a body
                    Need a body cry?

Susan.   Gin and toddy
                         Make a body
                    Walk about awry,
                         And a roddy
                         To your body
                    Some one should apply.

Capt. (*hazily*)   For auld lang syne, my friend,
                         For auld lang syne.

Susan. (*angrily*) Oh! bring this nonsense to an end
                    For you've had too much wine.
                    (*He attempts to clasp her round the waist.*)

Capt.   Be mine. (*hurried music*)[30]

Susan.   Unhand me, monster.

Capt.   Hold your row!

---

[29] *Welch rabbit* Broiled cheese on toast, often served with beer, red wine, or port; also called Welsh rabbit or Welsh rarebit.

[30] *hurried music* Musical underscoring in a melodrama to imply the rapid passage of time: i.e., to 'hurry' the play to the next important plot development.

Susan.	Help! William, help! (*shakes off* CROSSTREE, *and runs down to* L.—*then makes as if about to attempt passing him to* R.U.E.)

Capt. (R.C. *up. Sneeringly*) Oh, yes! Help! help! but how!
(*seizes her and drags her towards* C. *and* R. *as* WILLIAM, *followed by* SAILORS, GNATBRAIN, DOLLY, DOGGRASS DAME, *enters* R.U.E.)

Wil. Susan! among the buccaneers! Die! (*runs* CROSSTREE *through with cutlass as* SUSAN *gets to* WILLIAM *and falls in his arms* R.) *Picture.*

Capt. (*falling* C.) Ow!

Dame. The Captain!

Dog. Ain't you been and done it now!

SCENE FOURTH.—Telegraph Office.

Enter SHAUN O'PLOUGHSHARE *and a Telegraphic Clerk* L.

Shaun. (L.) Bedad, I understand what ye requires—
Sure, 'tis an aisy thing to work thim wires.
'Tis a fine sight entirely! I suppose
Thim lines is for the clerks to dry their clothes—
Quite a line regiment! When will I begin?

Boy. (R.) Don't send no messages without the tin;
A guinea for a word, so just mind, old 'un!

Shaun. Silence is silver here, and speech is golden.

Boy. I'll leave you now. (*Exit* R.)

Shaun. Sure, there is much to larn,
And he laves me to wash the whole concern.

Enter DOLLY, R.

Dolly. You've heard the news? They're trying that poor Willum
On board by a court-martial.

Shaun. Och! they'll kill 'um.

Enter GNATBRAIN *with papers* L.

Gnat. (L.)   The lawyers say—they're right, depend upon't—
                  It's witnesses to character they want.

Dolly. (R.)   I'll go for one.

Gnat.   And so will I, for Bill.

Shaun. (C.)   What go for one! I'll go myself, I will;
                  I'll write to say we're coming. (*crosses to* R.)

                  (*Several telegraph bells ring suddenly.*)

Dolly. (*to* SHAUN, *who is going* R.C.)   That's the thing—
                  The telegraph. (*gets* L.C.)

Shaun. (R.C. *at back*)   Sure, when did that bell ring?

Enter SUSAN *distractedly*, R.

Susan.   What belle! don't talk of belles, with Will in fetters.
                  Can't I send to him—(*pointing to telegraph wires.*)
                                    By these Bell's letters?
           (*seizing* SHAUN) Where's the Atlantic line? do work it quick!

Shaun. (R.)   Sure! ye must pay.

Susan. (R.C.)   Pay! for the Atlan*tic*? (*crosses to* L.)
                  Oh! this is a hard struggle to go through,
                  When I would send my Bill a *billy-doo*![31]

Dolly. (R.)   He wants a guinea for one word!

Susan. (*to* SHAUN, C.)   Let's run
                  The twenty words I'll send him into one.

Gnat.   You'd spin a sort of yarn.

Shaun. (*at back* C.)   Oh! mighty fine!

Susan.   A string of words, to make a single line!
                  To save my William, say you will befriend him?
                  Or else another single line will end him.

---

[31] *billy-doo* Pun on *billet doux*, a love letter; literally, a 'sweet note'.

Shaun.   The boy said they must pay, before he went hence,
Ten words rolled into one won't stop his sentence.

Susan.   My Will must have two witnesses.

Shaun.   Then pay!

Susan. (C.)   Wherever there's a will there's a way.
Yet while I'm talking words to fill a volum,
My William's undergoing *sus. per collum*:[32]
And because all my lucre's gone,
I'll be a passive, wretched looker-on.
Oh! I could wring his nose! (SHAUN *runs to corner*.)

Dolly. (R.C.)   Best try the tip!

Susan.   I can't. How can I get to William's ship?
I'm going mad; I feel it; and my hair,
Which being my own I have a right to tear—
I will, till but one single hair you'll see.
A *single hair* performance that will be;
And I, who once upon a time could make
Up for the pretty 'Lady of the Lake,'[33]
Will now make up for all that's gone and shock
You, who'll call me the *Lady of the Lock*.[34]

Dolly.   I fear she doesn't know what she's about.
      (SUSAN *crossing to her, wildly*. GNATBRAIN *gets to* L.)

Susan.   I don't look in my mind: so you look out:
I might do something that you wouldn't like,
And make a stunning hit with my *Long Strike*.[35]

(*turning towards* SHAUN, *who is* L.C., *and gets behind* GNATBRAIN.)

Gnat.   What noble mind is here o'erthrown![36]

---

[32] *sus. per collum* Abbreviation for *suspensus per collum*, to be hung by the neck.

[33] *Lady of the Lake* A figure in Arthurian legend, also known as Niume. In Tennyson's epic poem *Idylls of the King* (1859), as in Sir Thomas Malory's *Le Morte d'Arthur* (c. 1478), the Lady of the Lake presented the sword to King Arthur.

[34] *Lady of the Lock* Pun on *Lady of the Lake* (see n. 33, above) referring to Susan's vow to pull out the 'locks' of her hair. Additional pun on the homophone 'loch', the Scottish word for 'lake'.

[35] *Long Strike* A factory melodrama by Dion Boucicault. Adapted from novels by Elizabeth Gaskell (1810-65), it was first produced at the Lyceum Theatre in 1866.

[36] Cf. Ophelia, 'O, what a noble mind is here o'erthrown!' (*Hamlet* 3.1.151).

Susan.   That's you;
    I'll overthrow a noble body, too. (*walks down* GNATBRAIN,
          who gets round, L. SHAUN *gets* L.C.)
    I've caught an air—stop! I will sing a catch.
    Oh! Vive l'amour, cigars, and Colney Hatch.[37]
    And by the pricking of my little thumbs,
    I feel that something wicked this way comes.[38]

       Enter HATCHETT *and* RAKER, R., *dressed as River Police, with*
       DOGGRASS *between them, a prisoner.*

Hatch.   We've cotched a landshark, skulking on a shoal.

Susan.   Landshark!

Rake. (R., *corner*)   He's here!

Susan.   Oh, my prophetic soul!
    My uncle!

Dog.   Well, niece, you seem very gay.

Susan.   My nunky: Nunky dorum, doodle cum day!
    And you—(*to* HATCHETT.)

Hatch.   Hold up, since we've cut our trade,[39]
    River police, miss, us two have been made;
    And so we've set to work, miss, werry hearty,
    And to begin, we've taken up this party.

Gnat.   What has he done?

Rake.   Hold up! Nuffing par-ticular,
    But everything in general; he's no sticklar—
    Nor *we* in this case.

Hatch.   Which we give great care to.

Rake.   I'll charge him.

---

[37] *Colney Hatch* Middlesex County Lunatic Asylum in north London, popularly known in the nineteenth century as 'Colney Hatch'. Its name became synonymous with mental illness. Prince Albert laid the cornerstone in 1849, and the first patients were received in 1851.

[38] Cf. Second Witch, 'By the pricking of my thumbs,/Something wicked this way comes' (*Macbeth* 4.1.44-5).

[39] *cut our trade* Abandoned our former line of work.

Hatch.   Yes; and what you say, I'll swear to.

Dog.   You see, these gentlemen are so impartial.

Hatch.   So telegraph at once to the court-martial.
              Say, send a boat—the first thing they can rig—
              Say, a fast screw.
                              (SHAUN *bothered at needle*.)

Susan.   Add, in the captain's gig,
              Then we'll all go.

Shaun.   Yes, when the tin I've got.

Hatch.   This chap here shall be purser for the lot.
              (*takes purse out of his pocket.*)

Susan.   Yes, Nunky pays for all. (*pays* SHAUN.)

Dog.   All! 'tis a haul!
              This is a change indeed!

              (SHAUN *bothered by everything.*)

Gnat. (*taking purse*)   The change is small.

Dog.   But first—
                  (*The others are engaged in telegraphing.*)

Hatch.   Be quiet: we'll take no denial,
              Whatever you observe will, on your trial,
              Be used against you; so you'd best behave—

Rake.   And come with us young William for to save.

Susan.   Where's the Atlantic line? Quick, quicker be.
                  (*Harp chord, and bell rings.*)
              Oh! here it is, of course! The *chord of Sea*.

Shaun.   Now, there. (*bang*) It's gone. (*needle works wildly.*) And
                  there's the needle playing.[40]

Susan. (*in agony*) He says—

---

[40] *And there's the needle playing* In a needle telegraph, a galvanometer needle would
swing left or right to signal dots or dashes when different polarities of voltage were
placed on the lines. Needle telegraphs were used primarily on railways in England and
were obsolete by 1844.

Shaun. (*attempting to follow needle*) He says—he can't hear what I'm saying.

Susan.   Use the large letters.
     (*The needle suddenly whirls round and then stops.*)

Shaun.   Here's a situation,
     Och! 'tis all over with communication—
     'Tis no good trying messages to send off,
     Some spalpeen's been and cut the other end off.
     (*crossing to* L.)

Gnat. (*rapping*) Why can't you answer to a question? Won't you?

Dolly.   You call these clerks the *civil* servants, don't you?

Susan.   Agony! (*clutches* HATCHETT, *who clutches* DOGGRASS,
          who clutches RAKER, *who hits him on the head with
          his staff.*) I'm on pins and needles!

Gnat. (*seeing a sudden flash illuminate the clock for a moment*)   Shaun?

Shaun.   Ah! here's a spark at last. Hoorah!
     (*The face is illuminated with the words* 'BOAT GONE!')

Susan (*horrified*)   Boat gone!
               (*the words disappear*)

Gnat.   There's some mistake, I see it at a glance, sir.

Dog.   It answers, but it doesn't seem to answer.

Susan.   Don't let the boat go, say, 'Hi!, wait a minute,'
     Say a policeman's coming—to go in it.

Hatch. (*seeing the clock illuminated again suddenly, and as suddenly the light
          vanishes—chord*)
     The telegraphic letter you wrote
     Won't pass—

Susan. (*agonised*)   Because—

Hatch.   It's too like a *flash note*.[41]
          (*lights up quickly.*)

Gnat. Oh! here we go again.

---

[41] *flash note* Counterfeit banknote.

Shaun.   They want a bating.

Susan. (*horrified*) Ship weighing anchor—No!

(*Only the word 'weigh' appears at first, then the whole message, 'Weasel's Weighting.'*)

CONCERTED PIECE.
'The Mouse Trap', then 'The Adele Waltz'

Susan.   Let us be off to the ship on the sea
                      For the boat's waiting for you and for me:
                      Sweeter by far than raspberry jam
                      Will come See-usan to her Willi*am*.
Gnat.   Sailing or rowing I feel no alarm,
                      Sing Rule Britannia while it is calm.
Shaun.   And, to renew an old joke rather late,
                      Sure I hope that Britannia will rule the waves straight.
Susan.   Oh, my! never say die.
                          Why—why should any one cry?
                      Sweeter by far than raspberry jam
                      Will come See-usan to her Willi*am*.
Chorus   Oh, my! &c.

Dog.   On board the ship we're expected to go.
Rake.   Why you're singing an old song, I know!
Gnat.   'Tis Vilikins and his Dinah, popular in its day;[42]
Dog.   And William and Susan may end the same way.
Hatch.   End the same way.
H.D.R.   End the same way.
Susan.   Chorus of indignant loviers!
                          Oh, my! never say die.
                          Why—why should anyone cry?
                      Nunky! my words I'll once again say.
                      Nunky Dorum, doodle cum day.
Chorus   Oh, my! never say die:
                          Why—why should anyone cry?
                      Angry with Nunky, all we can then say
                      Is—Nunky Dorum, doodle cum day!

---

[42] *Vilikins and his Dinah* Popular nineteenth-century ballad, principally identified with the burlesque actor Frederick Robson. Dinah, who loves Vilikins, poisons herself to avoid marrying the suitor named by her father.

'*Hunkey Dorum*'

Susan.	Yes, we mean by Nunkey, you,
All.	Nunky Dorum doodle cum day;
Dog.	Put my monkey up, you do.
All.	Monkey Dorum doodle cum day;
Hatch.	Governmental Flunkies two,
All.	Hunkey Dorum doodle cum day;
Rake.	You look funky—rather blue—
	Tunkey Dorum doodle um day.
Chorus.	'Twill be as sweet as raspberry jam,
	When Susan comes to her Willi*am*:
	We'll turn all colours from white to brown,
	When the boat goes up, and the boat goes down.
	(*dance and off*)

SCENE FIFTH.—*The deck of H.M.S. Polly Phemus.*[43]   *Court-martial*—LORD HIGH ADMIRAL *and* ADMIRALS *discovered*—WILLIAM *a prisoner*—*two* MARINES *bring down tub* R.

Lord.   That you killed Captain Crosstree is quite settled.

Adm. 2.   Sent him to *grass*, in fact, when he was *nettled*.

(*Laughter on board, in which the prisoner joins, as does everyone except the* LORD HIGH ADMIRAL.)

Lord.   Hem! Admiral of the Blue![44] I think you spoke,
                   This ain't an occasion for a joke.

Adm. 3.   His jokes are no joke. (*business*)

Lord.   Admiral of the Yellow:
                   Excuse me—you're a very stoopid fellow!
                   Another word, I'll flog you till you *beller*,

---

[43] *Polly Phemus* In Greek mythology, Polyphemus was the Cyclops blinded by Odysseus; also, a type of moth.

[44] *Admiral of the Blue* The rank of an admiral in the Royal Navy was denoted by colour. The ranks, in ascending order, were Admiral of the Blue, Admiral of the White, Admiral of the Red, and, finally, Admiral of the Fleet. The colours are taken from the Royal Navy's three principal squadrons. An Admiral of the Yellow is an officer promoted for ceremonial purposes only, and who is effectively decommissioned (i.e., 'yellowed'). This system of ranking was abandoned in 1864. Burnand invented the Admiral of the Black, a role which was played in blackface.

And change your name to Admiral of the *Yell*er,
Now I will read a word upon this head.
            (*reads from an enormous book, &c.*)

Wil. (*in tub,* R.) Ah, yes! I see you're Admiral of the *Red*.

Lord.   Hallo! I'm Lord High Admiral, Mr. Prisoner,
             I'm the talker, you must be the lis'ener.

Adm. 2.   I'll read.

Adm. 3.   You won't.

Adm. 4.   I'll make a speech.

Lord.   You'll what—
             Am I the Lord High Admiral, or not? (*looks at book*)
             What's the first Article?

Wil.   Well, I should say,
             Your honours, the first article is 'A'.

Lord. (*to* WILLIAM) As soon as look at you,
             If you're not quiet, I will throw this book at you.
          (*enquiringly*) You did kill Captain Crosstree, William?

Wil.   Why,
             Ain't that the werry question we're here to try.

Lord.   We settled that you did.

Wil.   Stop! not so fast!
             I claim a trial by a jury mast. (*shake of heads*)
             You shake your heads, I see your eyes a rollin',
             You'll send me up aloft, like poor Tom Bowlin'.[45]
             A mate on a screw steamer, whom I knew,
             Was always thought the darling of his *screw*.
             But, my dear eyes! I wish to be respectful;
             And of my chances not at all neglectful.
             But if your honours have the smallest doubt
             About my case, why don't you fight it out?
             Such an opinion as, my luds, I've got of you
             Ain't much. I don't mind if I fight the lot of you.
                                  (*comes out of tub.*)

---

[45] *Tom Bowlin'* In 1789, Charles Dibdin (1740-1814) wrote *Tom Bowling*, also known as *The Sailor's Epitaph*, after the death of his eldest brother Thomas. The song is a lament for Bowling, a dead sailor—i.e., one who has 'gone aloft'.

Lord.   Horse Marines! cover us for our protection.
      (MARINES *come down and point at Admirals.*)
      Turn your guns in the opposite direction.
      We've all agreed! (MARINES *put* WILLIAM *in tub, and then go up stage.*)

Adm. 2.   I'm not.

Lord.   And who are you?
      Marines, remove the Admiral of the Blue.
      Or—silence! Where's my spectacles? (*preparing to read sentence*)

Wil.   Refuses
      My *mus*cles, and his barnacles he chooses.

Lord.   No witnesses to character, I note.

Voices. (*without*) Ho! ship ahoy! (*all lift telescopes with one jerk.*)

Lord.   Perhaps from Cowes. Alongside comes a boat.

Wil. (*seeing* SAILOR *throw rope, R.*) Make that fast round your rowlocks.
      From Cowes! and they are making for our bulwarks.

Enter HATCHETT, DOGGRASS, *and* RAKER, *over bulwarks.*

Hatch.   Witnesses in a boat for you to call.

Dog.   'Twas quite a toss-up we were here at all.

      (HATCHETT *goes down and stands with* DOGGRASS, R. *of* WILLIAM; RAKER, L. *During the above,* GNATBRAIN, DOLLY, *and* SHAUN *have entered, and are bowing to the Admiral.*)

Lord.   He's in a scrape; your bows there is no use in.
               (*They go down.*)

Susan. (*without*) Where is he?

Wil.   Ah! that voice!

Susan. (*rushing in*)   My William!

Wil.   Seeusan!

(*Embrace. Everyone unmanned.*)

Susan.	Cheer up, my Willy! I've been reading for yer,
	This book of 'Every Woman her own Lawyer;'
	Flotsam and Jetsam—Rules made for the Navy.
	You'll hear me make those fellows cry 'peccavi'.[46]
Lord.	Now, then, young woman, if you please, sit down.
Susan.	I'm his counsel—don't you see my gown?
Lord.	But where's your wig?
Susan.	Insult me, don't you try it.
Wil.	Never say die!
Susan.	I don't; I never dye it.

(*goes up to the C. end of table; talks to* ADMIRALS. HATCHETT
takes WILLIAM *back to his tub. DAME tumbles up with
difficulty.* ADMIRALS *look at* DAME *through telescopes.*)

Dame.	Oh, dear! If safe again I get to shore,
	You'll never catch me on the sea no more.
Wil.	Mother cheer up!
Dame.	I can't cheer up. Bad luck! It
	Feels (*they offer her a bucket to sit on; she upsets it*)
	As if I was going to kick the bucket.
	Ill omen! ill o' woman.
Lord.	Sit to leeward.
Dame.	Could you oblige me with a glass of—steward?
	(*sits at corner of table, and is attended by the Admiral*)
Susan.	I've studied for the bar. I give my calm aid
	To William.
Dame. (L.)	Lor! here's Susan as a barmaid.
Wil.	Now you have all embarked, the case begins.
Dame.	Embarked, you call it, I've em-barked my shins.

---

[46] *cry 'peccavi'* To acknowledge one's sins. *Peccavi* is Latin for 'I have sinned'.

Susan.   Now witnesses to ch'racter. Gnatbrain can
                    Speak to him.

Gnat. (*crosses to* R.C.)   William, how d'ye do, my man?

Lord.   Address the prisoner, we must forbid it.

Gnat.   I thought I was to speak to him, and did it.
                              (*stands on an inverted pail.*)

Susan. (*as counsel*) How do you like him?

Gnat.   Like him? pretty well.

Susan.   Stand down, call Doggrass.

Hatch.   Doggrass.

Susan.   You're to tell
                    Something, but only truth the law allows.

Dog.   Thank you, I'm the uncle to his spouse
                    Susan—you'll see the likeness in my phiz.[47]

Susan.   Of William—

Dog.   A nice young man he is.

Susan.   You've known him—

Dog.   Know him well, ten years about.

Susan.   You've always found him—

Dog.   Always found him out;
                    He's very bad.

Susan.   Stand down. (*business*)

Rake.   Stand down.

Wil.   I see
                    There's not much good you're standing up for me.
Susan.   Call Shaun O'Ploughshare.

---

[47] *phiz* Face, short for 'physiognomy'.

Rake.	Shaun—
Hatch.	O'Ploughshare, where?

Shaun. (*crossing to* R.C.) 'Tis soon to make a call upon a share.

Wil.	Speak up for me.
Shaun.	I will so, with facil'ty.
Susan.	Well, the accused you know?
Shaun.	Accused? He's guilty!
Susan.	As to his character, 'tis not a bad one.
Shaun.	Sure, good or bad, I niver knew he had one.
Susan.	Stand down!
Hat.	Stand down!
Lord.	Dame Hatley?

(*Small chair,* DAME *sits and puts her feet in bucket.*)

Dame. Right, old fellar!
Excuse me—I must take my umbrella.
This here young person is my only child,
Thank goodness! which he were a little wild.
I never saw in him the least improvement—
You couldn't stop the ship's unpleasant movement.
It's most important what I've got to tell,
But I can't do it if I don't feel well.
I feel as if I'd danced a too-quick waltz:
Ain't a sailor got a sniff of salts?
Oh, you bad boy, to bring me here. For one,
I hope you'll punish him for what he's done.

Susan. Stand down!

Dame. D'ye mean to execute him gents?
I hope it won't put me to expense,
For I'm his widowed mother; if the Crown
Would like to pension me—

Raker.	Stand down!
Hatch.	Sit down!

Susan.   He's served Britannia, she as rules the waves,
                And Britons never, never shall be slaves;[48]
                                              ('Hear, hear.')
                He's served her, man and boy, in her employ;
                He was a life-preserver when a boy,
                And saved the man whom now he's charged with killing:
                Just look at everybody's eyes a-filling.
                With tears.

Lord.   Then plead 'Not guilty.'

Wil.   No, old cock!
                I'm not an old hull lying in a dock;
                I'm not much in the speechifying way,
                Except shivering timbers and belay.
                Bless my dear eyes, and heave ahead! I could
                Dance you a hornpipe, if that's any good.

Lord.   'First article'—no hornpipes near the gunwale;
                Next—Smoking not allowed abaft the funnel.

Wil.   Susan! you're my sheet anchor. (*pulls out flag*)

Susan.   See his grief;
                And keep your eyes upon his handkerchief,
                While he keeps his upon it.

Lord.   Take that back;
                The prisoner's using out best Union Jack.

Susan.   Your Ludships! I've one witness yet to call:
                Jump up! He'll clear him—then, I think, that's all.
                Now, Serjeant Hatchett, speak! you'll be believed.
                      (*business with pencils and paper*)

Hatch.   My luds, from information I received,
                I went to London, where I saw a crowd,
                Near the Alhambra,[49] talking very loud.
                I saw, sir, in the centre of the men,
                A sight that horror-struck me, sir, and then
                I found that he's the boy who, I will swear

---

[48] *Britons never, never shall be slaves* Abbreviated lyric from 'Rule Britannia'. The chorus was first sung in a masque staged in 1740 under the patronage of the Prince of Wales.

[49] *Alhambra* Music hall in Leicester Square, central London.

Painted the statue, sir, in Leicester-square.[50]

All.	Oh!

(WILLIAM *disappears in tub.*)

Susan.	Up till now your worships have been told That he (the prisoner's) been as good as gold.
Lord.	That he's no longer gold, but guilt-y's clear, At least, I must say that is my idea. Now, gentlemen, you're charged, so you may doff Your hats.
Susan.	They're cocked, and they are going off.
Dame.	Well, they've gone off, and what is their report?
Lord.	Thus we record the sentence of the court.

ADMIRALS *with bones, banjo, fiddle, tambourine, &c.—clear off tables, &c.*[51]

All.	For he's a jolly bad fellow.
	For he's a jolly bad fellow (*bis*)
	     And so say all of us, *&c.*
	It's a way we have in the army,
	It's a way we have in the Navy (*bis*)—
	     Young William is guil*tee*.
	Hip, hip, hip, hooray!

Lord.	Now one cheer more we'll give him three times three.

(*All cheer, led by* LORD HIGH ADMIRAL, CROSSTREE *appears at the wheel.*)[52]

---

[50] *painted the statue* An equestrian statue of George II at the centre of Leicester Square had fallen into disrepair by the middle of the nineteenth century. The last act of vandalism was whitewashing the horse and then adding black spots so that the monarch appeared to be riding a cow.

[51] *bones, banjo, fiddle, tambourine* Instruments played by minstrel show serenaders. 'Bones' are percussive folk instruments—originally the bleached rib bones of animals, but later curved sticks of wood—that are struck against each other to simulate clapping hands or stamping feet.

[52] The foliation of the original manuscript is confused here (fol. 66), with two pages of dialogue placed in the wrong order. The acting edition corrects the error.

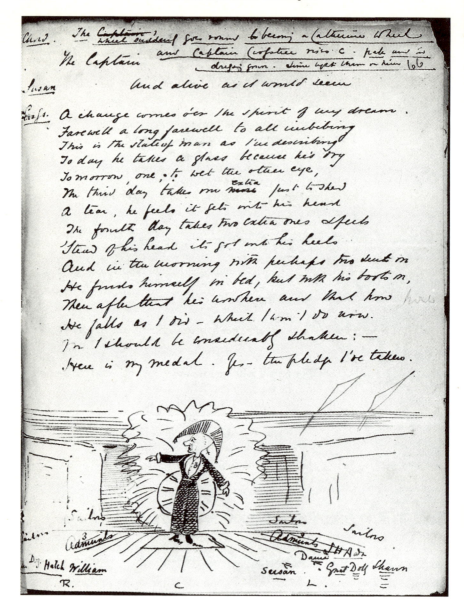

Chord. The Captain's wheel suddenly goes round to become a Catherine Wheel

The Captain and Captain Crosstree rises C. pale and is dressing gown. Lime light thrown on him 66

Susan. And alive as it would seem

Cross. A change comes o'er the spirit of my dream.
Farewell a long farewell to all imbibing
This is the state of man as I've describing
To day he takes a glass because he's dry
To morrow, one, to wet the other eye,
The third day takes one extra just to shed
a tear, he feels it gets into his head
The fourth day takes two extra ones & feels
Steam of his head its got into his heels
And in the morning with perhaps two dents on
He finds himself in bed, but with his boots on,
Then after that he's nowhere and that how
He falls as I did — which I am I do now.
For I should be considerably shaken; —
Here is my medal. Yes — the pledge I've taken.

11 Captain Crosstree at the wheel, with limelight shining upon him. Original manuscript of *The Very Latest Edition of Black-Eyed Susan* (British Library Add Ms 53,055 O, fol. 66)

The wheel suddenly goes round to being a Catherine Wheel and Captain Crosstree rises C., pale and in a dressing gown.[53] *Limelight thrown on him.*[54]

Capt. (*singing*)   Young William's *not* guil*tee*.

Chorus   The Captain!

Susan.   And alive, as it would seem!

Capt.   A change comes o'er the spirit of my dream.[55]
                  Farewell, a long farewell to all imbibing!
                  This is the state of man as I'm describing:
                  To-day he takes a glass because he's dry,
                  To-morrow, one to wet the other eye;
                  The third day takes one extra, just to shed
                  A tear—he feels it gets into his head;
                  The fourth day takes two extra ones, and feels
                  'Stead of his head it's got into his heels;
                  And in the morning, with, perhaps, two suits on,
                  He finds himself in bed, but with his boots on;
                  Then after that he's nowhere; and that's how
                  He falls, as I did—which I won't do now;
                  For I should be considerably shaken:—
                  Here is my medal. Yes—the Pledge I've taken.[56]

Lord.   Oh, this won't do at all. There is no flaw
                  In the indictment—you are dead in law,
                  And we'll soon settle matters if you're not,
                  I'll call out the marines and have you shot.

Hatch.   Stop! here's a letter.

Shaun.   Which he took from me.

---

[53] *Catherine Wheel* A firework in the form of a wheel that spins around from the recoil of the explosives placed along its circumference. The Catherine Wheel, typically used on Bonfire Night, takes its name from St. Catherine of Alexandria (d. 310 AD), who was tortured upon a spiked wheel.

[54] *Limelight* A brilliant white light produced when a block of quicklime was heated by a combined flame of oxygen and hydrogen. Focused limelight, such as was used in this scene, functioned as a primitive follow-spot before the use of electric stage lights.

[55] Cf. Lord Byron's 'The Dream': 'A change came o'er the spirit of my dream' (stanza 3, line 1).

[56] *the Pledge I've taken* To 'take the pledge' was to vow to abstain from drinking alcohol. Medals were given to those who took the pledge in token of their commitment to reforming their lives. The Victorian temperance movement inspired the dramatic sub-genre of 'temperance melodramas', such as T.P. Taylor's *The Bottle* (1847), intended to save the urban working classes from the perils of gin and beer.

Capt.	Which says that William, well, it says he's free.
Wil.	But Doggrass.
Dame.	Pitch him over.
Gnat.	Pitch, tar, feather him.
Shaun.	Give me five minutes with him, I'll leather him.
Wil.	So, Susan, it's all finished, let's get on'ard. You see your little Bill is not dishonoured.
Susan.	Dishonoured! No! and if our kind friends will But give their names to back our little Bill, Then we may safely say the thing is done, Thus taken up our little Bill will run.

FINALE. Air.—'Champagne Charlie is my name.'

Will.	Our Nautical Burlesque we end, The good old story's done.
Hatch.	And if their names our friends will lend, Our little Bill will run.
Capt.	Yes, if you're pleased, we hope you'll back Your Crosstree.
Dame.	And his Dame.
Susan.	And if you're asked whose Bill—then Black- Eyed Susan is the name. Black-eyed Susan is my name, If you say, 'tis good to-night, my boys, Then you'll come back again to see.
Chorus.	Black-eyed Susan, *&c., &c., &c.*

'Rule Britannia.'

Capt. (C.)	Rule Britannia Britannia rules the waves, For Britons always, always, always—
Lord.	Bless the Prince of Wales![57]

---

[57] *Bless the Prince of Wales* Apart from the obvious reference to the future Edward VII, perhaps also an allusion to the song's origins (see note 48, above). The chorus also

Chorus.	Rule Britannia,
	&c., &c., &c.
Capt. (C.)	Rule Britannia
	Britannia rules the waves,
	For Britons never, never, never—
Lord.	God Save the Queen!
Chorus.	Rule Britannia,
	&c., &c., &c.

CURTAIN.

suggests Susan's role in the original melodrama as a surrogate Britain: an icon of the empire itself.

THE CORSICAN 'BOTHERS'; OR, THE TROUBLESOME TWINS

H.J. BYRON
(1869)

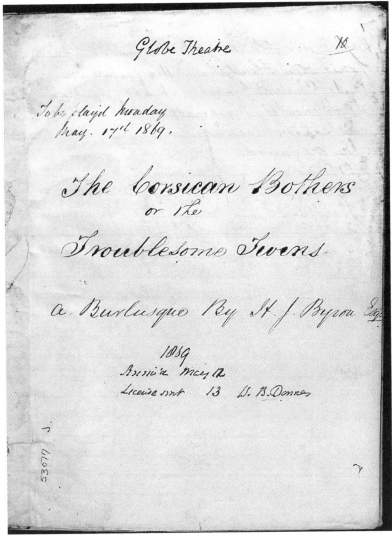

12 Title page of the original manuscript of *The Corsican 'Bothers'; or, the Troublesome Twins* (British Library Add Ms 53,077 J)

Editor's Introduction

The Corsican 'Bothers'

In February 1852 Charles Kean, actor-manager of the Princess's Theatre, produced Dion Boucicault's *The Corsican Brothers*, an adaptation of a popular French melodrama based up a novel by Alexandre Dumas *père*. The play took London by storm. Among its most ardent admirers was Queen Victoria: she saw it four times in eight weeks, commissioned E.H. Corbould to paint a scene from the production, and drew a sketch of the famous tableau of 'The Duel' in her journal. Sheet music for the play's 'Ghost Melody' sold thousands of copies. So popular was *The Corsican Brothers* that it quickly found its way into the repertoires of minor theatres in London and provincial theatres throughout the country. Although the starring roles of the twins Louis and Fabien dei Franchi were mostly closely identified with Kean—he played the parts more than 250 times before his death in 1868—they were also acted in London by Charles Fechter in the 1860s and Henry Irving in the 1880s.

The action of Boucicault's melodrama turns on the mysterious telepathic bond which allows each twin to sense when the other is endangered. Ingeniously, the playwright transforms symmetry of character into symmetry of plot. The play opens in Corsica, where Fabien feels a premonition that his twin has come to harm in Paris. As Fabien hastily writes to his brother seeking reassurance that all is well, the blood-stained spectre of the murdered Louis rises from the stage floor. To the haunting strains of violins, the ghost 'glides across the stage—ascending gradually at the same time'.[1] That scene, which gave its name to the stock 'Corsican Trap,' introduced the novelty of a ghost moving across the stage in a slow incline rather than merely floating upward and out of sight. The spectre then reveals to Fabien and his mother a tableau of the painting 'The Duel,' depicting his own death at the hands of the villain Chateau-Renaud in the forest at Fontainbleau.[2] The second act dramatizes the events in Paris leading up to the duel, and thus is meant to occur simultaneously with the first act. During a masked ball at the Paris Opera, Chateau-Renaud places a bet that he can persuade the virtuous Émilie de Lesparre to accompany him to a dinner party arranged by his friend Baron de Montgiron. He succeeds in luring her to the dinner party under false pretences. Louis, also at the party, comes to Émilie's aid and confronts the unscrupulous Chateau-Renaud. They arrange to duel the next morning. The second act closes with a tableau of the fateful duel, thus restaging the end of the first act. At the beginning of act three, Chateau-Renaud has fled Paris. Fabien, swift in pursuit of his brother's killer, catches up with him in the forest at Fontainbleau. The grieving Fabien avenges Louis's death, and Chateau-

Renaud dies on the very spot where he committed murder. As Fabien collapses in sorrow, Louis's ghost, now at peace, once again slowly rises from the stage floor.

'[T]his French piece of melodramatic ghostliness and blue fire', the *Era* presciently observed, 'is a fair subject for ridicule'.[3] Indeed, no fewer than nine burlesques of *The Corsican Brothers* were performed over the next four decades.[4] Parodic allusions to *The Corsican Brothers* occur in numerous Victorian burlesques and extravaganzas, including Planché's *The Discreet Princess* (1855) and Byron's *1863; or, the Sensations of the Past Season*, the latter of which is included in this volume. In keeping with the supernatural and pictorial appeal of the original play, the various burlesque versions of *The Corsican Brothers* centred on ghosts and tableaux vivants. In *O Gemini! or, Brothers of Co(u)rse* (1852), the ghost was ludicrously represented by a flowing white sheet with a turnip jack-o-lantern for its head. *The Corsican 'Bothers'* satirized the Corsican Trap by having the ghost fall over as it attempted to float across the stage. This 'spectre of travesty', the *Era* archly reported, 'is shown to have great difficulty in preserving his phantom perpendicularity'.[5] Byron's burlesque also offers a degraded version of the tableau by transforming the duel into a fistfight: the dignity of the rapier sacrificed for the coarseness of a bare-knuckle fight. Louis thus suffers not a mortal wound but merely a black eye, and Chateau Renaud, savouring his victory, does not wipe blood off his sword but casually smokes a cigarette.

Yet the more ingenious aspect of the scene is Fabien's reaction to the mysterious vision. In both the original and burlesque versions the tableau was revealed through a 'rise and sink'—theatrical jargon for simultaneously raising and lowering (i.e., 'sinking') the top and bottom halves of a painted backdrop to remove it from the stage. Actors already in place behind the backdrop thus appeared to emerge from nowhere. In illusionistic plays—such as *The Corsican Brothers*—characters do not call attention to the workings of stage machinery. In *The Corsican 'Bothers'*, however, the situation is rather different. As the bottom half of the backdrop is lowered beneath the stage a frightened Fabien exclaims that his 'house is sinking'. The burlesque character mistakes the physical actuality of the performance ('sinking' the scenery) for the events represented within the performance ('the house is sinking'). Byron thus calls into question the believability—indeed, the acceptability—of increasingly elaborate stage effects. We can read the satiric vision scene in *The Corsican 'Bothers'*, then, as a form of metatheatrical criticism. By obliging its audience to remain aware of the performance *as* a performance, the burlesque refuses to allow spectators to succumb to the wonders of technologically created illusions; instead, it demands that they acknowledge how those illusions are manufactured.

Most burlesques of *The Corsican Brothers* featured theatrical parody, topical references, and cross-dressing. In *O Gemini! or, Brothers of Co(u)rse*, the popular comedian J.B. Buckstone portrayed the twins as united by a 'sympathetic cold' which made them both sick at the same time. Buckstone's nasal intonations (which consisted chiefly of substituting 'd' for 'n') were not only a ludicrous character trait but also a parody of Kean, whose much-ridiculed speech impediment made him sound as if he suffered from a permanent head cold. Similarly, in *The Corsican Brothers and Co., Ltd* Edward Royce impersonated Irving's 'conduct of all the chief scenes of the melodrama', including his 'manner of eating a stage meal' and 'lighting a cigarette'.[6] The burlesque convention of localizing actions and characters is shown especially well in *The Camberwell Brothers*, which transfers the action from Corsica and Paris to contemporary London. Funky Franky and Fighting Franky, sons of a Camberwell milkman, substitute for the dei Franchi twins. Scenes originally taking place in Fontainbleau and the Paris Opera are relocated to the Cremorne Gardens and Greenwich Park. *The Corkonian Brothers*, trading on the stereotypic 'stage Irishman', moves part of the play's action to Cork and so recasts the brothers as Tim and Pat Mulligan. (On the stage Irishman, see the introduction to Byron's *Miss Eily O'Connor* in this volume.) Of all these burlesque productions, *The Corsican 'Bothers'* incorporated the greatest amount of cross-dressing in the roles of Madame dei Flunki, Chateau Renaud, Montgiron, Martelli, and Meynard. Although it closely follows Boucicault's original plot, *The Corsican 'Bothers'* contains one twist. In the final scene Fabien avenges his brother's death by giving Émilie to Chateau Renaud. The act is hardly generous since, as Fabien misogynystically confides to the audience, Émilie's temper is 'fearful' and '[s]he'll turn his hair grey in a month'.

The text for *The Corsican 'Bothers'* is taken from Lacy's acting edition, collated with the British Library manuscript (Add Ms 53,077 J).

For biographical information on H.J. Byron, see the introduction to *Miss Eily O'Connor*.

Notes

[1] Dion Boucicault, *The Corsican Brothers* (New York: Samuel French, n.d.), p. 20.
[2] Since a single actor played both brothers, the play's vision scenes required the use of two doubles: one to play the ghost and one to play the mortally wounded Louis.
[3] *Era* 18 April 1852.
[4] Other burlesques of *The Corsican Brothers* include Gilbert Abbot à Beckett and Mark Lemon's *O Gemini; or, Brothers of Co(u)rse* (Haymarket 1852), Hugo Vamp's (pseud. John Robert O'Neill) *The Arcadian Brothers; or, the Spirit of Punch* (Marionette Theatre 1852), Charles Selby's *The Camberwell Brothers* (Olympic 1852), the anonymous *The Corkonian Brothers* (Strand 1854), F.C. Burnand's *The Corsican Brothers and Co., Ltd* (Gaiety 1880), *The Coster Twin Brothers* (Philharmonic Theatre 1880), *The New Corsican Brothers* (Prince of Wales, Liverpool, 1889), and *The Corsican Brothers-babes-in-the-wood* (1881).
[5] *Era* 23 May 1852.
[6] *Theatre* 1 December 1880.

The Corsican 'Bothers;' or, The Troublesome Twins

First performed at the New Globe Theatre (under the management of Mr. Sefton Parry), on Monday, May 17th, 1869.

An Original Burlesque Extravaganza, founded on a famous Romantic Drama, entitled, the,

CORSICAN 'BOTHERS;'
Or, THE TROUBLESOME TWINS

Characters

Louis dei Flunki..........(*the Brothers! very much alike*.........Mr. J. Clarke
Fabien dei Flunki...............*especially Louis*)............................."....... .
M. de Chateau Renaud (*a Roué, a Libertine, a Blackleg, an Adventurer, a Darling, a Lady Killer, and a Gentleman Killer*)..Miss Maggie Brennan
The Baron Montgiron   }......(*too awful swells*)..........Miss Sylvia Hodson
The Baron Martelli   }.......................................Miss Jessie Anstiss
Orlando............(*the Raw Material*)..............................Mr. H. Andrews
Colonna...........(*the Staple Commodity*)............................Mr. Tindale
Antonio…(*an excellent Judge, who not making any observation, may be said to reserve his Sentence*)................. Mr. Beak
M. De Meynard (*his Parents' first and Fabian's second*)
....Miss Rose Behrend
Griffo (*anything but a* dumb-*estic*)...........................Mr. W.J. Hurlstone
    A Head Waiter   A Corsican Cabman   A Native Doctor

Madame dei Flunki (*Maternal Parent of the Troublesome Twins— Pity and Forgive Her*)...........................Mr. E. Marshall
Marie (*a Waiting Maid—and great shame she should wait too*).......................................Miss Clara Thorne

Emilie de Lesparre (*a Grass Widow, but by no means*
            green)..Miss Hughes
Coralie   }.........(*three Young Girls of the Period,*............Miss Ashton
Celestine }..........*who make everybody else* smart...............Miss Wilson
Estelle   }..........*as well as themselves*)......................Miss J. Fountain
Girls of the Period   ...   Misses Varcoe, Ashton, Bennett, Wilson,
    Fountain, Thorne, Knight, and Thorpe
Young Gents of the Period   ...   Misses Pardon, Grosvenor, Westfield,
    Prentis, Braithwaite, Anstiss, Robinson, and Leclerq.

Programme of Scenery.

SCENE I—THE RESIDENCE OF THE DEI FLUNKI FAMILY IN CORSICA.

Arrival of a Visitor in hot haste, who gets a cool reception. Anxious enquiries for Louis, and extraordinary revelations concerning the wonderful sympathy between the Twin-born interrupted by the cancelling of an old Vendetta, to the mutual satisfaction of Colonna and Orlando. How one gives his bird, and the other his word, and how Fabien received a mysterious intimation that his Brother has come to grief and has received a *Fontain-blow* on his eye, and how he determines in a *second* to set *fourth*, and how he frightens his mother and starts himself.

THE BROTHER'S GHOST!

SCENE II—THE OPERA LOBBY.

THE PET! THE NET! THE SET! and THE BET!

SCENE III—MABILLE.

Grand Ballet of Ladies and Gentlemen of the Period
By a distracted troupe of attractive Artists.

How the Ladies shew their partiality for *Real Pleasure* and *Champagne*, and how Louis proves himself an anomaly, for though the least drop upsets him, he can *stand* any quantity of Wine. Champagne *cuplets*...How Chateau Renaud wins his Wager, and Emilie de Lesparre expresses a strong opinion of his conduct in a *cuss-ary* manner, and how Louis takes up the affair and takes down de Renaud, and how the Scene, notwithstanding the General Row, ends with immense Harmony in the shape of an arranged Fight and a Concerted Piece.

SCENE IV—CORRIDOR OF A PARIS HOTEL.

How Madame dei Flunki with her Retinue makes up her mind that the hostile meeting shall be interrupted, and at 'this juncture the Police shall arrive upon the scene.'

THE FAMILY BREAK UP, AND THE DOMESTIC BREAK-DOWN!

SCENE V—THE FOREST OF FONTAINBLEAU.

Chateau Renaud's Post-horses break down, but his *re*-morse is strong enough, and he feels his crime is literally of the blackest nature, as does Fabien, who having travelled for five days and nights is not quite awake to his danger, and how he puzzles de Renaud by a *double a cross stick*, and how the weapon fails through its snap action, and how the Mother is struck by her Boy, but recovering from the stroke of the Son is enabled to forgive everybody, whilst Fabien avenges his Brother by presenting Emilie to Chateau Renaud, thereby securing his Enemy's discomfort for an unlimited period, and how he determines to write a comprehensive account of the whole mystical business, and enclose it to Professor *Black-eye*.

GRAND CLIMAX!

SCENE VI—THE RETURN OF SPRING-TIME AND THE BIRTHDAY OF BEAUTY!

SCENE FIRST.—*Apartment at the Dei Flunki's.*

*Chimney-piece, R.; over it a picture, two goggle-eyed little boys in frills
    exactly alike; under it in large letters, 'The Masters Dei Flunki;'
    door of entrance, R.U.E.; doors, R. and L.; clock, R.; table, C.; writing
    table, L.; chairs.*

Curtain rises to the tune of 'The Twins'—MARIE *discovered spinning at
    a wheel, R., and* GRIFFO *brushing boots, R.C.—*GRIFFO *half
    footman in his dress.*

Griffo.   How are you getting on, my dear?

Marie.   Tol-lollish.[1]

Griffo.   That's what I call a most superior polish.
                 Your face this boot reflects—there, look again.

Marie.   It shews it lovely.

Griffo.   Yes, it shews it plain.
                 Beats all your rubbish sold as perfect leather.
                 (*brushing*) Would you and me could brush along together.
                 Come leave off spinning, dear, my love's no flam:
                 Come, cut the *weal*, remember who I *ham!*

Marie.   You *Ham* indeed! *Ham common.*[2]

Griffo.   Be my wife,
                 Or else remain a spinster all your life.
                 'In spring,' says Tennyson, 'a young man's fancy
                 Turns lightly,' and it's true, 'to thoughts of Nancy.'[3]
                                 (*a loud knock, both frightened*)
                 What's that?

Marie.   Go, look!

---

[1] *tol lollish* Tolerably well.

[2] *Ham common* Pun on Griffo's lower status ('I am common'). Ham Common is a
parkland near Richmond, outside London.

[3] Cf. Tennyson, *Locksley Hall* (1842): 'In the spring a young man's fancy turns to
thoughts of love' (line 20). Tennyson was Poet Laureate when *The Corsican 'Bothers'*
was performed.

Griffo.   Indeed! I beg your pardon,
          Talking of Tennyson, don't *he knock hard 'un!*[4]
          He's one of those obtrusive sort of chaps
          Who think that they can entrance gain per *raps*.[5]
          Come, *let him in*, he's footsore I've no doubt.

Marie.   Suppose that he's a cab—

Griffo.   Then *let him out!*
          I'm quite afraid of draught or else I'd go.

Marie.   Yes, draughts have very often laid you low.

Music.—she opens door—enter MEYNARD *followed by* CABMAN, *half
     Corsican half Londoner—*MEYNARD *carries small valise, thin
     umbrella, and light travelling rug.*

Cabman.   Here, this won't do; we're far beyond the radius, sir.

Meynard. You won't get any more than what I've paid you, sir.

Cabman.   Come now, be generous to a party, *do*.

Meynard. Shut up!

Cabman.   Another Tizzy!

Meynard.   *Tizzy vous*.[6]

Maynard. Vanish!

Cabman. (*at door*)   You can't afford to ride about;
              May all the maledictions—(*going to doorway,* R.)

Griffo.   There, get out!
          Exit CABMAN, R.U.E.

---

[4] *he knock hard 'un* Pun on Tennyson's poem *Enoch Arden* (1864).

[5] per *raps* Punning reference to the contemporary vogue for spirit 'rapping': i.e., ghosts who seem to knock (or 'rap') on a table during a séance to signal their presence to the living.

[6] *tizzy vous* Corruption of the imperative *taissez-vous* ('shut up').

Meynard.	My rug! (*hands it to* GRIFFO) My—Bag—Umbrella! Where's your missus?
	A queer ramshackle sort of domus, this is!
	Nice girl though. (*pinches her chin*) Didn't notice you were
present.	
	(*kisses her*) Excuse me.
Marie. (R.)	Their French manners are so pleasant.
	Oh, sir!
Griffo. (L., *aside in a rage*)	Revenge!
Meynard. (C.)	Just mention that I'm here.
	Take up my card at once to her, my dear.
Griffo.	Missus is going p'rhaps to bed, sir.
Meynard.	What?
Griffo.	Yes, Missus is *retiring*; you are *not*.
	(*aside*) Ha! Ha! I had him there!
Meynard.	Don't try to quiz;[7]
	Besides, if I mistake not, here she is.

Music.—Enter MADAME DEI FLUNKI, *door, L.*

Madame. (L., *to* MARIE)	Why don't you mind your work, you idle hussy.
	I've a good mind—a stranger! Lawks a mussy![8]
	If you're the taxes we are not at home.
Meynard. (*bowing*, C.)	I'm *not* the taxes, Madame, but have come
	To tax your hospitality. In *me*
	The bosom friend of your son Louis see.
Madame. (*staggering*)	My son—oh, no—
Meynard.	A gentleman most rare.
Madame.	You know my boy! Pray take a chair—*mon chère*.[9]

---

[7] *to quiz* To banter.

[8] *Lawks a mussy* Minstrel dialect for 'Lord, have mercy'.

Meynard.   We are great pals—in fact we never differ.

Madame.   I'm charm'd—prepare him the best bed room, Griffer.

Meynard.   Really, I—

Madame.   At his name the tear-drop trickles—
                    You must be peckish. Here! cold meat and pickles!

Exeunt GRIFFO *and* MARIE—*and return with tray,* R.

Meynard. (*aside*) With cold meat she her son's best friend is greeting.
                    This ain't a *warm reception*—this *cold meeting!*

Madame.   We're hospitable folks!

Meynard.   You really touch one.

Madame.   Also bring forth the family cheese—the Dutch one.

Concerted Piece—'*Go a-head.*'

Madame.   I hope you'll make yourself at home, *mon chère,*
                    We're homely sort of folks, as you're aware.
                            You're welcome to
                            Our best home-brew.
Meynard.   Your courtesy is rare!
Griffo. (*aside*)   These foreigners are very seldom seen
                    To tip a servant—they're so very mean!
Madame.   Though humble folks,
                            It us provokes,
                    If all ain't nice and clean.
                            Soon you will larn,
                            Though it's a barn,
                            All is 'cummy fo.'[10]
                    Bring the cheese of Holland forth,
                            The butter fetch also;
                            Go ahead

---

[9] *mon chère* The acting edition, in using a masculine adjective to modify a feminine
noun, is perhaps alluding to the actress playing the part of Meynard *en travestie.*
[10] *cummy fo* Corruption of *comme il faut* (proper; as it should be).

And bring the pickled gherkins too,
        And don't forget the bread,
    Then if you've got an appetite,
        Why go a-head.

Madame.	Soon you will larn, &c
Griffo.	ꞌꞌ
Marie.	ꞌꞌ

Meynard.	Soon I shall larn, &c.

Meynard.	I haven't any appetite at all;
	But in the morning early me you'll call,
	At breakfast I,
	Madame, will try
	Your senses to appal.
Marie.	He really is a pleasant little chap;
	To-morrow I'll put on my Sunday cap.
Griffo.	Now if I winks
	At her I thinks
	My claret he will tap.[11]

Madame. (*with great expression repeats*) Though it's a barn, &c.
All.   (*repeat as in verse*)

    MEYNARD *and* MADAME DEI FLUNKI *dance up*—GRIFFO *and*
    MARIE *dance off,* R.U.E.

Meynard. (*coming down,* R.C.) Will Fabien dei Flunki soon return?
        To see him with anxiety I burn,
        Because I hear he is so like his brother,
        You couldn't at a glance tell one from t'other.

                    (*Music, 'The Twins,' piano*)

Madame. (L.C.) It's that confused me. I've at times gone mad
        When I've thought one boy was the other lad;
        But, lawks, in disposition they're the same,
        Both of the dears are very fond of game;
        Each hates a blowing-up—I speak no gammon—[12]

---

[11] *my claret he will tap* He will draw my blood; from the boxing slang expression 'to tap claret'.

[12] *gammon* Exaggeration or humbug.

> Both have a partiality for salmon;
> When children, both liked toffey—cried at whipping,
> Which they oft got, because of lessons skipping—
> Were in the habit both of story-telling—
> Would never take their medicine without yelling—
> Would both their clean boots plunge in the same puddle;
> At times said words as made their ma's blood 'cuddle;'
> Would mutually punch each other's head,
> And always howled when they were sent to bed.

Meynard. (R.C.) Remarkable, indeed!

Madame. (C.)   He comes—my Fabi-ang!
                          (MEYNARD *crosses*, L.)
          I know his footsteps very well; Oh, *tray-biang*.

         Music.—Enter FABIEN, R.C. *opening.*

          Embrace your mother.

Fabien. (R.)   Bother! I'm knocked up;
          I want my tea, so brew a strongish cup.
          Halloa! (*sees* MEYNARD)

Madame.   A friend of your dear brother Louis.

Fabien. (*starting*) A friend, you say, of Louis? (*crosses to* L.C.)
                                              How de *do-ee*?
          (*shakes his hand—aside to him*)
          When did you see him last?

Meynard. (L.)   Three weeks ago.

Fabien. (C.) What were his spirits like?

Meynard.   Extremely *low*.

Fabien. (*aside*) I knew it—I was sure of it—I said it.

Meynard.   We'd drunk them all, and none of us had credit.

Fabien.   I felt that there was something wrong—

Meynard.   Explain!

Fabien.   Wherever Louis is—in France, in Spain,
                In England, or America—wherever
                He may proceed—the distance doesn't sever
                The strange communication.

Meynard.   My dear host,
                I s'pose you are alluding to the post.
                It is convenient—

Fabien.   Young man, don't chaff[13]—
                It's instantaneous.

Meynard.   The telegraph?
                'Messages sent to all parts of the—'

Fabien.   Bother!
                The telegraph between me and my brother
                Is magical and keeps us ever near.
                My darling brother Louis!

Meynard.   Is it dear?

Fabien. (*comes down*, C.) Listen, and you shall hear the wondrous mystery
                Involved in our extremely moving history.
                A flute accompaniment best will do,
                The song's on *twins*—the flute's notes go, *too, too*.

                        Song.—'The Twins.'

                You've heard a good song called *The Twins*, a strangeish case
                        it be,
                The case, however, of my brother Louis and of me
                Is more involved considerably, because you see with us,
                He is twin *one*, and I'm twin *two*, which makes it rather wuss.[14]
                We cut our tiny teeth together at the age of three;
                He took the measles and the measles instantly took me;
                The same disasters simultane-ous-ly us befell;
                He never took a pill as *ill*, but I took one as *well*.

---

[13] *chaff* To joke.
[14]*wuss* Corruption of 'worse' to accommodate the rhyme.

We always made the same mistake when adding up our sums;
We both were nigh succumbing to a plethora of plums;
We liked the same good things to eat, from roast beef to ragout,
Which made it rather awkward when there wasn't enough for two.
Our thoughts all run in couples, dual objects we behold,
We are so single-minded, but our boots are double-soled;
For fruit we both eat pairs, and thoughts of *Dublin* each allures,
But if we settle down in France, we mean to live at *Two-ers*.[15]

Meynard.   Mere fancy—change of air and change of scene
                 Would set you and your brother all serene—
                 Russia—France—Turkey—anywhere at all.

Fabien. (*dreamily*) We thought of trying the Egyptian Hall.[16]
                 The air they say is mild there.

Meynard.   No, it's chilly.
                 It's high.

Fabien.   What?

Meynard.   Mountainous.

Fabien.   Why?

Meynard.   Piccad-*hilly*.
                 Still it agrees with twins. (*shouts without*) What means that
shout?

Fabien.   A rabble rout. (*crosses*, L.)

Meynard.   More of the *bawl* than the *rout*.
         (*crosses*, L.)

Music.—GRIFFO *enters, dragging in* ORLANDO, *a fearful-looking ruffian,
         covered with every kind of offensive weapon*, L.U.E.

Griffo. (L.C.)   Please, sir, this here's Orlando.

---

[15] *Two-ers* Pun on the French city of Tours.

[16] *Egyptian Hall* Popular exhibition hall in London's Piccadilly Circus. Built in the
early nineteenth century, it resembled an ancient Egyptian temple. Panoramas and magic
acts were among its more popular offerings.

Fabien. (C.)   Here you see
                    Of Corsica the stock commodity—
                    Nice-looking article—one ceaseless rage—
                    A robber—just come to his brigand-age;
                    A thief throughout. Not hard to understand it,
                    As you perceive, his very *legs* are *band-it.*

                    (*Music.*—MARIE *lugs in* COLONNA, R.U.E.—*another ruffian, armed*
                    with carbine and daggers, &c., down, R.)

Fabien.   Specimen Number Two. They're both indigenous.

Orlan.   Indigenous! That rascal robbed my *pigeon 'us,*
                    That is, his vile ancestor did; the same.
                    And now I want to see his *little game.*[17]

Fabien.   He means the pigeon.

Orlan.   Mind you, no evasion,
                    It must be white, and of the male persuasion.
                    A male white pigeon—strictly to the letter,
                    No hen, or there's *no hend* to our Vendetta.

Meynard.   You hear—a really interesting sight—

Colon. (R.)   I've got the bird!

Orlan.   A male?

Colon. (L.)   A male.

Orlan.   And white?

Colon.   I've got him in this bag.

Orlan.   Half dead, no doubt;
                    Open your *male* bag, then, and let him out.

Madame. (*a little up,* L.C.) How sweet it is to see two rival houses,
                    Forgetting mutual hate and murderous *vowses,*

---

[17] *little game* Trick or dodge.

Drowning their enmity in friendship's cup,
Rough man's rude nature softened, and—

Orlan. (*turning fiercely on her*)   Shut up!
    (*treads on her toe*—MADAME DEI FLUNKI *retires up to*
        GRIFFO, *alarmed*)

Fabien.   Now, then, be friends—shake hands—stretch out your wrists.
(*he draws them towards each other*, C.—*both make fierce ejaculations, and move
threateningly towards each other*)
        Look here! I said 'shake hands,' and not shake fists.

Orlan.   His great grandfather's father's great grandfather
        Stole my an-cestors' white male pigeon.

Colon. (*conceitedly*)   Rather!

Orlan. (*rushing towards him with drawn dagger*)   Ha!

Colon. (*repeating action with enormous carbine*)   Ha!
        (*as they do,* MADAME DEI FLUNKI *interposes and gets
        crushed between them*—GRIFFO *leads her up to the back,*
limping)

Orlan.   Shall I shake hands with him?

Colon.   I shan't with *you!*

Orlan.   There's one more killed of us than—

Colon.   Very true!
    There is, ha! ha!

Orlan.   Ha! ha! (*business of daggers, &c., repeated*)

Fabien.   Come, let this cease,
    Enter Antonio, Justice of the Peace!

Music.—Enter JUDGE, R.U.E., *ludicrously made up with several olive
    branches—male and female peasants—*ALL *sing.*

Chorus, 'Voici le Sabre'.

All.   Here is the Justice—
                                 The Justice—
                                 The Justice;
           Here is the Justice—the Justice of the Peace.

           This case the wust is—
                                The wust is—
                                The wust is
           Ever yet known; so make it up,
           And let your quarrel cease.

          (*this must be sung grandiloquently, and by all in unison—
                  bang at conclusion—*JUSTICE *goes to table and
                  arranges papers*)

Fabien.   Here, take that olive branch in your fist. (*to* ORLANDO, *who
                  takes it, and crushes it in his grasp*)
         Now, why the *Dickens* give the *olive a twist?*
         Come, sign your name. (*gives* ORLANDO *pen*—GRIFFO
                  smooths out paper for signing*)

Orlan.   You're sure the pigeon's white?
        I feel that I do wrong.

Fabien. (L.)   Do *wrong?* do *write!*

Orlan.   There! (*dashes a long stroke*)

Fabien.   Come, Colonna. (*approaching him,* R.C.)

Colon.   If I do I'm shot!

Fabien.   Well, that you p'raps *call honour*—I do not.

Colon.   Can't write.
        (MARIE *swings him round to* FABIEN, *and* FABIEN *swings
        him round to table, and pushes his nose on the
        table—bang on drum*)

Fabien.   Then make your mark!
        (COLONNA *slashes pen twice across paper, and goes,* R.C.)

Orlan. (L.)   Now then—the bird.

Colon. (*with grimace*) I've sat upon him once or twice!

Fabien.   Absurd!

Colon. (*giving it from bag*) Come out!

Orlan.   You dog! The pigeon you would smother?
                            (COLONNA *raises it to strike* ORLANDO)

Fabien.   Come now you needn't *pitch into* each other.

Orlan.   I never yet clapt eyes on a more skinny un.
               Its wings don't match.

Fabien.   Mere difference of *a pinion*.

Orlan.   And one leg's longer than the other.

Fabien.   Grumbler!

Orlan.   He'll never walk—

Fabien.   Why should he? he's a *tumbler!*

                Concerted Piece—'*Happy, gay, and free, boys.*'

Madame.   And now as you have made it up, you both are free to go,
               As each is satisfied, why, now no one has cause to crow.
Orlan.   I'm not quite sure that I'm not done.
Meynard.   Pooh, nonsense! could it be?
Marie.   It's quite a sight to give delight.
Colon.   Well, that I don't quite see.
Fabien. (*with dancing action*) Be always gay and free, boys,
                    Take the time from me, boys—
                         Happy, gay, and free!
All. (*with action*) Be always gay and free, boys, &c.

Meynard.   I'll send a neat description of this interesting scene.
Griffo. (*aside*) But he won't pay the postage—those French chaps are always
                    mean.

Marie.   That's jealousy, and nothing else.

Madame.   My friends, you'll want your tea;
So pray don't wait, it's getting late.

Orlan. (*to* COLONNA) That is a hint for we.

Fabien. (*speaking to* ORLANDO *and* COLONNA) My worthy friends,
        when you have left us, do not forget the lesson you have
        learnt, and under any circumstances—

Colon. and Orlan. Yes, yes!

Fabien.   Under any circumstances—
        (*relapsing into tune again, with action of dancing*)
        Be always gay and free, boys, &c., &c.

        (*Chorus repeated—characters waltz off—*ORLANDO *and*
        COLONNA *waltz off together, very seriously, last, R.C.*
        opening. FABIEN *and* MADAME DEI FLUNKI *left on—*
        FABIEN *stands perfectly still, wrapped in thought.*)

Madame.   What means this gloom upon your brow? It seems
        As if your life was one long round of dreams!
        A good strong cup of tea your sense will shake up.

Fabien.   Ah! I must have a *strong cup* if I'd *wake cup*!

                  (*tremulous music*)

        Listen! This morning, yonder mountain I
        Was climbing, when suddenly—oh, my!
        I (and the feeling did with dread me fill)
        On that *big mountain* felt a *little hill*.[18]

Madame. (R.C.) That mountain is a breather, and the fact is
        In climbing mountains you are out of practice.

Fabien. (L.C.)   A pain here did my further footsteps hinder.

---

[18] *little hill* In the burlesque actor's customary Cockney accent, the initial '/h/' of 'hill'
would have been suppressed, thus making the word pronounced as if it were 'ill'.

Madame.   Shortness of breath—that *pain*, boy, was a *winder*.

Fabien.   I sought my watch; ten minutes 'twas to nine.
                 Behold! our clock has stopped—a certain sign
                 Louis' been hurt; infallible I've found it.

Madame.   I wound it up myself.

Fabien.   Poor Louis *wounded*!
                 The pain—this feeling strange—that warning clock—
                 He's got into a row and had a knock. (*comes down*)
                 Considering I go in for quiet greatly,
                 And feel each blow he gets immediately—
                 For fighting folks, his great propensitee,
                 Comes now and then a little hard on me;
                 I don't complain, but when he gets such knocks,
                 If he *will* fight, I wish he'd learn to box!
                 I'll write to him.

                              (*Ghost Melody played in eccentric variation*)[19]

Madame.   You'd better go to bed.

Fabien. (*at table*, L., *writing*) 'I feel that somebody has punch'd your head;
                 You've got a blow—I'm sure of it—a stunner!
                 Because I felt a corresponding "oner,"[20]
                 Also a stitch upon the mountain side.
                 A stitch in time saves *nine*, of course, I knew it,
                 That's why the clock stopped just *ten minutes to it*.
                 If you're alive and well, don't let us doubt it;
                 If dead, you needn't bother p'raps about it.'

Madame. (R.)   What thought, and what consideration, too!
(*figure of LOUIS, in his shirt sleeves, and with a very black eye
   rises*, R., *and glides slowly towards FABIEN*)[21]

---

[19] *Ghost Melody* A reference to the music composed for the ghost's entrance in the original 1852 production of *The Corsican Brothers* at the Princess's Theatre.

[20] *oner* (pronounced 'wun-ner') A knockout punch in a fight: i.e., the 'one' punch thrown to end the match.

[21] For an explanation of the burlesque's 'ghostly' effect, see the introduction to this play.

Fabien.	[']And so no more at present, but adoo.[']²²

Fabien. ['] And so no more at present, but adoo.[']²²
Listen! What's that?

Madame.   My dear, I wasn't speaking.

Fabien.   What is the meaning of that hideous creaking?

Madame.   Griffo's new boots, p'raps—I don't hear it, dear.

Fabien.   I do, and now it's getting very near.

Madame.   What are you talking of?

Fabien.   That sound again!
But let me seal the letter, and—

*(the figure by this time has got behind him, and gives him
a very decided punch on the head—drum—FABIEN
tumbles out of his chair)*²³

Now then!

(turns) If you do that again!—My brother—!

*(takes stage, L.C.)*²⁴
Madame.   What?

(figure sinking—FABIEN takes stage, L.)

Fabien.   See there—his eye—he must have had it hot!

Madame.   There's nothing there—you're wandering, my chick.

Fabien.   Don't you see Louis?

---

²² *adoo* Colloquial pronunciation of 'adieu' to complete the rhymed couplet.

²³ In the original melodrama the ghost touches Louis on the shoulder just as he is about to seal the letter.

²⁴ *takes stage* To 'take [the] stage' means to cross the stage in a particularly commanding or intense manner. Taking the stage not only throws focus on the moving actor but also balances the entire stage picture. In this instance, Fabien moves stage left, thus placing him directly opposite the ghost of Louis on stage right.

(*figure sinks*)

Madame.   You're a *loui-natic*.

(*the back of the chamber sinks*)

Fabien.   Look there! The whole side of the house is sinking!

Madame.   It's evident my poor boy's took to drinking.

Fabien.   The scene is moving, mother, don't you see!

Madame.   This is a very *moving scene* to me.

                 (Fabien *staggers back with a half shriek, as picture is
                 revealed of* LOUIS *on ground with a black eye—*
                 CHATEAU RENAUD *with a single-stick in
                 hand smoking a cigarette—the others grouped
                 in imitation of the famous tableau*)[25]

Enter DE MEYNARD *and* GRIFFO, MARIE, ORLANDO, *and* COLONNA,
     R.U.E.

Fabien.   Look there! Some heavy blows have plainly passed,
                 And brother Louis has been heavily grassed,[26]
                 Or rather mowed—[27]

Meynard. (R.)   What is the matter?

Fabien. (C.)   What!
                 (*to group in picture*) Leave him alone, you snobs[28]—I'll fight
                      the lot! (*vision closed in*)
                 Griffo, my horse! my bag! I'm off to Paris!

Meynard.   Really! what means this mental Mr. Harris?[29]

---

[25] For a discussion of the entire episode, see the introduction to this play.

[26] *grassed* To be knocked to the ground, especially in a fistfight.

[27] *mowed* Cut down, used to make the pun with 'grassed'.

[28] *snob* University slang for a townsman (as opposed to a gownsman), with the implication of vulgarity and coarse manners. Fabien's implication is that Chateau Renaud and his cronies are not gentlemen. Fabien breaks the theatrical frame once more by treating figures in a supernaturally induced vision as if they were actually present.

Fabien.   Brothers should stick together when they can,
                Although in thought and feeling we're one man,
                We've *two fists each*—that's four.

Madame.   I'm quite alarmed!

Fabien. (*with arms extended*) They'll find our motto is forewarned—*four-armed.*

                Concerted Pieces—'Dusty Bob.'

Madame.   He's off to Paris. What can the matter be with him?
Fabien.   I'm off to Paris before the break of day!
Meynard.   What a strange chap! I'd sooner live two days than three with
                    him.
                Really, he's got an extraordinary way.
Fabien.   I'm off to Paris!
[Meynard.]   He's off to Paris—
                He's off to Paris at once without delay!
                    Ri fol de riddle ol,
Fabien.   Whack fol de riddle ol,
Griffo   Ri fol de riddle ol, wack fol ol de day.

                Air—'Drinking Song'—(Grand Duchess.)

Meynard.   He'll go away,
                He'll go, he'll go away;
                    Away, away, he'll go.
                To Paris he will speedilee,
                    As he has let us know.
All.   To Paris he, &c.

Marie.   Away, away,
                Without delay,
                    Aboard a ship he pops;
                To Paris, city of the gay.
                    So famous for its shops.
Fabien.   It is a pretty sort of place,
                Amusing quite in any case;
                Delightful to the human race,
                And those who're fond of *boulla baisse.*

---

[29] *Mr. Harris* Most likely a reference to George Harris, author of *Civilisation Considered
as a Science* (1861).

All.	It is a pretty sort of place, Amusing quite in any case; Delightful to the human race, The human race.
Meynard.	Oh, what can mean This dreadful scene? My senses quite it shocks; Who'd think to find Out here a kind Of foreign Box and Cox![30]
All.	Who'd think to find Out here a kind, &c., &c.
Marie.	Oh, master's quite Upset to night.
Meynard.	Well, is he often so?
All.	At all events, This pair of gents To Paris bound to go.
Fabien.	To Paris city, *toujours gai.*
Madame.	Where life is no work—all is play.
Marie.	Where dissipation's the O K.
Meynard.	Right sort of thing both night and day.
All.	To Paris city, *toujours gai*, &c., &c.

(*whilst they have been singing this,* GRIFFO *and* MARIE
    *have been singing operatically and in harmony with
    a repetition of previous words in the 'Dusty Bob'
    melody, played very piano—at conclusion, 'Dusty Bob'
    melody assumes the ascendancy—and just as scene is
    going to be closed in, the spectral clock,* R., *which has
    not previously moved, dances down in imitation of
    the 'Green' in Jack and the Green—*MADAME DEI
    FLUNKI, MEYNARD, &c., *dancing round à la 'My
    Lord and Lady' to it, but perfectly
    seriously—*COLONNA *and* ORLANDO, R. *and* L.
    corners, as clowns—closed in)[31]

---

[30] *Box and Cox* Two-person farce written in 1847 by John Maddison Morton (1811-91);
it was one of the most popular comedies on the Victorian stage.

[31] *My Lord and Lady* A comedy by Planché, written in 1862.

SCENE SECOND.—*Box Lobby at the Opera. Placards up—- 'Large Fees to Box Keepers'—'No Seats secured after the doors are open'—'Pass-out cheques must be crossed "London and Westminster Bank"'—'The Free List is suspended in the Box Entrance'—'Places may be secured six years in advance'—'Refreshments'—'Pale Dry Biscuits of a delicate nutty flavour, and fine Old Crusted Cheese-cakes always ready'.*[32]

Lively music.—Two or three PEOPLE *enter and go into box;* BOX-KEEPER *showing them in—*BOX-KEEPER *made up with exaggerated white tie, black suit and comic wig, &c.—*MONTGIRON *and* MARTELLI *stroll on, R.*

Martel.	I say, it's rather jolly, don't you know; But, I say, Chateau Renaud doesn't show. How is it, eh?
Mont.	He is engaged in making Love to a lady—one who's rather taking. In fact, I'd cut him out there, 'pon my life, Only it's such a bore to have a wife. It ties a fella down so.
Martel.	Well, but he Isn't a marrying man exactly. She Has an old husband who's away. But stop! Madame de Lesparre, p'raps we'd better drop. Here is our friend—a most conceited pup.
Mont.	The subject drop, or he may take it up. De Renaud at all weapons is *au fait*.

Music.—Enter CHATEAU RENAUD, *L. 1 E.*

Chateau.	What about Chateau Renaud do you say— Abusing him?
Mart.	Oh, no!

---

[32] The placards refer, in part, to the difficulties of obtaining a good seat for a performance of a popular play. Box office staff were routinely given money under the table to secure a ticket. The 'Free List' was a roster of individuals such as newspaper critics and friends of the theatre manager who were to be given free tickets upon demand.

Chateau.   I'm glad; you see
I've fought this week some—let's see—twenty-three.
Yes, twenty-three young parties have I met,
Whom I've taught lessons that they won't forget.
Six fellows, when I didn't like it, winked—
The insult trifling—those I simply pinked;
Some interrupted me when speaking: that
I punished with a bullet through the hat;
Those more impertinent—as you have heard—
I made a point of winging, like a bird.

Martel.   Did you kill any?

Chateau.   Y-a-a-s; I think a pair.
One fellow asked me if I curled my hair;
The other said my cigarettes were bad:
I had to kill 'em both—it's rather sad.
But I'd let off a lot.

Martel.   Precisely so.

Chateau.   And one must keep one's hand in, don't you know!
But I am here to meet a lady.

Martel.   Yes!
Madame de Lesparre, come, my boy, confess.

Chateau.   The same.

Mont.   I don't believe it.

Chateau. (*coolly*)   Don't you? (*goes up*)

Martel. (*aside to* MONTGIRON)   Stop;
He'll shoot you!

Mont.   My dad kept a draper's shop,
And Chateau Renaud looks on trade as low,
And wouldn't fight with *me*, Martelli,—so
I can insult him!

Martel.   I'm a swell and can't.

Chateau.   And so you don't believe me? (*down*, C.)

Mont.   What's more—shant! (*conceitedly twists
            moustache*)

Chateau.   Ha, ha! Do you, Martelli?

Martel.   Oh, I never
            Doubt any gentleman.

Chateau.   My very clever
            And most amusing friend, let's have a bet:—
            Suppose, by my persuasion, I can get
            The lady named to join us at Mabille
            To-night at supper, will you join then?

Mont.   I *weel*. (*crossing*, R.)

Chateau.   Fifty Napoleons? (*crossing*, L.)

Mont.   All right, my hearty!

Chateau.   You'll find 'twill be a very *bona party*.[33]
                   Music.—MONTGIRON *and* MARTELLI *exeunt.*
            But here she comes—and agitated too!
       Enter MADAME DE LESPARRE *with mask in hand,* L.
            Most fascinating of your sex, how do?

Emilie.   Oh dear, if any one my features knew,
            They might enquire—

Chateau.   'Twould be a hopeless task!
            You they have let a mask—so *let 'em ask.*
            Enchanting one—

Emilie.   I said I'd meet you here
            To give you back your *billet doux*.[34]

Chateau.   My dear,
            You did.

---

[33] *bona party* Pun on Bonaparte; 'bona' is slang for good.
[34] *billet doux* Love letter; literally, a 'sweet note'.

Emilie.   And you'll return me mine?

Chateau.   Oh, stay!
Why do you treat me in this shameful way?
It's driving me half wild! I do declare
I take no pride in parting my back hair.
As for my tailor, he makes what he likes—
Beau Brummel's merged in Mr. William Sykes.[35]
A perfect *bore* appears the *Bore de Boulon*;[36]
Well-fitting gloves I now don't see the pull on;
My boots run big—in Yorkshire phrase, once 'pratty;'
My waist was *wasp*-like—now I'm scarcely *gnatty*.

Emilie. (L.C.)   Give me my letters back, and let me go,
Somebody will observe us.

Chateau. (R.C.)   Oh, dear, no!
You'd lose them; and I haven't got them here.
If at the gardens of Mabille, my dear,
You'll come with me, I'll give them to you there.

Emilie.   Mabille, indeed! I wonder how you dare—

Chateau.   Oh, every one goes everywhere.

Emilie.   Perhaps, but I'm not every one, you worst of chaps!

Chateau.   That dull old-fashioned failing of propriety's
Completely dying out in good society;
For dissipation's drown'd decorum's voice—
You pays your money and you takes your choice.

Emilie.   Not very choice, I think, nor yet delectable.
Give me the days when most folks were respectable,
When girls were kept at school whilst in their teens,
And people cared to live within their means;
When folks who really loved each other mated,
Although their spoons and forks p'raps might be plated,

[35] *William Sykes* The thief and murderer Bill Sykes from Charles Dickens' novel *Oliver Twist* (1838).
[36] *Bore de Boulon* Pun on Bois de Boulogne, a public park in Paris. It was redesigned in the early 1850s.

And didn't care at all to wait—not they—
For real silver—till their hair was grey;
When boys were boys, and gentlemen not 'gents;'[37]
When shops were shops, and not 'establishments;'
When servants dressed according to their station,
Not of their misseses an imitation;
Ere days of 'telegrams' and 'patent stoves;'[38]
And children weren't called 'kids' and 'little coves;'
When people didn't turn night into day, (*crosses* R.)
And 'twasn't *infra dig.* to pay your way![39]

Chateau.

Horribly slow and wretchedly unpleasant,
For my part, I think no time's like the present,
Except the future—that's when we shall meet
To night,—Mabille,—at nine, '*quel* jolly treat!'
Till then, a short affectionate farewell.
We meet at nine, and at *Mabille—ma belle.*

(*they go up and cross*)

Duet.—'Ben e Ridicolo.'

Chateau.

Life at Mabille they say,
Glides like a dream away,
Till the dawning of the day!
        Life is one spree;
Let us be joyous, pray,
Flinging dull care away,
I for the treat will pay;
        Only too glad.

Emilie.

Yes, I will meet you there,
Though I don't think it fair,
        Yet I will verily
        Go there with thee.
Folks there are never slow,
Knowing no care or woe,

---

[37] *gents* Uneducated men of the lower middle class who attempted to simulate gentility in dress and behaviour. The 'gent'—a sham gentleman—was a frequent object of ridicule.

[38] *patent stoves* Cast iron, wood-burning stoves used in Victorian kitchens.

[39] *infra dig* Beneath one's dignity.

Sighs may for the sad ones be—
          The sad ones be.
Mabille's a dreadful place,
I think in any case,
And I think verily
          You are too base!

Both.   Folks there are never sad.   *Exeunt*, R.

SCENE THIRD.—*Mabille. Statues and lamps about; Ballet to open Scene.*
CHARACTERS *retire up.*

Enter MARTELLI *and* LOUIS DEI FLUNKI, L.U.E. *who is made up something
like the 'Stranger,' and has a burlesque air of solemnity and inward sorrow.*[40]

Martel. (*down*, L.C.) Come wake up; you're a lively sort, friend Louis;
          You look, to say the least, uncommonly bluey.
          Do something:—

Louis. (R.C.)   I have tried, upon my word,
          The dissipation tea gardens afford;
          At bowls have really gone to any length,
          Have shot for nuts, been weighed, and tried my strength;
          Still these joys have failed to rouse me—she
          Is all I think about.

Martel. (R.C.)   Confide in me.

Louis.   I will. You've heard, no doubt, me and my brother
          Have both the same sensation as each other;
          And when he fell in love, I always did too—
          Kid Number One's love then was shared by Kid Two;
          Which made it rather awkward; so you see
          It came at last to—'Is it you or me?'
          That's ungrammatical—but means, you know,
          'Will you leave this to me?' or 'shall I go?'
          In the last case, in which we both were spoons,[41]
          We tossed—I lost—unluckiest of coons![42]

---

[40] *The 'Stranger'* Title character of August von Kotzebue's popular melodrama *The
Stranger* (1789).
[41] *spoons* Sentimental fools.

Cried 'Man.' To Fabien did hard fate allot her!
My brother cried out 'Woman,' and he got her.
(*crosses,* L.C.)

Martel.   Extremely sad!

Louis.   But short his triumph though;
        She married some one else.

Martel.   How very low!
(*music, 'Twins,' pianissimo*)

Louis. (*with intensity*) One day—'may that returning day be night,'
                To quote the poet—Renaud met her sight;
                Chateau Renaud, a sparkling chap he is,
                He might be Chateau *Margot* from his *fizz!*[43]
                I'll own it's handsome—Emilie de *Les*parre,
                Who, when her father said, 'You'll wed?' said, '*Yes*, pa.'
                Forgot her absent spouse, and me, her father,
                And Fabien! forgot herself, too, rather,
                And listened to the accents of this *roué*;
                But, scoundrel, there's a certain Monsieur Louis
                Who's *hovering* round you, my two turtle-doves.
                A case of *Friendship's hovering*, if not Love's.
(*crossing,* R.)

Martel.   He's first-rate at the small sword—dread the thrust of it,
               A crack shot also, Louis.

Louis. (*collapsing*)   That's the wust of it.
                If he could not fence and he couldn't shoot,
                I'd call him out this very day—the brute!
                But as he knows each weapon how to use it,
                It makes a fellow think twice ere he *doos* it.
(*lively music*—LOUIS *turns up, with the conventional
                tragic walk and with a profound air of
                settled misery*—MARTELLI *goes up*)

---

[42] *coon* A man. The word was not a racial slur in Victorian England.

[43] *Chateau Margot* High-quality red wine from the lower Medoc in France.
fizz A reference to the bubbles in champagne, but also a pun on *phiz*, a slang term for
'face' or 'looks'.

Enter MONTGIRON *surrounded by* MARIE, ESTELLE, CELESTINE, *and*
CORALIE, *all laughing, down* R.

Mont.   It's no use teasing me, I've not a sous;
                  I'm but a younger brother.

Celes.   Very true;
                  But still a pair of gloves, some scent, a fan,
                  Some trifle,

Coral.   Oh, Celestine, how you can!

Celes.   Madame, don't talk to me—

Coral.   To you indeed!

Estelle.   We are invited here to a grand feed—
                  Champagne *ad libitum*—where is it set?

Celes. and Coral. Hear! Hear!

Mont.   Ladies, we can't have supper yet.

Estelle.   Why not? I'm hungry!

Celes.   Yes, and so am I. (MONTGIRON *goes up*)

Coral.   How can you go on so, Celestine, fie!

Celes.   We've come here to enjoy ourselves—far be it
                  From me to mention wine—but I don't *see* it!
                      (MONTGIRON *who has been up, comes down*
                              with MARTELLI *and* LOUIS)

Mont. (C.)   You shall do, ladies. Let me introduce a friend.

Celes. (R.C., *curtseying low and laughing at* LOUIS) Chee-armed.

Cora.   Oh don't, you little goose! (LOUIS *goes up*)
                    I am quite surprised! (*pulling her dress*)

Celes.   You dare to touch me!—there!
                (*the two* GIRLS *slap at each other—general row, all*

talking—MANAGER OF GARDENS *comes forward fussily,* L. 1 E.)

Manager.   Here, I shall lose my license, I declare.

Mont.   It's all right.

Manag.   No, it ain't. You must keep steady.
                You owe me, too, a tidy lump already.
                If this goes on you'll have to quit the place.

Louis. (L.C., *who has come down, with an air of grandeur*)
        Supper for twelve.

Ladies.   Oh!

Manag. (*bowing*)   That's another case.

Louis.   Champagne—   (LADIES *clap hands*)

Manag.   Whose manufacture?

Martel. (*aside to* LOUIS)   You don't know it.
                Take my advice and cut it.[44]

Louis.   *Cut* it! (*to* MANAGER) *Mo*-it![45]
Manag.   Much honoured!

Louis.   Every kind expensive drink of, (LADIES *delighted*)
                And everything to eat that you can think of.
                        (*goes up—turns and walks up with the same
                                melancholy air*)

Celes. (*crosses,* R.C. *to* MARTELLI) Who is he?

Martel.   He's a twin—just like his brother!

Celes.   I must say I should like to meet the other.

Louis. (*coming down*) And whilst the supper is preparing, bring—

---

[44] *cut it* Hastily depart.
[45] *Mo*-it Pun on Moët, a leading brand of French champagne.

Celes.   Excuse me, champagne is the only thing
                I touch—yes, Perrier Jouet I love dearly,
                Or Cliquot.

Coral.   Nothing could be *Ruderer* really!

Louis.   You hear?   *Exit* MANAGER, L.

Martel. (*aside*)   I hope he's got enough to pay with him.

Louis. (*gives a deep sigh*) Ah, me!

Celes. (*aside to* MARTELLI)   Say, has he always got this jolly way with him?

Martel.   A blighted love has caused this melancholy.

Louis. (*with his hand on his breast, and in deep tones*)
                I vote for glasses round, and let's be jolly!
                Garçon!
WAITER *enters* L.1 E. (*exaggerated French Waiter*)
                               We would be merry—mirth is found
                In wine; so *donnez nous doo vang* all round.
                Hock, that's a wine that don't affect my nut,
                However much away the *hocks-I-put*.

Celes.   Champagne for us!

Louis, (*crossing, L.—aside to* GARCON)   That pink stuff that you sell
                At three and six, and ice it well.

          GARCON *puts his finger knowingly to his nose, and exits comically,*
          L.1 E.

          Medley—Concerted Pieces—'Cheer up, Sam.'

Marie.   Some folks may talk of claret,
                               Its virtues they maintain;
                          But give to me prime Sillery,[46]
                               Or any good Champagne.

---

[46] *Sillery* Superior dry white wine from Sillery in the champagne region of France, popular among the wealthy in nineteenth-century England.

However low your spirits are
 Depressed in sorrow's cup,
A sparkling beaker of champagne
 Will keep your pecker up!
 Cheer up, cham-
pagne will dispel every frown;
 Your care it will bury,
 And beats all your sherry,
The pale, and the dry, and the brown!

Chorus.   Cheer up, cham—
pagne will dispel every frown, &c.

Air (no symphony)—'Her Mincemeat Knife it went chop, chop, chop.'

Coral.   A drink divine,
 Is that sparkling wine!
Whenever one goes out to dine
You'll always see
That the companee
Wake up when it's introduced.
The ladies' eyes all lighten up,
 They do upon my word,
When the wire is snipped,
And the string is cut,
 And the pleasant pop is heard.
As the champagne bottles go pop, pop, pop,
Pop, pop, pop, pop, pop, pop!
A di'mond in every drop, drop, drop—
Drippety, droppety, drop!

Chorus.   As the champagne bottles go pop, pop, pop,
Pop, pop, pop, pop, pop, pop!
A di'mond in every drop, drop, drop—
Drippety, droppety, drop!

*Air—'The Glorious Vintage of Champagne' (no symphony—to be played
in the same time as above).*

Estel.   The glorious vintage of champagne
 Is a decided boon;
The best drink in the evening, and
 Likewise the afternoon.

At night, too, it is not so bad;
At luncheon 'tis a gain;
        For tea, I feel's,
        The only meal
At which *de trop*'s champagne.

Then let our song have this refrain—
The great advantage of champagne!
Then let our song have this refrain—
The great advantage of champagne!

Chorus.   Then let our song have this refrain—
The great advantage of champagne, &c.

        Air.— '*Susan, Susan, pity my confusion.*'—*(no symphony, same time)*

Louis.   It's well to have enough for one,
                            But if there should be two,
                        It's well to have enough for six
                            Of that delicious brew!
                        My servant's name is Susan, and
                            Rude folks might call her Sue,
                        And when I'm out of wine, I say—
                            As any one might do—
                        Soozan, Soozan, order half-a-doozen,
                            Of the best champagne that you can see!
                        Soozan, Soozan, I expect my coozan,
                            Which he is in the Ar-til-ler-ree.
Chorus.   Soozan, Soozan, order half-a-doozen,
                            Of the best champagne that you can see!
                        Soozan, Soozan, he expects his coozan,
                            Which he is in the Ar-til-ler-ree.

WAITER *enters, L.1 E., with champagne*—LOUIS *goes up with him. Music, waltz*—*at conclusion the* LADIES *go up with* MONTGIRON—LOUIS, *a little overcome with the wine down with* MARTELLI, *just before conclusion of waltz gets hustled about*—*music very piano through dialogue.*

Louis.   Don't leave us, ladies—(*staggers*)

Martel.   Hold up! you're unsteady.

Louis. (R.C.)   What's that there? (*reads*) 'Sherry cobblers always ready.'
(LADIES *laugh*) Let's—let's have a cobbler!

Martel. (L.C.)   No; it's near the hour.
            I thought he bragged too much about his power—

Louis. (*very drunk*) His power?

Martel.   Over Emilie Lesparre.

Louis. (*suddenly sober*) What! (*crossing, R.*)

Martel.   Jove! He didn't, though, for here they are. (*music*)

Enter CHATEAU RENAUD *with* EMILIE DE LESPARRE *on his arm,*
L.U.E.—*he bows to* MARTELLI—*does not perceive* LOUIS, *who is panting in*
horror at side, R., a little up.

Chateau.   The wager's mine—the tin, please, ready get—
            I've *found* my *Emilie*—you have *lost* your *Bet*!
            You see I'm up to time.

Emilie. (L.C.)   Is this a dream?
            I'm much too shocked and horrified to scream!
            Have I been bet upon? Am I brought here
            To—to—(*overcome with rage*)

Chateau. (L.C.)   To have a little supper with us, dear.
            We thought you were *ennuyée*, and I laid
            A wager—

Emile. (*boiling with rage*) May you never get it paid!
                May your best patent leathers crack when dancing,
                And may you get no partners but the 'prancing;'
                May you, when gloves you'd purchase a new pair
                Invariably forget the size you wear;
                May you be cut by those you'd wish to snub;[47]
                May you be 'pilled' at every West-end club;[48]
                When to your couch at dawn you may betake you,

---

[47] *to cut* To snub or to ignore someone.

[48] *pilled* Rejected on a ballot vote; in this case, voted down for membership in a club.
West-end Central commercial district of London.

May organ-men at eight o'clock awake you—[49]
Unless you'd catch a train at nine, and *then*
May they forget to call you until ten!
When you go out of town for changing air,
May you find *all* your creditors are there!
When well dressed, and it comes on rainy, may
Each Hansom cabman look another way!
And may you, when you dine on Richmond Hill,[50]
Be always let in to discharge the bill!!!

> (*this has been worked up with great intensity—
> slight pause—music ceases*)

Chateau.   Cease these anathemas.

Louis. (*crosses* L.C. *to* CHATEAU) Hem! This young *pussin*
Is my relation.

Chateau.   Is she?

Louis.   Yes, a *cussin*.
She's had enough of your society,
And will retire at once—

Chateau.   Halloa!
Louis.   With me.

Chateau.   Rubbish. Before we've had a glass of wine?
She won't *take any harm*.

Louis. (*taking* MADAME DE LESPARRE's *arm under his*) No, none but *mine*.
Come, Emily!

Mont. (*aside to* CHATEAU)   You won't allow this, surely?

Chateau. (*chafflingly to* LOUIS) Monsieur dei Flunki, you look somewhat poorly.
A little change of scene—ahem!—you know!
To-morrow morning—nine—at Fontain*bleau*.

---

[49] *organ-men* Itinerant street musicians, such as organ-grinders.

[50] *Richmond Hill* Area in Surrey, outside London, with a commanding view of the Thames and the city.

Louis.	*Blow* Fontain*bleau!* shan't go! I say, look here! (*to* MADAME DE LESPARRE) Look at the mess you've got me in, my dear!
Chateau.	Do you accept my challenge?
Louis.	No, I don't.
Chateau.	I call you out!
Louis.	Shan't come!
Chateau.	You won't?
Louis.	I won't!
Emilie.	You will be branded—have your name too stuck up.
Louis. (*aside*)	I must be *brandy'd* 'fore I get my pluck up.
Emilie.	He'll post you!
Louis.	*Post* me!
Emilie.	As a cur—get out!
Louis.	In the *dead* letter office, I've no doubt. (*crossing* R.C. *to* MARTELLI) You'll stand my friend? We are old pals—.
Martel.	I will. Should Chateau Renaud my friend Louis kill. (LOUIS *collapses*) Stand up! I'll tell your mother.
Louis.	Pooh, you flat,[51] That isn't acting as a friend, not that. If you would do your Louis a true service, Being, as you're aware, a trifle nervis, And you'd confer on him a lasting boon, (*in his ear*) Let the police know all about it soon!

---

[51] *flat* Fool or dupe.

Air.—'Come where the Moonbeams linger.'

Emilie.	Go where the moonbeams linger,
	Off, it is early morn;
	Or if you raise your finger,
	Surely as you were born,
	Chateau Renaud will beat you,
	Get your back to the light,
	Or badly he will treat you,
	He's such a fellow to fight!
Chateau.	At every kind of weapon,
	I am a dab, you know;
	And I can use my fists as well,
	Sure as I'm Chateau Renaud.
Emilie.	Go where the moonbeams linger,
	Get your back to the light,
	Or you will get a winger—
	He's such a fellow to fight! (ALL *repeat*)

Marie.	Oh! what a dreadful party;
	Who could imagine such?
Louis.	Louis admits in heart he's
	Weak, and his courage Dutch.
Mont.	Up in the early morning,
	He'll have to meet his foe;
Celes.	Danger and rheumatics scorning—
	Terrible Chateau Renaud.
Chateau.	It's his own fault, no other's,
	If he'll apologize,
	I shan't accept it—really—
	Certainly quite otherwise.
All.	Then don't apologize.
Emilie.	Go where the moonbeams, &c.
	(ALL *repeat—closed in as they go up*)

SCENE FOURTH.—*Corridor of an Hotel.*

Enter GRIFFO *and* MARIE *(as if after a journey),* L.

Griffo.	Was ever coachman so extremely dense?
	And why on earth call it a diligence?
	A slower coach was never seen, I s'pose,

	If that's the usual rate at which it goes.

If that's the usual rate at which it goes.
They call the coach a diligence—dare say
Because it dilly-dallies on the way.
None of your flirting with our two new flunkeys.

Marie.   Flirting, indeed!—a hideous pair of monkeys,
What missis was about to bring them—Well,

Griffo.   Missis's family is rather swell,
And so in livery she's popped Orlando,
Likewise Colonna—which they're rather grand—oh,
And though their rustic manners will peep out,
They'll both attract some notice I've no doubt.

Enter ORLANDO *and* COLONNA, R., *in exaggerated liveries,*
bouquets, white gloves and long sticks.

Orlan.   Here's a disgraceful shame; I feel so mean.

Colon.   My calves are not accustomed to be seen,
And they don't like it.

Orlan.   In the mountains we
Wore gartered bandages up to the knee;
Leggings which quite envelop-ed our pins,
Yes, covering a 'multitude of *shins.*'
Now as I walk along they cause remark.

Colon.   I shan't go out at all till after dark.

Orlan.   Up in the mountains we were happy—free.
It's true we seldom dined; but then our tea,
Though very weak and humble in its flavour,
Was honest, 'twas but seldom meat or gravy or
A vegetable passed our lips. For weeks
(Witness our wasted limbs and hollow cheeks,)
We've scarcely tasted food: whereas we now
Get four meals every day, and beer I vow
In buckets; then we've soft and downy beds,
Whereon to lay at night our powdered heads;
And every luxury—work! not a bit of it!
It's downright tyranny! Shall we submit to it?
Shall we be free again? (*this with great intensity*)

Colon.   Hooray!

Griffo.   Bosh this is.

Orlan. (*crosses,* R.) Away! away! to the mountain's brow!

Colon. (*collapsing*)   Here's missis.
   Enter MADAME DEI FLUNKI, L., *enveloped in travelling clothes—*
   furry and comic.

Madame. (*crossing,* C.) Where is my boy, my boy! has no one heard of him!
   Has no one been and said a single word of him!
       (ALL *turn aside as if in grief*)
   How could he leave his home at such a season
   To wander here—I *wander hear* the reason!
   I couldn't keep away from my two sons,
   Who're like each other as two penny buns;
   And so I—(*seeing the others*) What mean those averted heads?
 (ALL *groan*) I see;—the house is full, and there's no beds.
   In Paris there are others—(ALL *sigh*) Why that sigh?
   You've seen the scale of charges—they are high?
   But what of that, we've come to cut a dash,
   And I've a superfluity of cash;
   So it's—(ALL *groan*) Another groan! I tell you what,
   I'll give you all your warning on the spot
   If you don't—

Griffo. (*aside, crossing,* L.C.) Hem! Well, p'raps we'd better tell her.
   (*to* MADAME DEI FLUNKI) The fact is, Monsieur Louis—poor young
   feller. (*breaks down in tears*—ALL *howl*)

Madame. (*alarmed, crossing,* L.C.) What of him?

Marie.   Oh, ma'am, it's so very sad!

Madame. (C.)   The trouble that I've had about that lad.
   What's he done now?

Orlan. (*crossing,* R.C.)   You've heard of Chateau Renaud,
   A party to whom *no* girl could yet *say* 'No!'
   He's such a winning dog—there's no like him.

Madame. (*arranging her dress—aside*) I wonder very much if I shall strike him?
I'm not the girl I was, but parties say
I've got a sort of kind of queenly way;
A regal air and dignified address,
Which young things in their teens do not possess.
Go on. Go on!

Orlan.   Well, him and Monsieur Louis—

Colon. (*crossing,* L.C.) Fought, and De Renaud, who'se a reg'ler *roue,*
Got quite the best of it—his eye will shew.
He can't—for it's so very black you know.
Why, such a swordsman did your son incense, mum?
For—no offence, mum; what's he *know of fence,* mum?

Orlan. (*crossing* COLONNA) Well, hearing of this deed so very black,
Your other son's upon De Renaud's track,
Who's cut from Paris by a secret byway:
Fabien declares he'll catch him on the *eye* way.
We heard it 'cos they took post horses here;
De Renaud's frightened and looked rather queer,
Which, if his carriage breaks down on the road,
'Twill surely be a case of *eye* am *blowed*!
                    (*suiting the action to the word*)

Colon.   Rubbish, De Renaud is a dab at all swords,
From '*sarbers de mong pare*,' to pair o'small swords![52]
With rapiers he is up to dreadful tricks,
And the big broadsword blades of '*Brayvo 'Icks.*'[53]

Griffo.   De Renaud'll run him through, I'll lay a penny,
And treat his mountain buzzum like Mont *Senny.*
                    (ALL *groan and with pocket handkerchiefs to eyes*)

Madame.   What's to be done? The wood of Fontainbleau
Is where they always go and fight, you know.

---

[52] *sarbers de mong pare* Corruption of 'Le sabre de mon père', a song from Jacques Offenbach's *La Grande Duchesse de Gérolstein* (1867).

[53] *Brayvo 'Icks* Nickname for the popular melodramatic actor N.T. Hicks, whose most celebrated role was the thief Jonathan Wild in W.T. Montcrieff's *Jack Sheppard* (Victoria Theatre 1839). 'Brayvo 'Icks' is the phonetic rendering of a Cockney audience's cheer 'Bravo Hicks'.

We will be there. Prize-fighting's been put down;[54]
And if Joe Bloggs mayn't pitch into Bill Brown,
Why should this Chateau Renaud kill my son?
Go fetch a cab at once, a four-wheeled one;
Select a strong horse, Griffo, look alive!
Make the best bargain that you can for five.

Concerted Piece—'I'm her Pa.'

Madame.
Have you ever seen my son, mum?
Each is like the one, mum;
A couple of mischeevous lads
Away they both have run, mum;
Their mother is cut up, mum,
About each silly pup, mum.
She'll have a bill struck off she will,
   And offer a reward.

Marie.
Don't agitate yourself, mum,
Or throw away your pelf, mum,[55]
But take the matter quietly,
Resigned and quite piano.

Madame.
Oh, they both are teazers—reg'ler Julius Caesars!
They've curly hair—the lovely pair—
   Both born in Corsicah.
Their waists are both so slender,
They're both of the male gender,
And I always feel so proud,
   That I'm their ma!

Colon.
Take the matter easy,
Don't go on so breezy;
Depend upon't, before you want,
They'll both come back and squeeze ye!

Marie.
Then pray keep up your pecker,
Be manly, like Miss Becker;[56]

---

[54] Since prize fights were illegal—though hardly secret—they were typically held outdoors, as far away as possible from law enforcement officials. Indoor fights did not begin until the 1880s when boxing became a more gentlemanly sport.

[55] *pelf* Treasure or fortune.

[56] *Miss Becker* Lydia Ernestine Becker (1827-1905), a leader of the nineteenth-century women's rights movement.   In 1866, along with Emily Davies and Elizabeth

	Remember they've some property—
	Some landed propertie.
Madame.	They've had an education,
	Suited to their station;
	They both can toot upon the flute,
	And play on the pian-o.
	Oh, they both are teazers, &c.
All.	They both are teazers, &c. (*breakdown, off,* R.)

SCENE FIFTH.—*The Forest of Fontainbleau.*

'The Twins' played as Scene opens; CHATEAU RENAUD *seated on a broken trunk,* L.2 E. MARTELLI *looking off,* R.1 E.

Martel.	You want a pick-me-up—you're hipped.
Chateau.	I am.
	Hock is delusive, and how *false* is '*sham.*'
Martel.	Here is my flask—come now, one little sip.
Chateau.	Friend at a *pinch*, and also at a *nip*. (*takes flask*)
	The least drop in the world I do not mind;
	Cognac's a *noun* I never yet *declined*.
	It cheers one—gives one courage—
Martel.	Which you're out of.
Chateau.	That, my dear friend, there's very little doubt of.
	When I'm alone—when all alone—I vow—
	(And as you're nobody, I feel so now.)
	When I'm alone, remorseful visions rise.
Martel.	Well, if you will go in for Strasbourg pies,
	And *paté de fois gras* in mammoth heaps,
	You mustn't be astonished if your sleep's
	Not over tranquilizing, calm and placid;
	The Mabille sherry is a trifle acid;

Wolstenholme, she co-founded the Manchester Women's Suffrage Committee. The burlesque satirizes her work in feminist campaigns by describing her as 'manly'.

> Whilst the champagne, for which so oft you rung,
> Was not even *old* gooseberry—but *young.*[57]

Chateau. I only *tried* it.

Martel.   It with manners true,
Returned this compliment by trying *you!*

Chateau. This is the very spot—the very spot
On which poor Louis got it.

Martel.   No, it's not;
It's not exactly where he got it.

Chateau.   Why?

Martel. The spot on which he got it's on his *eye.*

Chateau. I feel for it remorse, likewise disgrace too;
  (*with great grief*) And when he'd said no hittings in the face, too!
              (*buries his head in his hands, and takes* R., *corner*)

Martel. Cheer up!

Chateau.   I can't—I'm overcome by fear!
Our carriage didn't, mind you, break down here
For nothing. (*going up,* C.) Oh, why did I punch his head so?
I yet shall rue the action.

          (*Music, three chords—is going* R.2 E. *when* FABIEN
                *enters suddenly—*CHATEAU *staggers back, and*
                MEYNARD *enters,* R.2 E.)
                         There! I said so.
     (*they take three steps down* R. *together*)
          Which of you is it? (*in horror to* FABIEN)

Fabien.   That you soon shall find.

Chateau. (*aside*) If it had been his ghost, I shouldn't mind.

---

[57] *old gooseberry* A chaperone for an engaged couple; more generally, to be the odd man out. The burlesque makes a pun on the familiar expression 'old gooseberry' and 'young gooseberry', meaning gooseberry wine that has not yet matured.

(*piano music*)

Fabien.   I'm Fabien dei Flunki—come away,
As fast as possible from Corsi*cay*.
You know the reasons, don't you? Five days back,
A certain eye grew suddenly quite black;
You know whose eye I mean, sir, I suppose—
(*with fervour, his hands clasped*)
It was my brother Louis' eye—*I nose*.

Chateau.   Your brother got what he deserved.

Fabien.   No doubt,
But now, sir, you and I must have it out!

Chateau.   Fight you! (*crossing, L., commences lighting cigarette*)

Fabien.   I felt the blow on my proboscis,
And instantly I ordered out post-*houses*;
Put on the steam, and travelled day and night.
I haven't slept for five days.

Martel. (*slaps him on the back*)   That's all right.
Five sleepless nights would knock up any fella!

Fabien.   I'd no companion but my umbrella!
Nor have I tasted food.

Martel. (*to* CHATEAU)   That's better still;
He'll be so weak.

Fabien.   You'll fight me?

Chateau.   Yes, I will! (*crosses, C.*)
But, understand, I don't fight any more.
Pugnacious relatives would be a bore.
And if they challenge me *ad infinitum*
I shall decidedly object to fight 'em! (*crosses, L.*)

Fabien. (*very pathetically*) Don't be alarmed! the feud will end with me:
I am the last leaf of my family tree—
So young, so beautiful! (*yawns heavily*) Excuse my ways.
But (*yawns*) I've not been in bed for several days.

Nevertheless—(*yawns, and leaning up against* MEYNARD,
appears to be gradually dropping off into a doze)

Chateau. (*crossing*, L.C.—*aside to* MARTELLI) I'll wait until he drops off in a
doze,
And then, sir, let him have it on his nose.

Meynard. (R., *remonstrating, to* FABIEN) I say, wake up! He's dozing, I declare.

Fabien. (*snores, dreamily*) If that's my shaving water, leave it there.
Bring me a cup of coffee when I ring.
(*subsides into slumber*)

Meynard.   I say—Revenge! and all that sort of thing.
(*rouses* FABIEN) A dreadful blow De Renaud did allot him.

Fabien. (*after slight yawn*) I beg my brother's pardon—I forgot him!
Really, I—

Chateau. (*aside*)   He's awake, and I confess,
I feel—(*aloud*) But we've no weapons.

Fabien. (*goes up*, C., *and pulls up sticks*)   Weapons?—yes.
Observe!—a fact perhaps you didn't know—
That single-sticks grow here at Fontainbleau.
Behold! (*chord*)

Chateau. (*taking* MARTELLI's *hand—aside and with intensity*)
His eye is hard upon me. Oh, why—why
Was I so hard upon his brother's eye?
I feel that I shall get the worst.

Martel.   The blues
Are overcoming you.

Meynard. (*crossing*, R.C., *handing weapons*) The weapons choose.

Chateau. (*comparing them*) This one's the knottier; for me 'twill do.
I'm certainly the *nottier* of the two. (MEYNARD *gives*
FABIEN *stick, and crosses*, R., *behind*)

Fabien. (*with stick*) Now are you ready? (*yawns heavily*)

Meynard. (*pushing him*) Here don't go to sleep so!

Fabien.   Excuse me, but you see I am on guard.

Chateau.   Keep so.
(CHATEAU *and* FABIEN *take off coats—aside to* MARTELLI)
I'm a gone coon—I ne'er shall leave this thicket.
A last gift, here's my watch—I mean the ticket;
You can redeem it for just two pounds three.
        (*wringing* MARTELLI's *hand with great feeling*)
May't make you happier than e'er it made *me*.
Nearly two pounds was on that ticker lent.

Martel. (*overcome*) It is too much!

Chateau.   It *is*, it never *went*.
Call on my bootmaker when all is past,
And tell him that I thought of him the *last*.
My tailor seek—mingle him with your woes,
And say I breathed his name just at the *clo's*.
My gunmaker I owe for caps. Call later,
And tell him I have paid the *det o' nator*.
To all my money-lenders also go,
They always took *such interest*, you know.

Fabien. (*asleep—*MEYNARD *shakes him—*FABIEN *shows muscle*) Time!

Chateau. (*takes Eau-de-Cologne from* MARTELLI) I'm prepared!
        (*they cross the sticks*)

Fabien.   Behold, we cross our *two* sticks!

Chateau.   Just so. (*after a little business* RENAUD *catches* FABIEN
                     on the ear)

Fabien.   Hullo!

Chateau.   A lesson in *acoustics*.

Martel.   Ear! Ear! Ear!

Fabien.   Ah! let him laugh who wins—I shall be winner!
        (*business repeated*)

Chateau.   Don't brag—it's very rude. (*catches* FABIEN *on the shin; he
                        howls*)

Fabien.   What's that? (*dancing with pain*)

Chateau.   A '*shinner.*'
                    How does it feel?

Fabien. (*hopping*)   It doesn't hurt a bit.

Chateau.   I hit your *shin.*

Fabien. (*rubbing it*)   Just so—don't men-*shin hit.*

Concerted Piece—'She's just about the age.'
(*enough movement kept up not to interfere with the words of the song*)

Chateau.   Oh, once I dearly loved to fight with swords.
Fabien.   I hate their whizz
                    Just pass your ears, and I prefer
                        A bout with fistis-*siz.*
                                The stick you hold
                                Is not too old,
                            Nor too young to engage.
                    It's made of coarsish wood, you know,
                            And it's just about the age.
Chorus.   It's made of coarsish wood, you know—
                                The wood you know—the wood;
                    It's made of coarsish wood you know,
                            And it's just about the age.
Chateau.   Oh, if your mother only had a notion you were out,
Fabien.   She'd go into hysterics, could she fancy what about.
                    I always would go fighting when a child, and come to tea
                    With one or two black eyes, you know—occasionally three!
                    But then, you know, I would, you know—
                            I would, you know—I would.
                    Pa said it did me good, you know,
                            I was just about the age.

Chorus.   But then, you know, he would you know,
                            He would, you know, he would.
                    Pa said it did him good, you know,
                            He was just about the age.

Chateau.	Now mind yourself, Dei Flunki.
Fabien.	And mind yourself, Renaud.
Martel.	Should Fabien fail,
	The dreadful tale
	His ma' you'd let her know.
Meynard.	I'd rather you,
	I hear it's true,
	Her temper's—
Martel.	Don't refuse.
Fabien.	She'd punch the party's precious head
	Who carried her such news.
Chateau.	I've really heard she would, you know,
	She would, you know, she would.
Fabien.	What's more she really could, you know,
	She's just about the age.
Chorus.	We really heard she would, you know,
	She would, you know, she would;
	What's more she really could, you know,
	She's just about the age.

Chateau. (*singing—recitative*) Now mind your eye.
Meynard.   You'd better mind your eye.
All.   (*harmonized*)   He'd (I'd) better mind his (my) eye.

Air.—The Chorus to 'Angelina was always fond of Soldiers.'

Meynard.	See, he lunges chiefly from the shoulder;
	The single-stick goes whizzing round your ears!
	To your fate pray be resigned—
Chateau.	'Tis an awkward trick, you'll find,
	And I learnt it from the Belgian Volunteers—
	Tap, tap!
	(*business through the above, finishing by two smart raps on* FABIEN's *head*)
All.	See, he lunges chiefly from the shoulder, &c.
	(*symphony played tremulously, throughout which they speak*)
Fabien.	I don't see half a chance, but *vicey versey*;
	(CHATEAU, *leaning on a stick, breaks it*)
	Halloa! You're now completely at my mercy.

> (*aside*) His stick in two—all chance for him is gone.
> (*heroically*) Louis, you yet shall be avenged! Come on!
> (*lunging, and threatening* CHATEAU RENAUD)
> Come on, and meet your doom!

Meynard.   Come, this won't do.

Fabien.   Mind your own business—what is it to you?

Meynard.   A duel must be equal.

Fabien.   I don't see it.

Meynard.   And so, of course, you'll break your stick.

Fabien. (*sighing—breaks it*)   So be it.[58]
        (*aside to* MEYNARD) You're a nice friend, you are.

Chateau. (*aside*)   He funks! He flinches!
        (*swaggering*) This stick's quite long enough. A dozen inches
                Are quite enough to *incher* as you'll see. (*snow falls*)

Fabien.   I'm in the forest and I'm up a tree.
                At it he really seems *au fait—oh, fate!*

Meynard.   Quick! Recollect your brother.

Fabien.   He can wait.
                I say, look here, it's coming on to snow.
                Suppose we put it off a year or so?

Chateau.   No—no—no—certainly not.
Meynard.   " "
Martel.   " "

Meynard.   Remember Louis!

Fabien.   You said that before,
        (*aside*) Louis' becoming somewhat of a bore.
                (CHATEAU *has wrapped his handkerchief round his bit*

---

[58] In the original play, Fabien does not have to be goaded into such honourable
behaviour. The scene's humour renders the revenge plot absurd.

> *of stick, holding in the other hand the broken short*
> *stump of a sword, à la combatants in 'Huguenot*
> *Captain')*[59]

Chateau. Come, I'm prepared!

Fabien. I'm not. (*backed up*) Well, if you will,
Here goes!

> (*a short fierce fight—*FABIEN *blown—*MEYNARD *gives him*
> *drink from case bottle—*CHATEAU RENAUD *walks round*
> *à la boxer and stands prepared—*FABIEN *staggers towards*
> CHATEAU RENAUD *and rushes at him, meeting* MADAME
> DEI FLUNKI *who falls,* L.C., FABIEN *falling,*
> R.C.—MADAME *is raised by* ORLANDO—*she slaps his face,*
> *and falls fainting in his arms—*FABIEN *is raised by*
> MEYNARD, *who holds him up in a state of collapse*)

MADAME DE LESPARRE *enters,* R., *with* ORLANDO, COLONNA, MARIE
and GRIFFO—*Picture.*

Madame. Your loving mother would you kill?

Emilie. (*coming down,* R.C.) Oh, Fabien! I've discovered that my spouse,
When he exchanged with me his marriage vows,
Already had a wife! and so you see,
As he committed—

Chateau. Gracious!

Emilie. Bigamy!
I'm free.

Fabien. More free than welcome.

Chateau. (*aside*) What's he say?

Fabien. (*leading her to* CHATEAUD RENAUD) Take her—be happy!

---

[59] *Hugenot Captain* The French opera *Les Huguenots* (1836) by Giacomo Meyerbeer
(1791–1864). In Act IV, the Count de Nevers breaks his sword, vowing not to participate
in the Catholic plan to massacre Huguenots.

Emilie.   What is this?

Fabien.   And may
        Your future be a bright one, and a cheerful:
        Bless you, my children! (*aside to* MEYNARD)
                Why, her temper's fearful!
        She'll turn his hair grey in a month. (*going up*)

    Enter GHOST *of* LOUIS, L.U.E., *with a comforter round his neck, and a violent cold.*

Fabien. (*staggers back*)   Halloa!
        My brother Louis!

Louis. (L., *this is spoken by* FABIEN *with his back to the audience,*
        LOUIS *moving his lips and gesticulating*)[60]
                I should like to know,
        If it don't interfere much with the plot,
        Whether I am to be avenged or not?
        It's freezing! Cease these mutual appealings:
        Even a wretched spectre has his feelings. (*sneezes*)

Fabien.   Alas, poor ghost![61] Take that. (*places his cloak over
                LOUIS, who sinks down trap after manner of the
                disappearance under the extinguisher trick*)[62]

Chateau.   Say, dearest Emilie, will you be mine?

Emilie.   Under the circumstances, can't decline.
        I'm yours.

---

[60] This moment of ventriloquism mockingly refers to the necessary double casting when both brothers appear onstage. Clarke, although he was playing Fabien, spoke Louis's lines while a 'double' mimed Louis's actions.

[61] Cf. Hamlet, 'Alas, poor ghost' (*Hamlet* 1.5.4).

[62] *disappearance under the extinguisher trick* One of Harry Houdini's magic tricks in which his son, Emile, seemed to disappear from a table on which he had been placed. The table contained a trap door through which the 'disappearing' person escaped. The original manuscript concludes here, with the stage direction 'Concerted Piece and Transformation' (British Library Add Ms 53,077 J, fol. 63.)

Madame.	I say, it's very cold out here, Ain't you a going to come home, my dear?
Fabien.	Yes.
Chateau.	But before you go—before our scene Changes from winter to the all serene, Isn't there something, eh?
Emilie.	Of course. Don't frown Upon our efforts when the curtain's down. Your smiles will warm our wood of Fontainbleau, And all its cold and dismal winter's snow Will melt away—a break-up quite immense, Beneath your bright and glowing influence. You won't be hard on those who've tried their best?
Madame.	You'll make a wretched parent ever blest. Bless'd if you don't!
Meynard.	Of course, they can't be hard on us. Any one can condemn; but come, *you'll* pardon us.

Orlan. (L., *fiercely*) If they do not—

Colon. (R., *fiercely*)   Ha! ha!

Fabien.	Shut up! (*to audience*) I say, Don't be severe upon our little play. Shew by a kindly ringing cheer or two, That the *Twin Brothers* haven't *troubled* YOU.

TRANSFORMATION[63]

Finale—'Pretty Little Flora.'

Emilie.   When the curtain's fallen,

---

[63] *TRANSFORMATION* A spectacular effect of scenery, lighting, and music, typically associated with pantomimes, in which a domestic scene magically turned into one of fantasy. Transformations were accomplished gradually, and could take fifteen or twenty minutes to complete. Designed by Julian Hicks, this concluding scene represented 'The Return of Spring-Time and the Birthday of Beauty'.

	Don't you go away,
	Don't you go away,
	And speak unkindly.
Chateau.	Say a civil something
	Of our little play.
	Treat our very many errors blindly.
Fabien.	Louis asks for pardon;
Emilie.	Emilie as well;
Meynard	And Chateau Renaud also, and each little swell.
Martel.	Our acting don't be hard on, say a pleasant word.
Mont.	All our errors pardon—many have occurred.
Fabien.	Pity little Fabien
	And his wretched ma.
Madame.	Which she will start home, first thing to-*more-er*.
Emilie.	And when she's returned again to Corsicah,
	There's sure to be some Pity little *fore* her.
All.	Pity little Fabien, &c., &c.

CURTAIN.

THE POET AND THE PUPPETS

CHARLES H.E. BROOKFIELD and J.M. GLOVER
(1892)

THE POET

AND

THE PUPPETS.

A TRAVESTIE SUGGESTED BY

"LADY WINDERMERE'S FAN."

* * * * * *

BY

CHARLES BROOKFIELD,

MUSIC BY

J. M. GLOVER.

* * * * * *

Have you heard the argument? is there no offence in't?
No! no! they do but jest, no offence i' the world.

13 Title page, *The Poet and the Puppets* (British Library, C.193.b.21)

Editor's Introduction

The Poet and the Puppets

The Poet and the Puppets takes its name from the header which the *Daily Telegraph* placed above a letter from Oscar Wilde which it printed on 19 February 1892. Wilde denied the newspaper's report that in a recent speech at the Playgoers' Club he had asserted that 'the stage is only a frame furnished with a set of puppets. It is to the play no more than a picture-frame is to a painting, which frame has no bearing on the intrinsic merit of the art within'.[1] The comic actor Charles H.E. Brookfield quickly sensed the satiric potential of the phrase used by the *Daily Telegraph*. He suggested to Charles Hawtrey, then actor-manager of the Comedy Theatre, that they produce a burlesque of Wilde's *Lady Windermere's Fan*, which had just opened at the St. James's Theatre. They enlisted Jimmy Glover to compose the music. The resulting burlesque sketch was duly titled *The Poet and the Puppets*.

Lady Windermere's Fan, Wilde's first theatrical success, was set in modern-day London. On the day of her twenty-first birthday party, Lady Windermere learns that for the past six months her husband has been keeping company with Mrs. Erlynne, a notorious 'woman with a past'. Windermere, when confronted by his wife, not only protests that the relationship is entirely innocent but seeks his wife's aid in restoring the well-born Mrs. Erlynne to society. Against his wife's wishes, Windermere invites Mrs. Erlynne to attend the party. A distraught Lady Windermere confides in Lord Darlington, who returns the confidence by declaring his love for her. After overhearing her husband agree to a financial settlement which will allow Mrs. Erlynne to marry Lord Augustus, Lady Windermere vows to leave her husband for Lord Darlington. But the explanatory note she leaves him is accidentally discovered by Mrs. Erlynne, whom we now learn is Lady Windermere's mother. Meanwhile, Lady Windermere (who knows nothing of her mother's identity) waits for Lord Darlington at his home. Mrs. Erlynne soon arrives there, determined to sacrifice herself to save her daughter's marriage. Throwing the intercepted letter into the fire, she promises that if Lady Windermere returns to her husband she will disappear from their lives. When Lords Darlington, Windermere, and Augustus are heard approaching, Mrs. Erlynne instructs Lady Windermere to conceal herself behind a curtain and flee when she can. Windermere quickly recognizes his wife's fan and immediately assumes that she is hiding in the room. To everyone's surprise, the concealed woman turns out to be Mrs. Erlynne. Lady Windermere has fled unnoticed. Retrieving the fan, Mrs. Erlynne casually explains that she had taken it by mistake and then exits. She visits Lady Windermere the next day to return the fan and to bid the Windermeres farewell. In a series of private conversations with husband and wife,

Mrs. Erlynne persuades each not to reveal any secrets to the other. After her departure, the Windermeres learn that she has agreed to marry Lord Augustus on the condition that they live abroad. The comedy thus ends with all marital relationships intact and no immorality exposed.

During the first run of *Lady Windermere's Fan*, Wilde learned that Brookfield, Hawtrey, and Glover intended to burlesque him as well as his comedy. So pointedly personal a burlesque was unusual since the Lord Chamberlain's powers of censorship effectively prevented blatant parodies of individuals. (For exceptions, see the section on censorship in the Introduction to this volume.) At Wilde's urging, Edward F.S. Pigott, the Examiner of Plays, instructed Brookfield and Glover to read *The Poet and the Puppets* aloud to Wilde himself. And so they did. Surprisingly, Wilde objected only to the punning refrain 'To make Oscar O'Flaherty—Wilde' in the play's opening song. (O'Flaherty was Wilde's middle name.) To placate the offended dramatist, the refrain was rewritten 'To make neighbour O'Flaherty's child'. After voicing this single reservation, Wilde listened to the remainder of the script with condescending amusement. As Glover recalled,

> while cigars were burned, the poet puffed, and punctuated each page as it was read with such phrases as 'Delightful!' 'Charming, my old friends!' (His calling Brookfield 'old friend' was touching.) 'It's exquisite!' etc. etc. As he showed us to the door he just gave us this parting shot: 'I feel, however, that I have been—well—Brookfield, what is the word?—what is the thing you call it in your delightfully epigrammatic Stage English? eh? Oh, yes!—delightfully spoofed.'[2]

With only minor changes to the script, *The Poet and the Puppets* opened at the Comedy Theatre on 19 May 1892 as an unmistakable satire of *Lady Windermere's Fan*, which had just passed its one hundredth performance. Like Byron's *1863*, Brookfield and Glover's burlesque opens with a dramatist struggling to find a topic for his play. The 'Poet'—Hawtrey, impersonating Wilde—enlists the aid of a fairy to help him 'invent' a play that is already 'well known and successful'. The suggestion of plagiarism was hardly idle since Wilde was charged by the theatrical press for blatantly incorporating the situations and plot contrivances of well-known plays into *Lady Windermere's Fan*. Among Wilde's apparent 'sources' were Sheridan's *The School for Scandal*, melodramas about 'women with a past', and the French plays of Eugène Scribe, Sardou, and Alexandre Dumas *fils*.[3] The fairy, played by Lottie Venne, conjures up apparitions of Shakespeare, Ibsen, Sheridan, A.W. Pinero, and Henry Arthur Jones, all vowing to provide the Poet with an 'occasional conventional idea or common-place situation, just to leaven the exquisite unexpectedness of [his] entire work'. Secure in his reliance upon these dramatic eminences, the Poet writes his play—about a 'wise child who doesn't know her own mother', an obvious allusion to Lady Windermere's ignorance of her mother's identity—and then instructs his puppet-actors how to perform their parts. (In the burlesque, however, Lady Winterstock does know that Mrs. Earlybird is her mother.) Throughout the play-within-the-play, which forms the burlesque of *Lady Windermere's Fan*, the Poet freely dispenses advice to his puppet-characters. Brookfield thus keeps Wilde himself in sharp satiric focus. The production's 'best hits', the *Era* attested, were aimed at Wilde, 'one of the most successful self-advertisers of the age, who has consistently pursued the principle of making himself conspicuous in order to secure notoriety'.[4]

Apart from Hawtrey's clever impersonation of Wilde, Brookfield parodied Nutcombe Gould's performance as Lord Darlington, Eric Lewis imitated George Alexander as Windermere, and Lottie Venne suggested Marion Terry's mannerisms as Mrs. Erlynne. In the first part of the play, Brookfield also impersonated Pinero and the actor-managers Herbert Beerbohm Tree and Squire Bancroft.[5] 'Those who have seen *Lady Windermere's Fan*', the *Theatre* heartily advised, 'should on no account miss the travestie'. Though not a financial success, *The Poet and the Puppets* held the boards at the Comedy Theatre for ten weeks, closing at the end of July 1892.

Wilde's demand that Piggott censor the burlesque was ironic in the extreme since only a few weeks later the Examiner of Plays banned Wilde's *Salomé* on the grounds that biblical characters could not be represented on the stage. Wilde publicly denounced Piggott as incompetent and entered into no behind-the-scenes negotiations to rescue his own play. Instead, he complained that Pigott

> panders to the vulgarity and hypocrisy of the English people, by licensing every low farce and vulgar melodrama. He even allows the stage to be used for the purpose of the caricaturing of the personalities of artists, and at the same moment prohibited *Salomé*, he licensed a burlesque of *Lady Windermere's Fan* in which an actor dressed up like me and imitated my voice and manner!!![6]

William Archer, a firm opponent of state censorship, rose to Wilde's defence in a letter printed by the *Pall Mall Gazette*. Contrasting *Salomé* with *The Poet and the Puppets*, Archer lamented that a

> serious work of art, accepted, studied, and rehearsed by the greatest actress of our time [i.e., Sarah Bernhardt], is peremptorily suppressed, at the very moment when the personality of its author is being held up to ridicule, night after night, on the public stage, with the full sanction and approval of statutory infallibility.[7]

The irony became even more bitter three years later. In 1895, Hawtrey and Brookfield created the roles of Lord Goring (often regarded as a surrogate for Wilde) and his servant, Phipps, in Wilde's *An Ideal Husband*. Brookfield could barely tolerate being required to memorize the playwright's dialogue. Uncharacteristically, he requested a minor role so that he could remain as detached from the production as possible. That same year both actors amassed evidence of Wilde's association with male prostitutes and then conveyed the damaging information to one of the Marquis of Queensberry's detectives. On the day when

Wilde was convicted at the second trial, Brookfield and Hawtrey hosted Queensberry at a celebratory dinner. At the time of his conviction Wilde had no idea of the actors' part in the conspiracy against him.

The text for *The Poet and the Puppets* is taken from the script in the British Library (Add Ms 53,499 M), which is identical to the version published in London by Mitchell in 1892. The manuscript originally submitted to the Lord Chamberlain—i.e., the one which Brookfield and Glover read to Wilde—has not survived.

CHARLES H.E. BROOKFIELD (1857-1913) was the son of a former royal chaplain and a lady-in-waiting to Queen Victoria. His father counted Tennyson, Dickens, and Thackeray among his friends. Brookfield himself was the godson of the distinguished historian Henry Hallam. A graduate of Trinity College, Cambridge, he abandoned an intended legal career for the stage. In 1879 he made his debut in a revival of Tom Taylor's *Still Waters Run Deep* at the Haymarket under the Bancrofts' management. He remained at that theatre throughout the 1880s, appearing in revivals of *Money*, *Masks and Faces*, *Society*, and *Ours*. After ill health forced him to give up acting, he turned to playwrighting. His speciality was short comic pieces, including the revue *Under the Clock* (1893) and the burlesque *A Model Trilby* (1895). In 1902 he published his memoirs, *Random Reminiscences*. The quintessential poacher turned gamekeeper, Brookfield began his career as a parodist and ended it as the Examiner of Plays. In 1911, shortly before his appointment was announced, Brookfield wrote in the *National Review* that the golden age of drama had ceased with Ibsen's *A Doll's House*. From the stage of the Savoy Theatre, Harley Granville-Barker (who had played a minor role in *The Poet and the Puppets*) declared Brookfield unqualified to serve as the government's theatrical censor. Brookfield's controversial tenure in the Lord Chamberlain's Office was brief, for he died less than two years later.

J.M. GLOVER (1861-1931), born in Dublin, was a musical conductor and composer. Glover studied music in France, later becoming orchestra conductor at the Olympic, Empire, Drury Lane, and Palace Theatres in London. He was also a composer for ballets, dramas, and pantomimes. As a music critic he wrote for *The Sun*, the *Daily Mail*, and the *Daily Telegraph*. He published two memoirs, *Jimmy Glover, His Book* (1911) and *Jimmy Glover and His Friends* (1913).

Notes

[1] *Daily Telegraph* 19 February 1892.

[2] J.M. Glover, *Jimmy Glover, His Book* (London: Methuen, 1911), p. 20.

[3] As the *Theatre* remarked, Wilde's play did not benefit from 'complete novelty of its incidents' (1 April 1892). Peter Raby has more charitably remarked that 'Wilde seems to have absorbed, and to reflect, a number of theatrical traditions' in the play 'and yet succeeds in formulating a distinctive style and method'. Peter Raby, Introduction, *'The Importance of Being Earnest' and Other Plays* (Oxford: Clarendon Press, 1995), p. viii.

[4] *Era* 21 May 1892.

[5] *The Theatre* 1 June 1892.
[6] Oscar Wilde, a letter to William Rothstein, July 1892, quoted in *The Complete Letters of Oscar Wilde*, ed. Merlin Holland and Rupert Hart-Davis (New York: Henry Holt and Co., 2000), pp. 531-2.
[7] *Pall Mall Gazette* 1 July 1892.

The Poet and the Puppets

Immortals

A Poet	Mr. C.H. Hawtrey
A Moralist	Mr. Charles Brookfield
An Author	Mr. Eric Lewis
A Realist	Mr. Ernest Cosham
A Bard	Mr. W. Philp
An Optimist	Mr. J. Phipps
The Spirit of Fair Arbitration	Mr. Charles Brookfield
A Fairy	Miss Lottie Venne
Hamlet	Mr. Charles Brookfield
Ophelia	Miss Lottie Venne

Mortals

Lord Winterstock	Mr. Eric Lewis
Lord Pentonville	Mr. Charles Brookfield
Lord Gonbustus Often	Mr. James Nelson
1st Young Man	Mr. Ernest Cosham
2nd Young Man	Mr. W. Philp
3rd Young Man	Mr. G. Barker
4th Young Man	Mr. Charles Milton
Parker (a Yeoman of the Guard)	Mr. W. Wyes
Lady Winterstock	Miss Cynthia Brooke
The 'Duchess'	Miss Lizzie Ruggles
Mrs Nicey-Nicey	Miss E. Goss
Mrs Lummy-Lummy	Miss E. Gordon
Mrs McNaughtie-Naughtie	Miss Lizzie Wilson
Mrs Willoughby Myndear	Miss Violet Austin
Mrs Welly Nearly	Miss Florence Wilson
Mrs Earlybird	Miss Lottie Venne

SCENE I	The Poet's Study.
SCENE II	Lady Winterstock's Ball-room.
SCENE III	Lord Pentonville's Smoking Room.
SCENE IV	At Lady Winterstock's.

SCENE I.—*The Poet's study. Lights down. The* POET *discovered at his writing-table* L. *burning midnight oil. Mysterious music which gradually resolves itself into an Irish jig. To which the* POET *presently sings.*

> 1.—When first I was hurled on the face of this world
> People thought 'twas a thunderbolt fallen.
> But when they found who had arrived a Hurroo!
> Rent the air—faith 'twas something appalling!
> Then a crowd came along many thousand men strong
> To gaze on this wonderful child.
> For they knew by his cry and the fire in his eye
> It was neighbour O'Flaherty's child.[1]

> *Chorus—*
> They may bubble with jest at the way that I'm dressed
> They may scoff at the length of my hair,
> They may say that I'm vain, overbearing, inane,
> And object to the flowers I wear.
>   They may laugh till they're ill but the fact
> remains still,
> A fact I've proclaimed since a child.
> That it's taken, my dears, nearly two thousand years
> To make neighbour O'Flaherty's child!

> 2.—While at Oxford I took every prize and I shook
> The whole College from attic to basement.
> When I got up to show them my Newdigate poem
> My master was dumb with amazement.
> Then he cried: 'I don't need this effusion to read—
> 'I return your MS. undefiled.
> 'Your success I proclaim on account of your name,
> [']Mr. neighbour O'Flaherty's child.[']

> 3.—When I came up to town I soon made a renown
> I dazzled folk with my variety.
> Philosopher—artist—and general impartist
> Of cynical views on society.
> I set London ablaze, and you'll find now-a-days
> Aristocracy's tea tables piled
> With voluptuous poems bound in delicate tones,
> All by neighbour O'Flaherty's child.

---

[1] On Wilde's objections to the original lyric, see the introduction to this play.

Poet.   I'm really and truly afraid I work too hard. I don't nurse myself nearly as tenderly as I should. I am so foolishly fertile. I ought to follow the example of the Aloe, and present to the world once in a hundred years an exquisite leaflet crimson with song. Now, whom shall I summon to my aid? Not a Muse! There's a vulgar sound about a Muse! And she's always offended if you don't address her by her full vocative. Oh! Muse! No! I'll call in some bright little fairy off a child's Christmas tree. Some little stag-eyed elf who delights in the young, and who will be impressed and enchanted with me. (*Music*)

<blockquote>
Fairy of yellow, of green, or of white,
Queen of the Tree!
Quit for an evening your realm of delight,
Wait upon me.   (*Gong*)
</blockquote>

(*He blows a cloud of smoke through which a fairy appears*)

Fairy.   You called? Behold I come. On tinsel wing
I poised aloft—then swiftly stooped to bring
Quick as the lightning's shaft—

Poet.   My dear child, now do be nice and natural and charming! It is such a mistake to introduce anything so prosaic as verse into anything so poetical as everyday life. To employ your oratorical resources in private conversation is like going to bed in your evening clothes.

Fairy.   I'm extremely sorry if my mode of expression is distasteful to you. Of course, meeting anyone for the first time, and with really no introduction, one hardly knows—knows—

Poet.   Please—please—don't speak of me as if you didn't know me. Surely the fairies are not so ignorant as to be unacquainted with me. Why, I invented fairies. You had only been myths before I wrote about you. A beautful book, published by Bogus—which ran through five editions. Have you never read the story of the 'Giant's Causeway'?

Fairy.   It's some time since I read it, but I remember I was charmed with it at the time.

Poet.   Ah, so was I!

Fairy. (*aside*)   It'll never do to let him know that fairies can't read.

Poet.   Well, you know I have a new idea. I've invented Art and Flowers and Fairies. Now I'm thinking of inventing plays and actors and actresses. I'm sure they'd be a delightful resource when one's bored.

Fairy.   What kind of plays and actors?

Poet.   Oh, they must all be well-known ones. I can't afford to invent anything that isn't well known and successful.

Fairy.   But I don't understand.

Poet.   That's why you're so charming. That's why I delight to surround myself with the young and fairy-minded. It would be so dull to be understood. The greatest pleasure in life is to be misunderstood.

Fairy.   Then I'm very glad that I'm making you happy, because I can't understand a word you say. Why did you summon me?

Poet.   To help me with my play.

Fairy.   If it's going to be some one else's why don't you help yourself?

Poet.   I'm so tired of helping myself.

Fairy.   What's the play about?

Poet.   It's about a wise child who doesn't know her own mother.

Fairy.   What do you want me to do?

Poet.   Well, I want you—to do the work.

Fairy.   What about terms?

Poet.   Terms?

Fairy.   Yes. How shall we divide the fees?

Poet.   Oh, I'll take the fees; but if you do all the work I'll give you a beautiful full-blown sunflower covered with soft pollen which you can make into a sweet little frock, and full of golden honey.

Fairy.   I'd sooner far I took my share in money.

Poet.   Dear, dear! There you are, dropping into verse again, and getting human and mercenary. Why can't you be fairy-like and unsuspecting—as I am? It would be so much pleasanter for me.

Fairy.   Well, I'll help you if I can. I don't much believe in you, but there's a kind of plausibility about you which is rather disarming—I might say, even attractive. Would you like a little expert advice about your play?

Poet.   If you'll kindly make the expert vanish as soon as he begins to bore me, I shall be delighted to give him an interview. And that's a concession, for I generally sell my interviews.

Fairy.   Right you are.

> Thalia's High Priest, whether live or dead[2]
> Greatest of playwrights, thou, whose bay-crowned head
> In centuries to come, when all have said,
> Shall spire supreme above the rest! Great Seer!
> Whoe'er thou art, from Shades or Club, appear.

(*Enter simultaneously a* BARD, *a* MORALIST, *an* AUTHOR, *a* REALIST, *and an* OPTIMIST. *They all speak together.*)

Author.   Mr. Poet, your most obedient.

Optim.   I'm sorry if I'm late—my horse shied at a steam-roller, and I—

Moral.   I shall be much obliged if you can see me first, as I have a night rehearsal at—

Bard.   At thy service, good Monsieur Poet.

Real.   I was passing through London with a Cook's ticket to inspect the hospitals which I was so fortunate—

Fairy.   Good heavens! Who *are* all these?

Bard, Author, Real., Optim., Moral. I heard your summons—you want me I think?

---

2 *Thalia* Muse of Comedy.

Poet. (*aside*)   The man I thought would come was Maeterlink.[3]
(*to* FAIRY) Now, which of these excellent folk do you think we had better consult?

Fairy. (*aside*)   For goodness sake don't ask me. Not one of them looks quite what
I expected. One doesn't want to be rude to them, poor things, after coming all this
way. I daresay some of them have come quite a long journey. (*Goes to* L.)

Poet. (*affably*)   So you good people are all writers of comedies, eh?

Bard.   We steal by line and level, an't like your grace.[4]

Moral. (*aside to* OPTIM) A most improper remark.

Optim.   If you desire to learn to write a play,
                     I think you'd better let me have my say.
                     Literature is the most important factor,
                     The play is always ruined by the actor.[5]

Moral.   I think the fault's sometimes the author's own.
                     You want a really nice domestic tone,
                     To give across the flote a homely glimpse
                     Of cosy covered teapot, cress and shrimps.
                     Of dypsomaniacs who've had reverses,
                     Of lion-hearted lads who marry nurses.[6]

Real.   One or the other of the pair you paint
                     Should have, I think, some little family taint
                     To make them beautiful.[7]

---

3 Maurice Maeterlinck (1862-1939) Belgian poet and symbolist playwright. Many
contemporary critics believed that Wilde's *Salomé* was heavily influenced by the symmetry
and simplicity of Maeterlinck's dramatic language.

4 *The Bard* Shakespeare.

5 *The Optimist* Playwright and essayist Henry Arthur Jones, who believed that theatregoers
paid too much attention to celebrity performers and too little attention to plays themselves.

6 *The Moralist* Arthur Wing Pinero. At this point in his career, Pinero was best known for
farces and sentimental comedies such as *The Magistrate* (1885) and *Sweet Lavender* (1886),
written in the tradition of T.W. Robertson's 'cup and saucer' domestic comedies of the late
1860s and early 1870s.

7 *The Realist* Henrik Ibsen, whose shockingly realistic plays included such 'family taints' as
hereditary syphilis (*Ghosts*).

Moral.   Why, what d'you mean?

Real.   I mean that I should introduce a scene
               In which the lad forces himself to leave her
               Because she's consanguineous hay-fever;
               Or that when worried or in any other bother
               She flies to brandy like her sainted mother.

Bard. (*aside to* AUTHOR) If they should question me, why I'm undone.

Author.   How so?

Bard.   I never wrote a play but one.

Author.   How?

Bard.   Hush! Your finger on your lips I pray.
               Henry VIII. is my only genuine play![8]

Fairy. (*to* AUTHOR) Won't *you*, sir, teach us how to write our rhymes?

Author.   Faith, dainty spirit, I'm behind the times.[9]
               Were I in '92 to court acceptance
               I'd give my Lady Teazle song and step-dance.
               And Charles, in corduroy of East-end cut,
               Should boast his conquest of a Lambeth slut.[10]

Poet.   Then I take it all you good people will assist at my first night?

All.   We will.

---

[8] *Henry VIII* A reference to the elaborate production of Shakespeare's history play produced at the Lyceum in 1892 with Henry Irving as Cardinal Wolsey and Ellen Terry as Queen Katharine.

[9] *The Author* Richard Brinsley Sheridan.

[10] Sheridan, as 'The Author', updates his characters Lady Teazle and Charles Surface from *The School for Scandal* (1777) to suit the performance conventions of the minor theatres and music halls in the working-class neighbourhoods of south London (e.g., Lambeth) and the East End.

Poet.   How I envy you. And if I should require an occasional conventional idea or common-place situation, just to leaven the exquisite unexpectedness of the entire work, you will not fail me?

All.   Rely on us.

Song—
Each Author polite who has come here to-night
Can return to his favourite haunt.
We will not detain you, we frankly had fain you
Were off, for we've all that we want.
You've each had your say as to what makes a play,
And we'll bear what you said in our mind,
We give you good greeting to our next merry meeting,
You've all been exceedingly kind.

Chorus—
You mean that we're all in the way,
All right then we'll hurry away;
If you're in a hurry we'll all of us scurry
And let you get on with your play. Good day,
We'll all of us hurry away.

SCENE II.—*Lord Winterstock's Ball Room. Six ladies lying in a heap like marionettes. Enter* POET L. *shown on by* PARKER.

Poet. (*glances at audience—to himself*) The House Beautiful. (*sees ladies*) How deliciously sybarite. Now, how can I rouse these charming ladies into life? Music might do it—but not the terrible music one hears from orchestras! It must be some delightful Orphean music coaxed from tambour and pan-pipes. (*pan-pipes and drum strike up outside*) Ah, that's delightful! Heavenly! (*down R.*)

(*Figures gradually rise and dance.*)[11]

Song—

[Ladies.]   We are tiny puppets here to dance and sing,
We will do our best if you will pull the string.
Tell us which way we're to poise and swing,
We're at your command till morning.
We've not much to say, but in our little way

---

[11] The figures danced in the style of 'automata or puppets' (*Theatre* 1 June 1892).

We assist the play, and help to make it pay,
Keep the public gay, not yawning.

(*Exit* POET. *Enter* LADY WINTERSTOCK R.)

Park.   And is your ladyship at home to-night?

Lady W.   Parker! Of course! Oh, by the way, you might
When you announce my guests make every name
A double one. It sounds more *crême de la crême*.
But, Parker, why this dazzling costume? [12]

Park.   It gives a tone of colour to the room;
The guard has struck me off the Yeoman's roster,
And so I get my living as a poster.
(*announces*) Lord Pentonville of Pentonville, my lady.

(*Enter* LORD PENTONVILLE)

Lady W.   A dazzling character, and oh! so shady.

Pent.   How are you, Lady Winterstock, my poppet?

Lady W.   Not quite so free, my lord—now just you drop it.

Pent.   Ah well, perhaps you're right and I was hasty,
But really, chaff apart, you do look tasty.

Lady W.   I can't allow such talk, you wicked man!

Pent.   When woman says 'I can't, she means I can.'
Nothing is so ennobling as crime.
No one is spotless who has not done time.

Lady W.   And have you really been in gaol, my lord!
Really and truly?

Pent.   Yes, upon my word.

---

[12] Parker appeared in the dress of a Yeoman of the Guard, as a mocking reference to Gilbert and Sullivan's operetta *The Yeoman of the Guard* (1888).

Lady W.   What was it for?

Pent.   A trifle, that's the pity.
        A foolish little business in the city.
        And e'er my pals and I had time to off it,
        They copped us and the swag[13]—I mean the profit.

Lady W.   But wasn't that a leetle bit tyrannical?

Pent.   How fascinating—and how puritanical!

Lady W.   Will you take tea? They're sure to bring it soon.

Pent.   Thank you, if you can trust me with the spoon.
        But—*badinage* apart—I paid this visit
        To bring a piece of gossip.

Lady W.   Well, what was it?

Pent.   It's rumoured that your husband, Winterstock,
        Goes almost every day towards five o'clock
        To Mrs. Earlybird's—and stays for tea.

Lady W.   Call on a woman I've refused to see?
        On my mamma? Oh, I'll not believe you.

Pent.   Well, having giv'n my news I think I'll leave you.

Lady W.   Don't go—Lord Pentonville, you'll be my friend.

Pent.   I will indeed—until the bitter end.

Lady W.   This woman—my mamma—this low enchantress,
        Was daughter of a common Temple laundress.[14]
        I wouldn't—not for all the wealth of nations,
        Receive a woman with such low relations.

---

[13] *swag* Unlawful gain or acquisition; booty.

[14] *Temple* Legal district of London which includes the Inns of Court, Lincoln's Inn, and the Inner and Middle Temple.

Pent.   In principle I really think you're right.
                     What shall you do, though, if she comes to-night?

Lady W.   I'll keep mamma outside at any hazard.
                     Should she come in—I'll land her o'er the mazzard.
                     Just hold my fan, my lord, I shan't want that.
                     One don't want weapons [t]o destroy a cat!

                                                    (*Gives fan*)

Pent. (*aside*)   Now, shall I sneak this fan?

Poet.   Well, I think not.
                     For if you do, you'll alter all the plot.[15]

Pent.   The one thing I can't resist's temptation.[16]
                     I'm off—to my avuncular relation. (*Exit* L.)

Poet. (*to* LADY W.) Now all the interest depends on you.
                     You've got to find out if this story's true.

                     (*Enter* LORD W., R.)

Lord W. (*aside, cross to* L.) I've got my cheque-book and I'm going to lock it
                     Up in my desk.

Lady W. (*aside to* POET)   Where is it?

Poet. (*aside*)   In his pocket.

Lady W. (*aside*) My silly heart is going pit-a-pat.
                   (*she picks his pocket, goes down* R.)

Lord W. (*perceives what she has done*) Oh, Margaret, you shouldn't have done that.

                     (*Exit* POET)

---

[15] The plot of *Lady Windermere's Fan* turns on Windermere's discovery of his wife's fan lying on a table in Lord Darlington's rooms.

[16] A joke on Lord Darlington's quip to Lady Windermere, 'I can resist everything except temptation'.

Lady W.   So now, my lord, you're fairly run to ground
              (*reads*) 'To Mrs. Earlybird, ten thousand pound'!

Lord W.   That's nothing, I was only dining there
              And lost a little bit at *chemin de fer.*

Lady W. (*reads*) 'Thirty-five thousand pounds to Mrs. E.'

Lord W.   That was to give her two days by the sea.
              I really don't see why there's all this bother!
              It isn't my fault that you've got a mother.
              I rather like her, and I go to see her—

Lady W.   How ill weak-mindedness becomes a peer!
              Mamma is not a person we should know,
              If she's received here—understand—I go!

(Exit LADY W.)

Song, LORD W.—

1.—My hearth's wrecked, and all through my mamma-in-law,
The most charming woman that ever I saw,
I take tea there nearly every other day;
She can only come here when my wife's away.
(Which I think is really most unfortunate)
I have been beseeching and importunate,
But my wife is utterly unreasonable,
Nothing that I find to say seems seasonable.

Chorus—

Never recognize your ma-in-law at all,
And especially don't bring her to a ball;
If she's prettier than her daughter
You'll be sorry that you brought her,
Never recognize your ma-in-law at all.
Take my tip!
Leave your wife's relations in the hall.

2.—My wife has such curious ideas about
Whom one ought to know (I've not the smallest doubt
She's quite right) but still it is an awful bore
If one may not see one's own mamma-in-law!

I had been quite looking forward to the chance,
Which I thought I should have had to-night, to dance
With mamma-in-law who trips delightfully;
I wish my wife wouldn't act so spitefully!

3.—I can't understand—I can't, upon my life,
How a clever, charming woman like my wife
Can be so small-minded and ridiculous!
Still I'm placed in rather a periculous
Situation. If my wife refuses to
Recognize before folk and abuses to
Her face my mamma-in-law (she's bound to do)
I shan't be surprised to see a round or two!

Last Chorus—
I've a good mind not to show my face at all,
But to sit with Parker in the servant's hall!
Smoke my pipe and drink in my porter,
Finish up with gin and water,
Let my wife receive the gents and ladies all;
While I sip
Stout and gin and water in the hall.[17]

(*Exit* LORD W., L. *Enter* POET, R., *followed by ladies and gentlemen*)

Poet.   The difficulty, which I foresee, is how to make my play long
enough. One very charming method would be to stop every now and then, and play
little bits over and over again. But it's so commonplace to repeat one's self. No—I
think I'll introduce some delightful successful character from some long-forgotten
standard drama, who shall discourse to my puppets for a little and encourage them.
Hamlet, for instance, might give some advice.

Hamlet. (*without*) Ah, right you are! I'm with you in a trice.
                    (*enters*) How are you? (*shakes hands with* PARKER)[18]

Poet.   Herbert, wouldn't you rather come on centre?

_____

[17] The song 'Never recognize your ma-in-law at all' was performed as a music hall parody,
and concluded with a dance.
[18] Brookfield was costumed and made up to resemble Herbert Beerbohm Tree as Hamlet.

Hamlet.   No, that's where all the other Hamlets enter.
                   Friends, puppets, mountebanks, you ears lend—
                   I'm glad to see you all. You know, my friend
                   Has with less modesty perhaps than cunning
                   Written a play which he proposes running. (*sits*)
                   A play which, though the story's rather thin,
                   Should make fools laugh and the judicious grin.
                   Now, when you speak his lines, remember will you
                   They're never vulgar, though at times familiar.
                   If you as players fain would make your mark,
                   You each should ride an hour in the park.
                   Your nature's mirror should contain a host
                   Of invitation cards.[19] The *Morning Post*
                   Should chronicle your movements—and take heed
                   You never play small parts, but only 'lead'. (*rises*)
                   When such high-vaulting ends in over-reaching,
                   The unsuccessful player takes to teaching.
                   But who comes hither? Is't my father's shade?
                   No. 'Tis Ophelia, poor distracted maid.

                   (*Enter* OPHELIA L.)

Oph.   Hush! Hush! Hush!
                   Here comes the Bogey-man,
                   So go to sleep you babies,
                   He'll catch you if he can!
                   Here's bronze for you—now prithee go and grind
                   Your organ in some distant street. I find
                   I've sixpence less than I should have—I know!
                   I gave it to that German Band to go.
                   They nearly finished me with 'Annie Rooney'. (*sings*)[20]

Ham. (*aside*)   Popular airs have made this lady luney!

Oph.   And childish treble pipes the 'Whistling Coon.'

Ham.   Sweet piano organ! Jangled out of tune.[21]

---

[19] The image here refers to the custom of displaying invitations by placing them around the frame of a mirror. Also, cf. Hamlet, 'to hold as 'twere the mirror up to nature' (*Hamlet* 3.2.23).

[20] Lottie Venne parodied Mrs. Tree's performance as Ophelia.

Oph. (*sings*)   Hamlet, I'm waitin', waitin' alone down 'ere.
                  (*speaks*) I'm bound to go on lovin' yer, my dear, d'ye 'ear?
                  (HAMLET *whistles—business* HAMLET *and* OPHELIA)

Ham.   Alas! sweet lady, what imports this song?

Oph.   Say you? Dear lord it is the fav'rite ditty
                  Of our greengrocer's boy—the more's the pity!
                  Talking of which I see with consternation
                  That picotee—and pink—and fair carnation
                  Have lately turned a mawkish, envious green!
                  They've all been dyed you know with anyline! (*sings*)

                      'Ere I go there's just one lay
                      Which perhaps has had its day—
                      You know what I would say—

Ham.   Dear—grant one boon to-day.
                  Let's fly this city, redolent so strong
                  Of orange peel, fusee, and comic song!

                        (*Song and dance*)

                  1.—Come, sweet lord, I'll fly away with thee.
                  Yes, sweet maid, and fly away with me!
                  Far away from giddy ditties, disenchanting din of cities,
                  Westward ho, across the sapphire sea.
                  Far away together—you alone with me!
                              (*Gavotte*)
                  2.—There we'll find a happy land of rest,
                  Nobody to criticise us, catechise, and then advise us.
                  Far away we'll do as we think best,
                  You and I together in the far, far West.

                        (*Exeunt* L.)

(*Guests converse. Enter* CECIL, LORD GONBUSTUS *and* LADY W.)

---

[21] Cf. Ophelia, 'Now see that noble and most sovereign reason,/Like sweet bells jangled, out of tune and harsh' (*Hamlet* 3.1.118-19).

Mr. D.   Now I suppose—take it for all in all—
This is about the very dullest ball
I've been to all the season.

Lady W.   That's polite.

Mr. D.   I mean the most successful, brilliant, bright!
I didn't see, my lady, you were there.

Lady W. I think I'll go outside and take the air.
Parker, my fur-lined cloak is up the 'spout,'
Go round to 'Attenborough's' and get it out.

              (*Enter* LORD W., L.)

Lord. W. (*aside to* LADY W.) My darling, I'm sure you didn't mean
All that you said just now. Don't make a scene
When your mamma comes.

Lady W.   You leave that to me,
I'll pummel her until she cannot see.

     (*Goes on to terrace*)

Lord G.   They tell me Mrs. Earlybird's invited?

Lord W.   She's coming—yes.

Lord G.   Ah, that's right. I'm delighted!
I really don't know anything that's harder
To kill than what they call a *mauvais quatre d'heure*.

Lord W.   She'll soon be here, I know.

Lord G.   Well, that's consoling.

1st Lady.   Meanwhile, dear poet, keep the ball a-rolling.

Poet.   What shall I talk about?

2nd Lady.   How can you ask?
Yourself, of course!

3rd Lady.	Yes, while we sit and bask Here in the sunshine of your presence.

Poet.	Well! I like the picture, I confess.

4th Lady.	Now tell What made you take to writing plays instead Of patronizing Art?

Poet.	Because I've said All that has ever been said about pictures; The painter, too, has writhed beneath my strictures.

5th Lady.	But poet, dear, you haven't yet imparted A quarter what we want to know—what started That master-hand to link, with cunning zest, Well-tested epigram and hall-marked jest.

1st Lady.	Were you afraid the play would meet with coldness?

3rd Lady.	Oh, Mr. Poet, if you'll forgive my boldness, I wish, instead of telling us, you'd sing it: Your music, now, don't say you did not bring it.

Poet.	I'll sing the song from mem'ry if I can.

3rd Lady.	Oh, Mr, Poet, you are a funny man.

Poet.	All poets' voices have a fairy tone, A kind of lightish Rutland Barrytone.[22]

Song—

A Poet lived in a handsome style,
His books had sold, and he's made his pile,
His articles, stories, and lectures, too,
Had brought success, as everybody knew.

---

[22] *Rutland Barrytone* The singer Rutland Barrington. Hawtrey imitated Barrington singing 'The Silver Churn' from Gilbert and Sullivan's *Patience* (1881). On opening night, the song was encored twice.

But the Poet was tired of writing tales
Of curious women, and singular males;
So soon as he'd finished his Dorian Grey,[23]
He set to work at a four-act play.

Chorus—

A four-act play, (*solo*) a four-act play,
A most aesthetic, very magnetic fancy, let us say;
He'd filled his purse by writing verse, why not a four-act play.

His young disciples expressed surprise,
They said 'dear, dear! Do you think it wise?'
The Poet-author made no reply,
Merely winked his left pellucid eye.
The piece came out, and it stood the test,
For he'd borrowed only the very best;
And those who came to scoff at the play
Had to hammer applause 'ere they drove away.

Chorus—

They drove away, (*solo*) they drove away,
While this magnetic, peripatetic author remains to say,
He was much delighted that those invited enjoyed his four-act
play.

(*During song* LADY W. *returns*)

Lady W. You have a charming timbre of voice, Sir Poet.

Poet. (*rises and goes down* R.) The poet's voice is beautiful, I know it.
(*music*)

Park. H'm—Mrs. Earlybird!

(*Enter* MRS. EARLYBIRD L.)

---

[23] *Dorian Grey* Wilde's novel *The Picture of Dorian Grey* (1890). Wilde had also published *The Portrait of Mr W.H.* (1889), *The Soul of Man under Socialism* (1891), and *Lord Arthur Savile's Crime and Other Stories* (1891) before he wrote *Lady Windermere's Fan*.

Lord W. (*aside*)   Now, will they fight?

(LADY W. *puts her tongue out at* MRS. E.)

Mrs. E.   How very charming Margie looks to-night.
                 (*aside*) She's really looking very cross and soured.

Lady W. (*aside*) I cannot strike her! I am such a coward.

(*Exeunt all, except* POET, LORD G. *and* CECIL.)

Mrs. E.   Come, Arthur, introduce me to the Johnnies.[24]

Lord. W.   Allow me—Mrs. Earlybird, Cecil.

(*All bow*)

Mrs. E.   Well, sonnie,
                 I'm glad to see you. Isn't that old Tuppy?

Dummy. Yes, but he's dyed a different colour.

Lord. G.   Puppy!
                 Delightful lady, can you spare a dance?

Mrs. E.   Dear Lord Gonbustus—give me but the chance.
                 I'll dance with you through life, I'll never leave you.

Lord G.   I only wish that I could dare believe you.
                 But 'ere I'd hope of such a prize attaining,
                 I *think* just one or two things want explaining.

Mrs. E. (*aside*) I've struck my gudgeon—now you'll see me hook it.
                 My Lord, I simply saw my chance and took it.

Song—
1.—When I was a little tiny child,
Fortune hardly every on me smiled,
Early up and very late to bed,
Slaving hard to earn a crust of bread.

---

[24] *Johnnies* Young men about town.

My one fault was that I loved to cram
Sweets, confectionery, strawberry jam.
I saw some upon the kitchen shelf,
So I clambered up and helped myself.

Chorus—
I saw my chance and took it! I took it! I took it!
By hook or crook I took it!—do you think I was to blame?
I couldn't overlook it! I saw my chance and took it!
If you felt now as I felt then, I know you'd do the same.

2.—Some years later I was helping ma
Minding chambers close to Temple Bar.
Our young gentleman had lots of tin,[25]
Mother told me to go in and win.
So I set my little neat white cap
Fairly at him, till he came, poor chap,
Clasped me closely in a fond entwine,
Whispered tenderly, 'My sweet—be mine!'

3.—Our married life (I grieve to tell)
Went not 'merry as a marriage bell.'
Till at last, upon a nice fine day,
My young lord and master slipped away.
Then I chose a moment opportune,
And petitioned Mr. Justice Jeune.
He at once pronounced a wise decree—
Settled half my husband's wealth on me.

4.—Now I want to find (that's if I can)
Some nice, sensible, discreet old man,
Who'll relieve me of my anxiety,
Launch me fairly in Society.
I would care for him most tenderly,
Love him, too—tho' p'rhaps but slenderly—
I'd—provided he insures his life—
Make him quite a little pattern wife.

---

[25] *tin* Money.

Last Chorus—
When my chance comes I'll take it! I'll take it! I'll take it!
Make no mistake, I'll take it!—do you think I'd be to blame?
If it don't come I'll make it! I'll make my chance and take it!
Some day, perhaps, you'll feel like me, and then you'll do the
    same.

Lord G.   Sweet lady, that explains the whole d——d thing.
                 D——d clubs, d——d cooks, d—n climate—everything.

Mrs. E.   Dear Lord Gonbustus, I accept your escuage,
                 I like your sentiments—
                     (*Enter* LADY W.)
                                 but bar your language.

Lady W.Now, where on earth's that kleptomaniac peer?
                 He's pinched my fan.

Lord W.   Well, never mind, my dear,
                 I'll go and ask him for it. As for you,
                 You'd better have a nap.

Lady W.   No, I'll go, too.

Mrs. E.   No, Lady Winterstock, you'd better pass,
                 Your hand's not strong enough.

Lady W.   I like your brass.

Mrs. E.   Don't talk like that, it isn't quite well bred!
                 I really think it's time you went to bed.
                 I'll go and see Lord Pentonville instead.
                 Your place, dear Lady Winterstock, is bed.
                 What matter if Lord Pentonville has fled?
                 The fact remains—your place is in your bed.
                 Oh, you don't know the wretched life I've led.
                 I know the whole game through from A. to Z.
                 I know, dear, how you're feeling—you've a dread
                 Of being thought provincial. Though your head
                 Is splitting, and your eyelids feel like lead,
                 Yet you would sit up. Rubbish—go to bed.

(*Enter Ladies and Gentlemen,* L. *and* R.)

Lady W. (*rises*)   You speak, mamma, as if you had a heart.
                    I do feel tired.

Mrs. E.   Well, then make a start.

Lord W.   I'm certain Mrs. Earlybird is right.

Lady W.Well, mind you get my fan. I'll say good-night!

Good-night chorus—

Go to bed and save your beauty—'tis an obvious social duty.
Till to-morrow, dear, good-night!
Go upstairs and disencumber, wrap your fairy form in slumber.
Wake to-morrow fresh and bright. Dream of fairies, sweet good-night!

SCENE III.—LORD PENTONVILLE's *smoking room. Enter* LORD W., YOUNG
MEN, LORD G., *and* POET.

1st Y.M.   I say, Tuppy, shut that door!

Lord G.   What door?

1st Y.M.   Why, *that* door!

Lord G.   I don't call that a *door*.

1st Y.M.   What d'you call it then?

Lord G.   *I* call it a *jar!* (PARKER *laughs*)

Poet.   My dear Tuppy, you're much too old to make that kind of repartee.

Lord G.   Old be d——d! Why, how old are you?

Poet.   Twelve, when I'm with young people, and a-hundred-and-twenty,
when I'm with old ones.

Lord G.   You don't look it.

Poet.   A-hundred-and-twenty?

Lord G.   No! Twelve.

Poet.   So I was told the other day by a tiresome railway official.

Park.   Have a drink?

All.   Hear, hear!

1st Y.M.   Any fellow can make a man drink; but forty can't make him take to water. I saw old Miller to-day.

Lord W.   What old Miller?

1st Y.M.   Why—old Joe Miller.[26]

Lord W.   Don't know him.

Poet.   Dear me! He's one of my dearest friends!

1st Y.M.   He was wearing a white hat.

Lord W.   What, at Sandown?[27] Did he fancy it was fashionable?

1st Y.M.   No; he fancied it kept his head warm.

                         (PARKER *laughs.*)

Poet. (*to* LORD G.) That's a very clever young man!

Lord G.   What do you call a very clever young man?

Poet.   A youth who knows how to dispense in the nursery the plums he has picked up in the dining-room.

Lord W.   You mean a kind of juvenile Deipnosophist?

Lord G.   What's a Deipnosophist?

---

[26] *Joe Miller* Slang for a stale joke; refers to the Joe Miller joke books first published in the 1740s.
[27] *Sandown* A fashionable racetrack that opened in 1875.

Poet.	A true philosopher whose maxim is 'no supper—no song.'
1st Y.M.	Who robs Mr. Peter of his stories to pay Mrs. Paul for her dinners.
Lord G.	I'm still in the dark!
Poet. position.	Never mind, Tuppy, a very wise lawyer was once in the same
Lord G.	Whom do you mean?
Poet.	Moses—when the light went out!
Lord G.	Oh dear! Oh dear! Oh dear!

Song—
'Dat sun's a-slanting.'

1.—Nigger mighty happy when he's layin' in de corn.
Chorus.—Dat sun's a-slanting.

Nigger mighty happy when he hear de dinner horn.
Chorus.—Dat sun's a-slanting.

But he more happy when de night draws on.
Chorus.—Dat sun's a-slanting.

Dat sun's a-slanting jest as sure as you're born,
And it's rise up Primus and give a mighty yell;
Dere's de old dun cow der a tinkling of her bell,
And de frogs churning up for de dew down fell.
Good-night, Mister Kildee! we wish you mighty well,
We wish you mighty well.

Chorus.—Good-night, Mister Kildee! we wish you mighty well.
(*Repeat*)

2.—De corn'll be ready by dumplin' day.
Chorus.—Dat sun's a-slanting.

But nigger got to stop and to stick and to stay.
Chorus.—*Dat sun's a-slanting.*

Same as de bee martin watchin' of the jay.
Chorus.—*Dat sun's a-slanting.*

Dat sun's a-slantin' and a-slippin' away,
An' it's rise up Primus and give it to 'em strong;
De cows gwine home with a ding, dang, dong,
Sling another tetch upon the ole time song.

Chorus.—*Good night! Mr. Whippowill, don't stay long.*
(*Repeat*)

Poet. (*rises*)   Before we go, wouldn't it improve the scene
If we were to find some *lady*?

Lord G.   What do you mean?

Poet.   I mean, that in a play one's always certain
To find a victim hidden behind a curtain.
You hunt her out. (*all rise*)

Lord G.   I really think you're right.
So, as a matter of form—here, where's a light?
This problem is most easily determinable.
(*Draws aside curtain—discovers six ladies*)
Six Lady Teazle's, now, by all that's d———ble![28]

(*Dance*)

---

[28] Wilde was criticized for having relied too heavily upon the famous 'screen scene' in Sheridan's *The School for Scandal* when writing the scene where Lady Windermere hides behind a curtain in Lord Darlington's rooms. In Sheridan's comedy, Lady Teazle is discovered behind a screen. *The Poet and the Puppets* makes light of Wilde's allegedly derivative dramaturgy by imagining half a dozen Lady Teazles concealed behind a screen. It bears remembering, though, that Lady Windermere escapes detection (unlike Lady Teazle) since Mrs. Erlynne intercedes to provide a necessary diversion.

SCENE IV.—LADY WINTERSTOCK'S *Morning Room.* PARKER *discovered.*
Enter Lady W.

Lady W.   I *am* so glad I took mamma's advice
      And went to bed! I dropped off in a trice!
      And now this morning I feel *so* much better!
      Why, here's an odd-shaped parcel and a letter
      For Arthur! Now what can it be? I'll settle
      That question very quickly! Where's the kettle?

      (She opens the letter with steam from kettle.)

      What's this? A letter from mamma! 'Dear Arthur
      I've made Gonbustus—Margaret's step father!
      Our best man was the Yeoman of the Guards,
      We leave for Rome this afternoon. No cards.'
      I always *knew* mamma would marry smartly,
      I'm sorry now I spoke to her so tartly—
      And here's a lovely slice of wedding cake!

      (PARKER *goes back. Enter* LORD WINTERSTOCK)

Lord W.   Why, hullo Margaret, are you awake?
      I've got your fan. Pentonville said he'd carried it
      Home by mistake.

Lady W.   Arthur! Ma's married
      To Lord Gonbustus!

Lord W.   What d'you mean; just recently?

Lady W.   This morning!

Lord W.   Well, they *might* have done it decently!
      Where are they going to honeymoon?

Lady W.   At Rome.

Lord W.   Well, if she ever calls, you're not at home.

Lady W.   Oh Arthur! What a change! And can't I soften
      This iron resolve?

Parker. (*announces*)   Lady Gonbustus Often!

(*Enter* LADY *and* LORD G.)

Lady G.   Well, Margaret?

Lady W.   Mamma, I *am* so glad!

Lord W. (*aside*) To think she's married that inane old cad.

Lady G.   I've brought my little chatterbox you see!

Lady W.   A model husband I'm convinced he'll be!

Lady G.   Oh, bother models; *I* prefer a live 'un!
                     Here, Puppy! Go and dally with a siphon.
                     He is so *fond* of siphons.

Lady W.   Fond of drink?
                     Then you can *love* him, mother, do you think?

Lady G.   My dear, I had a husband once before him;
                     They're all alike! Of course I shan't adore him,
                     Or hate him either—women are such fools—
                     They're apt to come to grief between two stools!

                              Song—

Before I was a titled lady—I havn't been one long—
I never knew quite what was right to do, nor yet quite what was wrong.
I loved to have a crowd of swains, tho' p'raps it wasn't right.
It made me weep to hear them plead, and laugh to see them fight.
Surrounded by so many loves I found the one thing to do,
Was to neither this nor that but just between the two.

                              Chorus—
               Not too young, not too old, not too bashful, not too bold,
               Not too warm, not too cold, just between the two.
                              (*ad lib.*)

I meant to be extremely proper. If ever I was not
The simple reason was that in those days I knew not what was what.

If anybody kissed my hand, instead of looking black,
Or doing this, or doing that, I simply gave it back.
Without a worldly education, what on earth is one to do
Who is not too bad and not too good, but just between the two?

Lady G.   Well, Arthur, tell me what d'you think of that?

Lord W.   Don't speak to *me*—you seven-minded cat!
            I suppose you think such wayward conduct fascinates.
            I hate, myself, a mother-in-law who vacillates!

Lady G.   Come, Arthur, won't you tell me that you're glad?

Lord W.   I won't! I think you're everything that's bad.
            Adventuress! Decoy! Gossip promulger!

Lady G.   Now, please, don't call me names—it is so vulgar.
            What is the meaning of this outburst, sir?

Lord W.   It means—I like you better as you were,
            You brazen Circe!

Lady G.   Come now—just you stow it!
            I won't put up with this! Here, Mr. Poet!
            Will you kindly speak to this ridiculous young
            Man who doesn't know his own mind?

Poet.   But inconsistency is so charming. Don't you think so?[29]

Lady G.   This is all very well,[30] but if people are going to see-saw about in
their emotions like this—there's no reason why the play should ever end!

Poet.   But it never *should* end! I should like it to flow on and on for ever!

Lady G.   Well, I'm sorry to be rude, but I'm bound
            To say I don't see why it should ever have begun.

---

[29] Annotation in the orginal text: 'Here is Song Lord W.—4 lines/Lady G.—4 lines/Poet—4 lines.' (fol. 27).

[30] *This is all very well* The original line, crossed out, reads 'That may or may not be' (fol. 27).

I know the way to save the situation,
I'll call the Spirit of Fair Arbitration.[31]
>   (*The Spirit appears through trap*)

Spirit.   You called?

Lady G.   And will you help us?

Spirit.   That depends.

Lady G.   Dear Bogey, here's an author who contends
The play he's written should go on for ever.

Spirit.   I know the author, he's extremely clever.
If you want my opinion of his play,
I'll try and sing you what I have to say.

>   *'Spirit of Arbitration' Song*—

It is difficult to state off-hand the special kind of play
Most likely to give pleasure, and to ultimately pay.
The public seem to alternate 'twixt French liqueur and tea.
(I don't believe they really care for Norwegian anchovy)[32]
But, touching Lady Windermere, I think it's safe to say
The management will change the bill—when the people stay away.

>   But you mustn't blame the play!
>   While the public go
>   There must be merit in the show.
>   There are some who say 'It seemed to me a trifle slow.'
>   And others, 'It's the best I've seen.'
>   But, there isn't any harm in the play. Oh, no!
>   A charming play—as such plays go—
>   Since the poet was induced to let the audience know,
>   It's always been a good play since.[33]

---

[31] *Spirit of Fair Arbitration* The London Chamber of Arbitration was founded in 1892 at the Guildhall in the City of London.

[32] *Norwegian anchovy* An allusion to Ibsen, who was from Norway.

[33] Annotation in the original text: '15 lines here' (fol. 28); most likely a reference to the length of the song lyric.

There are some young men who like burlesque—who sit there in a row,
And gaze upon the nether limbs of someone they don't know.
And send her little missives—even diamonds and flowers,
And wait outside the stage door in the wind and snow for hours.
They don't do any mischief, therefore (*if it pleases them*),
Give the lad his mild excitement, and the *coryphée* her gem.[34]

> But you mustn't blame the play!
> When the public go
> There must be merit in the show,
> And what, perhaps, at fifty seems a trifle slow,
> Seemed very smart at seventeen.
> But I don't see any harm in burlesque—oh no!
> There was one which hardly seemed to go,
> Till they got a clever lady from the 'halls' to 'show,'
> They've always had a full house since!

Lady G.   Tell us, dear friend, your ultimate decision?

Spirit.   I think the House will favour a division.[35]
The poet's won the palm in every sphere,
He's chosen to invade—therefore—

Poet.   Hear! Hear!

Spirit.   Let him now sally forth, equipped and curled,
To make conquest of some further world.
I therefore give it forth as my award
That he exchange the Stylos for the Sword!

(*Enfant Prodigue March begins softly.*)

Lady G.   You'd make a lovely soldier.

Poet.   Yes, I know.

---

34 The stanza refers to young men like the Gaiety 'mashers' who dutifully attend the same burlesque night after night, smitten by the latest stage voluptuary. *Coryphée* was the more dignified name for a burlesque chorine.

35 *House* Pun on the House of Commons (or any deliberating body) and a theatre audience (the 'house').

Spirit.

There's one formality before you go:
Just sign this document—a promise never
To write another play—however clever.

Poet.

To bind myself is quite against my creed,
I will not promise—but I'll sign the deed.
                    (*Signs.*)
I'll tell you as a soldier what I'll do
I will invent the Battle of Waterloo!

Song, LADY G.—

E're we break up, I think we should
Thank our poet, beautiful and good!
Sound his praises loud on drum and fife,
Bless the golden day which gave him life.
We'll extoll him on the suave trombone.
(He's too modest, p'rhaps, to sound his own)
Of his own merits he's dumb,
(Beyond a whisper on the drum).

Chorus—

We'll play our trump and blow it, and blow it, and blow it!
(Assisted by the poet) we make a glorious name.
We'll let the neighbours know it
When once we take and blow it.
We'll blow our brazen trumpet loud as we march along to fame.

FINALE

Representative Victorian Burlesques

All theatres are in London unless indicated otherwise.

Anon. *Arrah-No-Brogue; or, The Girl of the Lips* (Sadler's Wells 1865)
  Calypso and Telemachus (Sadler's Wells 1865)
  The Corkonian Brothers (Strand 1854)
  Dido and Aeneas (Strand 1893)
  An Extraordinary Version of the Lady of Lyons; or, The Trials and Troubles of Claude and Pauline (Britannia 1860)
  George Barnwell; or, The London Merchant Tailor (Surrey 1844)
  The Heart of Midlothian; or, a New Trial of Effie Deans (Victoria 1863)
  Kenilworth (Strand 1866)
  The Lady of the Lake (Royalty 1862)
  The Lady of Lions; or, Clod, the Bellows Mender (Strand 1838; Olympic 1841)
  Mad-Fred (Surrey 1863)
  Mephistopheles (Sadler's Wells 1894)
  Oily Collins (Soho 1861)
  Our Traviata (Surrey 1857)
  Pizarro, the Great Tyrant (Britannia 1861)
  The Strange Case of a Hyde and Seekyll (Toole's 1886)
  The Ups and Downs of Deal and Black-eyed Susan (Marylebone 1867)

A'Beckett, Gilbert Abbott. *King John (with the Benefit of the Act)* (St. James's 1837)

A'Beckett, Gilbert Abbott and Mark Lemon. *The Castle of Otranto* (Haymarket 1848)
  O Gemini; or, Brothers of Co(u)rse (Haymarket 1852)
  The Knight and the Sprite (Strand 1844)
  St. George and the Dragon (Adelphi 1845)
  Saradanapalus, the 'Fast' King of Assyria (Adelphi 1853)

A'Beckett, Gilbert Arthur. *An Utter Perversion of the Brigand; or, Lines to an Old Ban-ditty* (Haymarket 1867)

Akhurst, W.M. *The Grand Duke of Camberwell* (Elephant and Castle 1876)

Allen, Oswald. *Ingomar the Idiotic; or, the Miser, the Maid and the Mangle* (Marylebone 1871)

Arnold, Henry Thomas. *Nobody's Child* (Cremorne 1868)

Barrie, J.M. *Ibsen's Ghost; or, Toole up-to-date* (Toole's 1891)

Bell, Florence. *Jerry-Builder Solness* (St. George's Hall 1893)

Bird, W.W. *Alonzo and Imogen; or, the Dad, the Lad, the Lord, and the Lass* (Richmond 1869)

Blanchard, E.L. *Antigone* (Strand 1845)
  The Cricket on our Own Hearth (Olympic 1846)

Brookfield, Charles H.E. *A Model Trilby; or—a Day or Two after DuMaurier* (Opera Comique 1895)

Brookfield, Charles H.E. and J.M. Glover. *The Poet and the Puppets* (Comedy Theatre 1892)

Brookfield, Charles H.E. and Seymour Hicks. *Under the Clock* (Court 1893)

Brough, Robert. *Alfred the Great; or, the Minstrel King* (Olympic 1859)

The Last Edition of Ivanhoe, with all the Latest Improvements (Haymarket 1850)

  Masaniello; or, the Fish-o'-man of Naples (Olympic 1857)

  Medea; or, the Best of Mothers, with a Brute of a Husband (Olympic 1855)

  The Siege of Troy (Lyceum 1858)

Brough, Robert and William Brough. *The Enchanted Isle* (Adelphi 1848)

  Frankenstein; or, the Model Man (Adelphi 1849)

Brough, William. *Ernani; or, The Horns of a Dilemma* (Alexandra 1865)

  The Field of the Cloth of Gold (Strand 1858)

  The Great Sensation Trial; or, Circumstantial Effie Deans (St. James's 1863)

  Hercules and Omphale; or, The Power of Love (St. James's 1864)

  Joan of Arc (Strand 1869)

  King Arthur; or, the Days and Knights of the Round Table (Haymarket 1863)

  Perdita; or, the Royal Milkmaid (Lyceum 1856)

Bruce, Harry P. *Faust Reversed; or, The Bells all Gone Wrong* (Hoxton 1888)

Buckingham, Leicester Silk. *Lucrezia Borgia at Home and all Abroad* (St. James's 1860)

  Pizarro (Strand 1862)

  La Traviata; or, the Lady Cameleon (Strand 1857)

  Virginius; or, the Trials of a Fond Papa (St. James's 1859)

  William Tell: A Telling Version of an Old Tell-Tale (Strand 1857)

Burnand, F.C. *Alonzo the Brave; or, Faust and the Fair Imogene* (Strand 1855)

  Antony and Cleopatra; or, His-tory and Her-story in a Modern Nilo-metre (Haymarket 1866)

  Ariel, a Burlesque Fairy Drama in Three Acts and Four Tableaux (Gaiety 1881)

  The Beast and Beauty (Royalty 1869)

  Claude Duval; or, The Highwayman for the Ladies (Royalty 1869)

  The Corsican Brothers and Co., Ltd (Gaiety 1880)

  Dido, the Celebrated Widow (St. James's 1860)

  Dora and Diplunacy; or, a Woman of Uncommon Scents (Strand 1878)

  E—liza—abeth; or, the Don, the Duck, the Drake and the Invisible Armada (Vaudeville 1870)

  Faust and Loose; or, Broken Vows (Toole's 1886)

  Faust and Marguerite: 'An Im-morality' (St. James's 1864)

  The Frightful Hair (Haymarket 1868)

  Guy Fawkes; or, The Ugly Mug and the Couple of Spoons (Strand 1866)

  Helen; or, Taken from the Greek (Adelphi 1866)

  Here's Another Guy Mannering (Vaudeville 1874)

  The Hunchback Back Again; or, Peculiar Julia (Olympic 1878)

  Ixion; or, the Man at the Wheel (Royalty 1863)

  Lord Lovel and Lady Nancy Bell (Cambridge University 1856)

Mazeppa (Gaiety 1885)

The O'Dora; or, A Wrong Accent (Toole's 1885)

Patient Penelope; or, the Return of Ulysseus (Strand 1863)

Paw Clawdian; or, The Roman Awry (Toole's 1884)

The Rise and Fall of Richard III; or, a New Front to an Old Dickey (Royalty 1868)

Robbing Roy; or, Scotched and Kilt (Gaiety 1879)

St. George and a Dragon; or, We are seven (Strand 1870)

Stage Dora; or, Who Killed Cock Robin? (Toole's 1883)

Tra-la la Tosca; or, the High-toned Soprano and the Villain Base (Royalty 1890)

Ulysseus; or, the Ironclad Warriors and the Little Tug of War (St. James's 1865)

Venus and Adonis; or, the Two Rivals and the Small Boar (Haymarket 1864)

The Very Latest Edition of Black-eyed Susan; or, The Little Bill that was Taken Up (New Royalty 1866)

Very Little Faust and More Mephistopheles (Charing Cross 1869)

Burnot, Walter. *The German Silvery King* (Elephant and Castle 1883)

Byron, H.J. *1863; or, The Sensations of the Past Season* (St. James's 1863)

Aladdin; or, The Wonderful Scamp! (Strand 1861)

Ali Baba; or, the Thirty-Nine Thieves (Strand 1863)

The Bohemian G'yurl and the Unapproachable Pole (Opera Comique 1877)

The Corsican 'Bothers'; or, The Troublesome Twins (Globe 1869)

Don Juan (Alhambra 1873)

Fra Diavolo Travestie; or, the Beauty and the Brigand (Strand 1858)

George de Barnwell; or, Harlequin Folly in the Realms of Fancy (Adelphi 1862)

The 'Grin' Bushes; or, Missis Brown of the 'Missis'sippi (Strand 1864)

Guy Fawkes (Gaiety 1874)

Handsome Hernani; or, The Fatal Penny Whistle (Gaiety 1879)

Ill-treated Il Trovatore; or, the Mother, the Maiden, and the Musician (Adelphi 1853)

Ivanhoe in Accordance with the Spirit of the Times (Strand 1862)

The Lady of the Lane (Strand 1872)

The Lady of Lyons; or, Twopenny Pride and Pennytence (Strand 1858)

Little Don Giovanni; or, Leporello and the Stone Statue (Prince of Wales's 1865)

The Maid and the Magpie; or, the Fatal Spoon (Strand 1858)

Mazeppa (Olympic 1859)

Miss Eily O'Connor (Drury Lane 1861; Strand 1862)

Robert Macaire; or, The Roadside Inn Turned Inside Out (Globe 1870)

The Very Latest Edition of the Lady of Lyons (Strand 1859)

William Tell with a Vengeance; or, the Pet, the Patriot, and the Pippin (Alexandra, Liverpool, 1867; Strand 1867)

Dutnall, Martin. *The Cooleen Bawn* (Surrey 1861)

French, Sydney. *Lucrezia Borgia* (Marylebone 1867)

Rob Roy (Marylebone 1867)

Gilbert, W.S. *Dulcamara! or, the Little Duck and the Great Quack* (St. James's 1866)

The Merry Zingara (New Royalty 1868)

The Pretty Druidess (Charing Cross 1869)

The Princess: a Whimsical Allegory (Olympic 1870)

Robert the Devil; or, The Nun, the Dun and the Son of a Gun (Gaiety 1868)

Rosencrantz and Guildenstern (Vaudeville 1891)

Gilbert, W.S ('F. Latour Tomline') and Gilbert Arthur A'Beckett. *The Happy Land* (Court 1873)

Halfourd, John. *Faust and Marguerite* (Strand 1854)

Halliday, Andrew. *The Colleen Bawn Settled at Last* (Lyceum 1862)

Kenilworth; or, Ye Queene, ye Earle, and ye Maydenne (Strand 1858)

Romeo and Juliet Travestie (Strand 1859)

Hayman, Philip. *All My Eye-vanhoe* (Trafalgar 1894)

Henry, Richard. *Frankenstein* (Gaiety 1887)

Jaunty Jane Shore (Strand 1894)

Lancelot the Lovely; or, the Idol of the King (Avenue 1889)

Monte Cristo, Jr. (Gaiety 1886)

Lee, Nelson. *Lady Godiva and the Peeping Tom of Coventry* (City of London 1848)

Leslie, Fred. *Ruy Blas; or, the Blasé Roué* (Grand Theatre, Birmingham 1889; Gaiety 1889)

Merivale, Herman. *The Lady of Lyons Married and Settled* (Gaiety 1878)

Muskerry, William. *Thrillby* (Richmond 1896)

O'Neil, John Robert ('Hugo Vamp'). *The Arcadian Brothers; or, The Spirit of Punch* (Marionette 1852)

O'Neill, Arthur. *William Tell; or, the Arrow, the Apple, and the Agony* (Sadler's Wells 1867)

Oxberry, William Henry. *Acis and Galatea* (Adelphi 1842)

Lucy of Lammermoor (Strand 1848)

Norma Travestie (Adelphi 1841)

Paulton, Harry. *Masse-en-yell-oh* (Comedy 1886)

Paulton, Harry and Joseph Paulton. *The Three Musket Dears, and a Little One In* (Strand 1871)

Planché, J.R. *The 'Birds' of Aristophanes* (Haymarket 1846)

The Camp at the Olympic (Olympic 1853)

The Drama's Levée (Olympic 1838)

The Golden Fleece; or Jason in Colchis and Medea in Corinth (Haymarket 1845)

Mr. Buckstone's Ascent of Mount Parnassus (Haymarket 1853)

Mr. Buckstone's Voyage Round the Globe (Haymarket 1854)

The New Haymarket Spring Meeting (Haymarket 1855)

Orpheus in the Haymarket (Haymarket 1865)

Theseus and Ariadne; or, the Marriage of Bacchus (Lyceum 1848)

Reece, Robert (E.G. Lankester). *Agamemnon and Cassandra; or, the Profit and Loss of Troy* (Prince of Wales, Liverpool 1868)

Brown and the Brahmins; or, Captain Pop and the Princess Pretty-Eyes! (Globe 1869)

Don Giovanni in Venice (Gaiety 1873)

Faust in a Fog (New Road 1870)

The Forty Thieves (Gaiety 1880)

The Lady of the Lake—Plaid in a Tartan (Royalty 1866)

The Lady of Lyons Married and Claude Unsettled (Royalty, Glasgow 1884)

Little Robin Hood; or, Quite a New Beau! (Royalty 1871; Gaiety 1882)

Martha; or, a Fair Take-in (Gaiety 1873)

Our Helen (Gaiety 1884)

Oxygen; or, Gas in a Burlesque Meter (Folly 1877)

Prometheus; or, the Man on the Rock (Royalty 1865)

Richelieu Redressed (Olympic 1873)

Romulus and Remus; or, The Two Rum'uns (Vaudeville 1872)

Ruy Blas Righted; or, the Lover, the Lugger, and the Lacquey (Vaudeville 1874)

The Stranger—Stranger than Ever (Queen's 1868)

The Vampire (Strand 1872)

The Very Last Days of Pompeii; or, a Complete Bulwer-tement of the Classical Drama (Vaudeville 1872)

William Tell Told Again (Gaiety 1876)

Young Rip Van Winkle (Charing Cross 1876)

Sala, G.A. *Wat Tyler, M.P.* (Gaiety 1869)

Selby, Charles. *The Judgment of Paris; or, the Pas de Pippins* (Adelphi 1846)

Kynge Richard ye Third; or, Ye Battel of Bosworth Field (Strand 1844)

The Loves of Lord Bateman and the Fair Sophia (Strand 1839)

Sims, George R. *Carmen up to date* (Gaiety 1890)

The Corsican Brother-babes-in-the-wood (Hull, 1881)

Faust up to date (Gaiety 1888)

Smith, Albert. *Guy Fawkes* (Marylebone 1849)

Spry, Henry. *Quasimodo, the Deformed; or, The Man with the Hump and the Belle of Notre Dame* (Grecian 1870)

Stephens, Henry P. *Galatea; or, Pygmalion Reversed* (Gaiety 1883)

Little Jack Sheppard (Gaiety 1885)

The Vicar of Wideawakefield; or, The Miss-Terry-ous Uncle (Gaiety 1885)

Stocqueler, Joachim *et al. Robin Hood and Richard Coeur de Lion!* (Lyceum 1846)

Talfourd, Francis. *Alcestis, the Original Strong-minded Woman* (Strand 1850)

Harlequin Black-Eyed Susan! (Strand 1855)

Macbeth Somewhat Removed from the Text of Shakespeare (Strand 1848; Olympic 1853)

The Miller and his Men (Strand 1860)

Pluto and Proserpine; or, The Belle and the Pomegranate (Haymarket 1858)

Shylock; or, the Merchant of Venice Preserved (Olympic 1853)

Sir Rupert the Fearless (Strand 1848)

Taylor, Tom. *Sense and Sensation; or, The Seven Saints of Thule* (Olympic 1864)

Tully, John Howard. *Sambodampalus* (Strand 1853)

The Very Earliest Edition of Il Trovatore (Royalty 1861)

Williams, Thomas J. *Medea; or, A Libel on the Lady of Colchis* (Adelphi 1856)

Yardley, W. *Our Toys* (St. James's 1895)

Very Little Hamlet (Gaiety 1884)

Younge, William. *The Lady of Lyons* (Imperial 1879)

Lucrezia Borgia (Lyceum 1879)

Bibliography

A'Beckett, Arthur William. *The à Becketts of 'Punch'; Memories of Father and Sons*. New York: E.P. Dutton and Co., 1903.

—*Green-Room Recollections*. London: Simpkin, Marshall, Ltd, 1896.

A'Beckett, Gilbert Abbott. *The Quizziology of the British Drama*. London: Punch Office, 1846.

Adams, W. Davenport. *A Book of Burlesque: Sketches of English Stage Travestie and Parody*. London: Henry & Co., 1891.

Allen, Robert C. *Horrible Prettiness: Burlesque and American Culture*. Chapel Hill: The University of North Carolina Press, 1991.

Altick, Richard D. *Punch: The Lively Youth of a British Institution, 1841-1851*. Columbus, OH: Ohio State University Press, 1997.

Archer, William. *About the Theatre*. London: T. Fisher Unwin, 1886.

—*English Dramatists of To-Day*. London: Sampson Low, 1882.

Bailey, Peter. *Popular Culture and Performance in the Victorian City*. Cambridge: Cambridge University Press, 1998.

Bancroft, Marie and Squire Bancroft. *The Bancrofts: Recollections of Sixty Years*. London: J. Murray, 1909.

—*Mr. and Mrs. Bancroft On and Off the Stage*. London: Richard Bentley and Son, 1904.

Barrington, Rutland. *Rutland Barrington, a Record of Thirty-Five Years' Experience on the English Stage*. London: Grant Richards, 1908.

Barton Baker, H. *History of the London Stage*. 2nd edn London: G. Routledge & Sons, Ltd, 1904.

Bedford, Paul. *Recollections and Wanderings of Paul Bedford*. London: Strand, 1867.

Blanchard, E.L. *Life and Reminiscences of E.L. Blanchard*. 2 vols. London, n.p., n.d.

Bond, Richmond P. *English Burlesque Poetry, 1700-1750*. Cambridge, MA: Harvard University Press, 1932.

Booth, Michael. *Prefaces to English Nineteenth-Century Theatre*. Manchester: Manchester University Press, 1980.

Booth, Michael (ed.). *English Plays of the Nineteenth Century*. 5 vols. Oxford: Clarendon Press, 1969-76.

Bratton, J.S., *et al*. (ed.). *Acts of Supremacy: The British Empire and the Stage, 1790-1930*. Manchester and New York: Manchester University Press, 1991.

Brereton, Austin. *The Life of Henry Irving*. 2 vols. London: Longmans, Green, and Co., 1908.

Burnand, F.C. *The 'A.D.C.' Being the Personal Reminiscences of the University Amateur Dramatic Club Cambridge*. 2nd edn. London: Chapman and Hall, 1880.

—*Records and Reminiscences*. 2 vols. London: Methuen & Co., 1904.

Buszek, Maria-Elena. 'Representing "Awarishness": Burlesque, Feminist Transgression, and the 19th-Century Pin-Up'. *TDR* 43.4 (Winter 1999), pp. 141-62.

Caesar, Terry. '"I Quite Forgot What—Say a Daffodilly": Victorian Parody'. *ELH* 51 (1984), pp. 795-818.

Clinton-Baddeley, V.C. *The Burlesque Tradition in the English Theatre after 1660*. London: Methuen & Co., Ltd, 1952.

Cole, John. *Life and Theatrical Times of Charles Kean, F. S. A.* 2 vols. London: Richard Bentley, 1859.

Coleman, John. *Fifty Years of an Actor's Life*. London: Hutchinson and Co., 1904.

—*Memoirs of Samuel Phelps*. London: Remington & Co. Publishers, 1886.

—*Players and Playwrights I Have Known*. London: Chatto and Windus, 1888.

Cook, Dutton. *Nights at the Play*. 2 vols. London: Chatto and Windus, 1883.

—*On the Stage: Studies of Theatrical History and the Actor's Art*. London: Sampson Low, 1883.

Cross, Nigel. *The Common Writer: Life in Nineteenth-Century Grub Street*. Cambridge: Cambridge University Press, 1985.

Davis, Jim. 'Androgynous Cliques and Epicene Colleges'. *Nineteenth-Century Theatre Research* 26.1 (Summer 1998), pp. 50-69.

Davis, Tracy C. *Actresses as Working Women*. London: Routledge, 1991.

—*The Economics of the British Stage 1800-1914*. Cambridge: Cambridge University Press, 2000.

—'Spoofing the "Master": Parodies and Burlesques of Ibsen on the English Stage and in the Popular Press'. *Nineteenth-Century Theatre Research* 13.2 (Winter 1985), pp. 87-102.

Dentith, Simon. *Parody*. London and New York: Routledge, 2000.

Dircks, Phyllis. 'James Robinson Planché and the English Burletta Tradition'. *Theatre Survey* 17 (1976), pp. 68-81.

Donne, William Bodham. *Essays on the Drama*. London: John W. Parker and Son, 1858.

Ellis, James. 'The Counterfeit Presentment: Nineteenth-Century Burlesques of *Hamlet*'. *Nineteenth-Century Theatre Research* 11.1 (Summer 1983), pp. 29-50.

Ellis, S.M. (ed.). *A Mid-Victorian Pepys. The Letters and Memoirs of Sir William Hardman, M.A, F.R.G.S.* London: Cecil Palmer, 1923.

Erle, T.W. *Letters from a Theatrical Scene-Painter*. London: Marcus Ward & Co., 1880.

Filon, Augustin. *The English Stage*. London: John Milne, 1897.

Fitzgerald, Percy. *Principles of Comic and Dramatic Effect*. London: Tinsley Brothers, 1870.

Fletcher, Kathy. 'Planché, Vestris and the Transvestite Role'. *Nineteenth-Century Theatre Research* 15.1 (Summer 1987), pp. 9-33.

Ford, Richard. 'The "Waverley" Burlesques'. *Nineteenth-Century Theatre Research* 6 (1978), pp. 63-70.

Glover, J.M. *Jimmy Glover, His Book*. London: Methuen, 1911.

Goodman, Walter. *The Keeleys On the Stage and at Home*. London: Richard Bentley, 1895.

Granville-Barker, Harley. 'Exit Planché—Enter Gilbert'. *The London Mercury* 25.149/150 (March and April 1932), pp. 457-66, 558-73.

Griffin, Penelope (ed.). *Ibsen's Ghost; or, Toole up to Date*. London: Cecil Wood, 1975.

Halliday, Andrew (ed.). *The Savage-Club Papers*. London: Tinsley Bros., 1867.

Hamilton, Walter (ed.). *Parodies of the Works of English and American Authors*. 6 vols. London: Reeves & Turner, 1885.

Hannoosh, Michele. 'The Reflexive Function of Parody'. *Comparative Literature* 41.2 (Spring 1989), pp. 113-27.

Harker, Joseph C. *Studio and Stage*. London: Nisbet and Co., 1924.

Hewitt, Barnard. 'Mrs. John Wood and the Lost Art of Burlesque Acting'. *Theatre Journal* 13.2 (May 1961), pp. 82-5.

Hicks, Seymour. *Twenty-five Years of an Actor's Life*. London: C. Arthur Pearson, 1912.

Hollingshead, John. *Gaiety Chronicles*. London: Archibald Constable & Co., 1891.

—*My Lifetime*. 2 vols. London: Sampson Low, Marston & Co., 1895.

Hutcheon, Linda. *A Theory of Parody: The Teachings of Twentieth-Century Art Forms*. New York and London: Methuen, 1985.

Hutton, Laurence. *Curiosities of the American Stage*. New York: Harper and Bros., 1891.

Jacobs, Henry E. and Claudia D. Johnson. *An Annotated Bibliography of Shakespearean Burlesques, Parodies, and Travesties*. New York: Garland Publishing, Inc., 1976.

Jump, John. *Burlesque*. London: Methuen, 1972.

Kendal, Madge. *Dame Madge Kendal; By Herself*. London: J. Murray, 1933.

Kitchin, George. *A Survey of Burlesque and Parody in English*. Edinburgh and London: Oliver and Boyd, 1931.

Levine, Lawrence. *Highbrow/Lowbrow: The Emergence of Cultural Hierarchy in America*. Cambridge, MA: Harvard University Press, 1988.

Mackinnon, Alan. *The Oxford Amateurs*. London: Chapman and Hall, 1910.

Mackintosh, Matthew. *Stage Reminiscences*. Glasgow: J. Hedderwick and Son, 1886.

Marston, Westland. *Our Recent Actors*. London: Sampson Low, 1888.

Mathews, Brander and Laurence Hutton (eds.). *Actors and Actresses of Great Britain and the United States*. New York: Cassell & Co., 1886.

McCarthy, Justin. *Portraits of the Sixties*. London: T. Fisher Unwin, 1903.

Meisel, Martin. 'Political Extravaganza: A Phase of Nineteenth-Century British Theater'. *Theatre Survey* 3 (1962), pp. 19-31.

Merivale, Herman C. *Bar, Stage, and Platform*. London: Chatto & Windus, 1902.

More, Elizabeth A. 'Henry James Byron and the Craft of Burlesque'. *Theatre Survey* 23.1 (May 1982), pp. 55-70.

Morley, Henry. *Journal of a London Playgoer from 1851 to 1866*. London: George Routledge & Sons, 1866.

Müller, Beate (ed.). *Parody: Dimensions and Perspectives*. Amsterdam: Rodopi, 1997.

Müller-Schwefe, Gerhard (ed.). *Shakespeare im Narrenhaus*. Tübingen: Francke, 1990.

Nicoll, Allardyce. *A History of Early 19th-Century Drama, 1800-1850*. 2 vols. Cambridge: Cambridge University Press, 1937.

—*A History of Late 19th-Century Drama, 1850-1900*. 2 vols. Cambridge: Cambridge University Press, 1946.

'One of the Old Brigade'. *London of the Sixties*. London: Everett & Co., 1909.

Pemberton, T. Edgar. *The Life and Writings of T.W. Robertson*. London: Richard Bentley, 1893.

Planché, James Robinson. *The Extravaganzas of J.R. Planché, 1825-1871*. 5 vols. London: Samuel French, 1879.

—*Recollections and Reflections*. 2 vols. London: Sampson Low, 1872.

Rinear, David L. *The Temple of Momus: Mitchell's Olympic Theatre*. Metuchen, NJ: The Scarecrow Press, Inc., 1987.

Robinson, Henry Crabb. *The London Theatre 1811-1866: Selections from the Diary of Henry Crabb Robinson*. ed. Eluned Brown. London: The Society for Theatre Research, 1966.

Rose, Margaret. *Parody: Ancient, Modern, and Post-modern.* Cambridge: Cambridge University Press, 1993.
—*Parody/Meta-Fiction.* London: Croom Helm, 1979.
Rowell, George. *The Victorian Theatre 1792-1914: A Survey.* 2nd edn. Cambridge: Cambridge University Press, 1978.
Rowell, George (ed.). *Plays of W.S. Gilbert.* Cambridge: Cambridge University Press, 1982.
—*Victorian Dramatic Criticism.* London: Methuen, 1971.
Roy, Donald (ed.). *Plays by James Robinson Planché.* Cambridge: Cambridge University Press, 1986.
Sala, G.A. *The Life and Adventures of George Augustus Sala.* London: n.p., 1895.
—*Robson: A Sketch.* London: John Camden Hotten, 1864.
Sands, Mollie. *Robson of the Olympic.* London: The Society for Theatre Research, 1979.
Schoch, Richard W. '"Chopkins, Late Shakespeare": The Bard and his Burlesques, 1810-1866'. *ELH* 67 (2000), pp. 973-91.
—*Not Shakespeare: Bardolatry and Burlesque in the Nineteenth Century.* Cambridge: Cambridge University Press, 2002.
Scott, Clement. *The Drama of Yesterday and To-Day* 2 vols. London: Macmillan, 1899.
Scott, Harold. *The Early Doors: Origins of the Music Hall.* London: Nicholson & Watson, 1946.
Sims, George R. *My Life: Sixty Years' Recollections of Bohemian London.* London: Eveleigh Nash Co., 1917.
Slater, Michael. 'The Transformations of Susan'. *Theatre Notebook* 50.3 (1996), pp. 146-75.
Stephens, John Russell. *The Censorship of English Drama 1824-1901.* Cambridge: Cambridge University Press, 1980.
Stuart, Charles Douglas and A.J. Park. *The Variety Stage.* London: T. Fisher Unwin, n.d.
Toole, J.L. *Reminiscences of J.L. Toole.* 2 vols. London: Hurst and Blackett, 1889.
Trussler, Simon (ed.). *Burlesque Plays of the Eighteenth Century.* Oxford: Oxford University Press, 1969.
Vanbrugh, Irene. *To Tell my Story.* London: Hutchinson & Co. Ltd, 1948.
Watson, Aaron. *The Savage Club.* London: T. Fisher Unwin, 1907.
Watson, E.B. *From Sheridan to Robertson.* Cambridge, MA: Harvard University Press, 1926.
Wells, Stanley. 'Burlesques of Charles Kean's *The Winter's Tale*'. *Theatre Notebook* 16 (1962), pp. 78-83.
—'Shakespeare in Planché's Extravaganzas'. *Shakespeare Survey* 16 (1963), pp. 103-17.
—'Shakespearian Burlesques'. *Shakespeare Quarterly* 16 (1965), pp. 49-61.
Wells, Stanley (ed.). *Nineteenth-Century Shakespeare Burlesques.* 5 vols. London: Diploma Press, 1977.
Wenckstern, Otto. *Saunterings in and about London.* London: Nathaniel Cooke, 1853.
Whyte, Frederic. *Actors of the Century.* London: George Bell and Sons, 1898.
Willson, Robert F., Jr. *'Their Form Confounded': Studies in the Burlesque Play from Udall to Sheridan.* The Hague: Mouton, 1975.
Yates, Edmund. *Edmund Yates: His Recollections and Experiences.* 2 vols. 3rd edn. London: Richard Bentley and Son, 1884.